SHIPS & GUNS

SHIPS & GUNS

*The sea ordnance in Venice and Europe
between the 15th and the 17th centuries*

edited by

Carlo Beltrame and Renato Gianni Ridella

Università
Ca'Foscari
Venezia

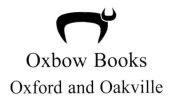

Oxbow Books
Oxford and Oakville

Published by
Oxbow Books, Oxford, UK

© Oxbow Books and the individual authors, 2011

ISBN 978-1-84217-969-7

This book is available direct from:

Oxbow Books, Oxford, UK
(Phone: 01865-241249; Fax: 01865-794449)

and

The David Brown Book Company
PO Box 511, Oakville, CT 06779, USA
(Phone: 860-945-9329; Fax: 860-945-9468)

or from our website

www.oxbowbooks.com

Library of Congress Cataloging-in-Publication Data

Ships and guns : the sea ordnance in Venice and Europe between the 15th and the 17th centuries / edited
  by Carlo Beltrame and Renato Gianni Ridella.
    p. cm.
  Papers presented to the international symposium "Ships and Guns," organized by the Dept. of
Sciences of the Antiquity and the Near East, Universit? Ca' Foscari, Venice, and held Dec. 11-12, 2008.
  Includes bibliographical references and index.
  ISBN 978-1-84217-969-7 (alk. paper)
  1. Ordnance, Naval--Italy--Venice--History--Congresses. 2. Ordnance, Naval--Europe--History--
Congresses. 3. Venice (Italy)--History, Naval--Congresses. 4. Europe--History, Naval--Congresses.
5. Underwater archaeology--Italy--Venice--Congresses. 6. Underwater archaeology--Europe--
Congresses. 7. Archaeology and history--Italy--Venice--Congresses. 8. Archaeology and history--
Europe--Congresses. 9. Venice (Italy)--Antiquities--Congresses. 10. Europe--Antiquities--Congresses.
I. Beltrame, Carlo. II. Ridella, Renato Gianni. III. Universit? degli studi di Venezia. Dipartimento di
scienze dell'antichit? e del Vicino Oriente.
  VF80.V36S44 2010
  623.4'18094530903--dc22
                                              2011000547

Printed in Great Britain by
Short Run Press
Exeter

Contents

Preface

Carlo Beltrame and Renato Gianni Ridella

The scientific articles gathered together in these proceedings represent most of the papers presented to the international symposium 'Ships and Guns' organized by the Department of Sciences of the Antiquity and the Near East, University Ca' Foscari, Venice on 11–12th December 2008. The symposium developed from the idea of a maritime archaeologist, Carlo Beltrame, and a specialist in historical ordnance, Renato Gianni Ridella, to put experts from the field of historic artillery in contact with one another and with underwater archaeologists engaged in the study of modern era wrecks, who often have to deal with cannons, bombards and guns – some of the most diagnostic and common finds on shipwrecks from the 15th century onwards.

Those who work in this field, in fact, think that it is very important to promote the dialogue between experts in artillery and maritime archaeologists for a mutual exchange of information. Often specialists in ordnance study these artefacts without a complete knowledge of the archaeological contexts from which they have been recovered while, even more frequently, archaeologists investigating their contexts have only a superficial knowledge of historic artillery.

Especially in the Mediterranean area, the ignorance and the indifference towards the history of the artillery are notable, often leading to incorrect interpretations of these weapons. In some cases we have truly grotesque situations; for example, the archaeological museum of Lipari where three 16th-century Venetian cannons (Beltrame in this volume) have been displayed to the public as 17th-century French guns belonging (as captured) to a Spanish ship, because we all know that every modern-era wreck with guns must be the remains of a Spanish galleon.

Apart from the lack of a serious dialogue between archaeologists and ordnance experts, this sector of maritime archaeology suffers also from the absence of specialist books, drawing on contributions from acknowledged experts, which can offer a well-researched and complete tool for working archaeologists and students. The only exception is the little volume *Guns from the Sea* (which had a limited distribution), a special issue of the *International Journal of Nautical Archaeology* (edited by Ruth R. Brown and Robert D. Smith in 1988), a collection of papers from the eponymous symposium held in London in 1987. Therefore, the present volume aims to, at least partially, fill this gap by including contributions from both ordnance experts and maritime archaeologists; the former mostly incline toward a technical study of historical artillery and the latter toward illustrating new, or less well-known, underwater sites indicated by the presence of guns.

In Italy, and in fact in most of the Mediterranean area, the study of ordnance is carried on by researchers not connected to institutions; this subject is entirely ignored by academic structures. This has led to a situation where research responds to events, rather than following a systematic programme. It is also hampered by a lack of funding, and, in some cases, research is undertaken by dilettantes who are often not adequately prepared for this task.

We come now specifically to the Italian territories which, until 1861, were divided into different states. Here it must be said that the few researchers competent on that subject were primarily interested in analyzing their own closest geographical regions. Thus, while we have sufficient coverage of the Republics of Venice and Genoa, the situation of the Spanish Viceroyalty of Sicily is, for now, still limited to primary investigation in the archives, while the study of the Dukedom of Tuscany is merely in its infancy. The other two pre-unification states with maritime affairs and navies, the Pontifical State and the Kingdom of Naples, are still unknown territories as far as historic artillery is concerned. It would therefore be a desirable situation for new, young researchers, with the help of acknowledged experts, to begin to fill this gap – one in which they could make valuable contributions.

Moreover, it would be of inestimable value to establish for Italy – as well as for Europe as a whole – a comprehensive picture of gun production. For example North European researchers have had some difficulties identifying pieces of ordnance from the Mediterranean, particularly in the case of civilian guns (as opposed to governments' guns) since often these did not bear recognizable coats of arms or significant inscriptions; in addition they might have weight marks in unusual units of measurement. The different weight systems in use across Europe are particularly confusing. One such difficulty can be found in the appreciable difference between the pound of 12 ounces used in Italy, roughly equivalent to 330 grams, and the 16 ounce pound used in Great Britain, France, the Germanic and Baltic Countries and Spain, that ranges from 400 to 500 grams. An example of such a misunderstanding is that of the scholar who identified a demi-cannon as a saker, mistaking the *cantaro* of Sicily (79 kgs) for the Castilian *quintal* (46 kgs). On the other hand cast-iron guns of English, French, Dutch and Swedish origins, recovered from many Mediterranean wrecks, are often a difficult matter for local experts who have little knowledge of their typology and are, of course, more at ease with the bronze pieces widely produced in Italy and Spain.

In this respect, it would be useful for the pieces always to be weighed in order to provide this very important information which, only too rarely, is available.

The numerous guns recovered from wrecks, particularly in these last few decades, have brought this category of artefacts to the attention of scholars dealing with maritime archaeology; artefacts that, we have to remember, represent one of the most important indicators of the presence of a modern-era wreck on the seabed because they are easily seen and recognised. However, to regard cannon as mere markers of modern wrecks would belittle these artefacts. On the contrary, in our opinion, they are objects throwing important light on the cultural context of their site. If, on the one hand, experts on ordnance can give important help in the interpretation of an archaeological underwater context, on the other, the material from maritime archaeology is furnishing equally precious information for the study of artillery. In the absence of dates engraved on pieces, the chronological contexts to which they belong, for instance, allow us to find new methods of dating guns. This is particularly useful for some types of pieces – such as swivel guns (*petriere*) – the chronology of which is still a matter of dispute. In addition, the characteristics of ships' hulls investigated in underwater excavations of modern-era wrecks can allow us to understand more clearly how guns were placed and used aboard, as well as how the improvements in ordnance have influenced the design and structures of the same ships. And now, a new and exciting development is the underwater finding of rare examples of gun carriages that, having mainly been built of wood, can be preserved in good condition in anaerobic aquatic contexts.

Here we have to remember what is the potential of the information we can learn from these products which represent the best in the metallurgical technology of their time. If the more obvious are those concerning the historical, technological and ballistic fields, we must not forget economically productive, commercial and finally artistic aspects; bronze pieces were often cast by true artists who decorated and personalized them with great skill. Speaking of the level of information that a piece of ordnance – *in lieu* of other archaeological data – can sometimes offer for identifying a ship, we may cite, as an example, the case of the two pieces displayed at Komiza in the island of Vis,

Croatia and their original owner. Beltrame (in this volume) puts forward the hypothesis that the initials and the family coat of arms borne by the guns suggest that their owner was the famous merchant *Alvise Gritti*, son of the illustrious doge *Andrea* and, in any case, without any doubt, are connected to the noble Venetian *Gritti* family.

Owing to the venue of this symposium, it is natural that much of it was devoted to Venetian gun production which undoubtedly played an important role, at least up to the 16th century, in the Mediterranean theatre. It deals with an aspect of the industrial and artistic production of the *Serenissima* Republic that is often neglected, all the more surprising since, on one hand, it has heavily contributed to making the Venetian fleets formidable to their enemies, while on the other it gave the Republic a marketable product much valued by the foreign powers, not only in the Mediterranean. The quite numerous papers from the conference about Venetian wrecks and guns confirm the historical weight of Venice's production evidenced by the amount of data, both archival and archaeological, at researchers' disposal; and this makes us hope for a greater institutional interest toward this subject, not only in the Venetian context.

In the same manner, in the other Italian and Mediterranean areas, as in the Atlantic and Baltic, studies concerning historical ordnance increased in parallel with the findings of new guns from the sea. We can remember here, as the most important examples, pieces recovered in the northern seas from the English *Mary Rose*, the Swedish *Vasa* and *Kronan* and in the Mediterranean those from the Sciacca wreck, in Sicily, and those from the Gnalić, Brsecine and Grebeni wrecks, in Croatia (Ridella in this volume).

However this apparently favourable situation is often obscured by the chronic lack of funds for research and the conservation of pieces and, above all, by the indifference of the authorities and even of many curators of museums holding historical ordnance. We know too well the difficulties of researchers, especially freelance or independent scholars, in obtaining information from some museums and collections and the not infrequent reluctance of these institutions to accept advice from experts concerning wrongly labelled pieces on display to the public.

We hope that the success of this meeting, though limited to a narrow circle of scholars, can help researchers to persevere in their studies and in their efforts to encourage and promote their knowledge of this neglected area to a wider audience.

Acknowledgements

The meeting has been possible thanks to the generous help of the Cassa di Risparmio di Venezia and of the Regione Veneto.

The editors of this volume are indebted to Ruth Brown and Robert Smith, authors of two articles, who have advised on the translations of most of the papers written by scholars for whom English is not their first language.

Carlo Beltrame, Renato Gianni Ridella
September 2009, Venice

Introduction

Ships, Guns and Historical Archaeology

Sauro Gelichi and Mauro Librenti

Maritime archaeology within post-Medieval contexts is a relatively recent development, probably in part due to advances within the discipline of the history of archaeology (Hall, Silliman 2006; Hicks, Beaudry 2006). Such approaches are also now being developed in Italy (Gelichi, Librenti 2007). However, it should be stressed that this phenomenon, as exemplified by a few important case studies, is limited by the relatively small size of the data-set and cannot therefore be used to present a complete history.

As the evidence below demonstrates, the attention given to the sites from this period cannot overcome the limited nature of the finds. However, the results which have emerged from this research do pull together a small number of key points: the structures of the ships or the armament and the categorisation of a few classes of well represented materials including pottery and glass, which were generally studied with a view to refining the chronologies of specific typologies.

At the Summer School on Underwater Archaeology which took place in Pontignano (Siena) in 1996, despite the fact that the audience were essentially aware of the main issues, the research presented on the circulation and economic value of underwater evidence stopped short at the Late Antique period (Volpe, ed. 1998). More recently, published maps of the Apulian shipwrecks also stopped in this Late Antique period (Auriemma 2004). This is a result of the priority, within historical and archaeological debates, given to issues relating to the dynamics of trade at the end of the Roman Empire and the fundamental characteristics of the economy in those transitional centuries (Volpe 1998).

Early medieval shipwrecks are known in the Mediterranean however: such references are clearly stated in Parker's 1992 volume (Parker 1992) which covers shipwrecks up to the 15th century (McCormick has also been working on this topic recently, though the work remains unpublished, and he directs his attention towards the examination of the early medieval shipwrecks).

Several recent papers have also stressed the problem of mapping Italian post-medieval shipwrecks, particularly in comparison to more active research in other countries, although despite this, the situation remains unresolved

(Galasso 1998; 1999). An important element, which merits further discussion, is an examination of the full potential of maritime archaeology. That is to say, not simply theoretical, methodological and technical issues, but also contextual aspects related to the specific environment of underwater investigations.

Some papers looking at the characteristics of under-water investigations highlight the fact that there is not enough differentiation between maritime archaeology and archaeology carried out in other environments. Gianfrotta and Pomey (1981, 10–11), for example, state that 'aims, methods and fundamental principles' also 'define archaeology as a historical discipline' (or if you prefer as an anthropological-historical one). It makes sense therefore to consider all these aspects together when considering the identity of maritime archaeology.

Let us turn to the intrinsic qualities and informative value of underwater contexts, which are the only ways to open up new and original perspectives on this specific type of archaeology. Some important points deserve reflection first of all. The initial point relates to the characteristics of the environment within which the investigation is undertaken, but not the issues linked to the excavation itself. The very nature of this research, linked as it is to the presence of water, produces a slightly unstable framework compared to the more solid characteristics of the actual evidence. To expand this point, the potentialities of these sites are not always clear, especially in the Mediterranean, as the recording systems are inevitably complex, and not the same as for a traditional archaeological survey. Galasso for example, who in 1998 set out a framework for the study of post Medieval underwater archaeology (Galasso 1998), stressed the disparity of the information available for these centuries, and the lack of attention given in general to the majority of these shipwrecks in Italy.

The evidence from these anaerobic contexts can potentially throw light on material culture from the post-Medieval period, but archaeologists seem to find it difficult to place this evidence within the known contexts from other excavations. For the modern age, comparisons between large groups of objects frequently end up being auto-referential, and are sometimes usable only through reference to iconographic and encyclopedic sources. However, the information potential is still very rich when compared to some contemporary situations from different types of archaeological contexts, and it highlights the fundamental importance of shipwreck evidence beyond simply providing chronological markers. Some specific characteristics exist within this discipline, such as lakes, lagoons, rivers, seas, port archaeology and even the archaeology of humid environments, which is largely characterized by the same basic denominators as underwater archaeology, such as the well preserved nature of perishable materials. Each of these characteristics needs to be considered independently according to the environment where they were deposited. Another issue, perhaps more significant, is represented by the historical value of the evidence. The nature of the underwater contexts of shipwrecks means they lack complex formation processes, but instead they have a special historical value which is frequently assessed through a combination of research instruments (archives, historical and archaeological sources) that take advantage of the well-known historical environments within which many important shipwrecks are placed. However, historical archaeology has investigated planes and recent war wrecks (such as the seaplane shot down in the first phases of the Pearl Harbor battle: see Rodgers, Coble, Van Tilburg 1998). In other words, the evidence from a documentary point of view often aids the analysis of the archaeological material gathered from shipwrecks.

The specific characteristics of underwater contexts, beyond the methods used for their analysis, are of course peculiar to the discipline and include rapidly formed stratigraphy, spoliation trenches only in specific cases, relatively closed contexts or at least those formed within a very brief span of time with very specific sets of characteristics informed by unique social, economic, military or technological considerations.

For instance the shipwreck recovered near Grado (Giacobelli 1997) was filled with wasters of Roman glass (2nd century AD) and the Serçe Limani shipwreck was filled with Islamic glass (Bass 1984). These contexts provide large assemblages of material which document the trade of glass wasters, almost on an industrial level and at the same time they present us with an exceptional view of the material in use during these periods that can also be studied from an archaeometric viewpoint. Exceptional situations aside, these cargoes interest scholars beyond the discipline of maritime archaeology, and inform us about processes of commercialization in the wider sense. For instance mapping the circulation of Roman amphorae in the Mediterranean is based on the integration of data relating to shipwrecks and data recovered from land excavations (Panella 1998). Sketching out the dynamics of trade is one of the main priorities for researchers dealing with larger archaeology questions. A recent study on this issue looked at Mediterranean trade during the Lombard and Carolingian ages, using material from the excavations of the port of Comacchio (Gelichi 2008; 2009). This investigation has

Figure 0.1. Stari Bar. Pottery from Deruta (after Gelichi ed. 2005, 29).

transformed our knowledge of the economy and society of Northern Italy during a poorly studied period in Italian history. In this case the structures of the port provided invaluable insights, despite the lack of methodology in the original investigation.

Underwater archaeology was not directly used here, but the site provides a framework for research in maritime archaeology. In particular the investigation of trade demonstrates wider economic patterns which can be traced in other Mediterranean contexts, and sometimes also in other geographical maritime contexts, highlighting political and economic phases of expansion or decline and relationships between different regions.

The excavations of the Ca'Foscari University in Stari Bar (an abandoned city in Montenegro) have revealed, for example, the economic character of the place through evidence of imported goods along the commercial maritime trade routes. These imports continued from the late medieval period until the 20th century, but little material evidence exists, in general only pottery and glass (D'amico 2005; Baudo, Grandi, Bagato, Fresia 2006). The economic contexts suggest a mechanism of distribution which, in the late medieval period and in the early modern period, sees intense activity in the triangle between Venice, Ancona and Ragusa (Anselmi 1969) (Figure 0.1).

But a comparison with the late 15th- and 16th-century material recovered from several shipwrecks on the Croatian coast (Brusić 2006; Radić Rossi 2006; Gluscević 2006) and above all with that of Gnalić (Gustin, Gelichi 2006) in the sea near Biograd, reveals a series of data which tell a different story. The Gnalić shipwreck, which is now well known due to the wealth of published information, was armed and loaded with reasonably common objects such as glasses, window furniture and pottery, as well as more luxury items such as lamps, fine glassware, drapes, trinket boxes, semi-finished materials and minerals

Figure 0.2. Coils of brass wire (after The Venetian Shipwreck at Gnalić, *2004, 74)*

Figure 0.3. Parts of the chandeliers (after The Venetian Shipwreck at Gnalić, *2004, 55).*

(Figure 0.2). This cargo tells us a lot about the economic context. For instance the quantity of semi-worked materials and metallic objects is exceptional and they probably come from outside Venice (Figure 0.3). This ship was active during a tense political period in the Mediterranean and the Adriatic, when politico-military issues connected to the Turkish occupation and the expansion of the European continental navy affected commerce and trade (Braudel 1976, 2239). This period also belongs to a new phase of oceanic trade, which saw expansion in a few decades and the inclusion of nations such as the English. Trade was transformed through the exportation of finished goods towards Asiatic ports and the exchange of goods from these territories. At this time the Italian economy was characterized by the exportation of semi-finished goods and raw materials, and by a decrease in the trade of finished goods (Romano 1998).

In a world which increasingly invested in mercantile activity, where private commercial organizations had a powerful effect on the human economy, and European governments had new issues to deal with (Sutton 2000), a progressive economic polarization seems to occur between Italy and other states of Europe, and a sort of militarization of political and economic activities. The specific characteristics of the goods traded provide useful indicators for tracing such economic patterns.

Among the countries which develop wider commercial networks, we see the exploitation of overseas areas within a conservative framework; others develop strong internal dynamics. Great Britain, for instance, saw a reorganization of agricultural property and national manufacturing activities in a mercantile and capitalistic sense (Johnson 1990).

In 1500, in Italy, land followed a process of re-feudalization (Cazzola 1987), and subsistence-living coexisted with wage incomes. This was to the detriment of a mercantile and productive economy, which instead until the end of the Middle Ages resulted in a degree of capitalistic development in some areas (Braudel 1976, 2114–2116).

We cannot use one single shipwreck to map out the dynamics of trade on an international level (similar shipwrecks are not yet fully published), but it is still useful for archaeology in a wider geographic sense to use this example to look at economic questions, though other significant issues linked to shipwreck evidence, such as the architecture and technology of the ships should also be considered. A final important aspect is the social complexity of the cargoes, where we see the goods for trade mixed up with the daily objects used by the crew. The evidence displays many different types of objects, and it is not always possible to distinguish the crew's property from the cargo in the mix of pottery, weapons and pewter.

To conclude, it seems that underwater archaeology interacts very well with other types of archaeological evidence, and can add significantly to the debate and analysis of fundamental questions. Clearly the logistics of underwater archaeology and its unique environment make analysis a very complex and expensive exercise, and few fully excavated shipwrecks exist for comparison. However it is surely better to exploit this valuable evidence where it exists than to relegate it to discussions on purely technical issues.

References

Anselmi, S. (1969) Venezia, Ragusa, Ancona tra Cinque e Seicento: un momento della storia mercantile del Medio Adriatico. *Atti e Memorie della Deputazione di storia patria per le Marche*, Serie VIII, vol. VI (1968–69).

Auriemma, R. (2004) *Salentum a salo. Forma Maris Antiqui.* Galatina, Congedo.

Bass, G. F. (1984) The Nature of the Serçe Limani Glass. *Journal of Glass Studies* 26, 64–69.

Baudo, F., Grandi, E., Bagato, C., Fresia, S. (2006) 3. The fortifications of Bar. Archaeological evidence from gate 112. In S. Gelichi (ed.) *The Archaeology of an Abandoned Town. The 2005 Project in Stari Bar*, 33–54. Firenze, All'Insegna del Giglio.

Braudel, F. (1976) L'Italia fuori dall'Italia. Due secoli e tre Italie In *Storia d'Italia*, 2, 2092–2248. Torino, Einaudi.

Brusić Z. (2006) Tre naufragi del XVII o XVIII secolo lungo la costa Adriatica orientale. In M. Guštin, S. Gelichi and K. Spindler (eds) *The Heritage of the Serenissima*, 77–84. Koper, Zalozba Annales.

Cazzola, F. (1987) Il "ritorno alla terra". In *Il tramonto del Rinascimento, Storia della società italiana*, vol. X, 103–168. Milano, Teti.

D'Amico, E. (2005) The excavation of UTS 161. The pottery. In S. Gelichi, M. Guštin (eds.) *Stari Bar. The Archaeological Project 2004. Preliminary Report*, 61–78. Firenze, All'Insegna del Giglio.

Galasso, M. (1998) Archeologia subacquea postmedievale: problemi di approccio e *status quaestionis. Archeologia Postmedievale* 2, 177–186.

Galasso, M. (1999) Archeologia subacquea post-medievale. Modelli culturali, Internet e bibliografia on line. *Archeologia Postmedievale* 3, 245–271.

Gelichi, S. (ed.) (2005) *The Archaeology of an Abandoned Town. The 2005 Project in Stari Bar*. Firenze.

Gelichi, S. (2008) The eels of Venice. The long eighth century of the emporia of the northern region along the Adriatic coast. In S. Gasparri (ed.) *774. Ipotesi su una transizione*, Poggibonsi 2006, 81–118. Turnhout.

Gelichi, S. (ed.) (2009) *L'isola del Vescovo,. Gli scavi archeologici intorno alla Cattedrale di Comacchio.* Firenze, All'Insegna del Giglio.

Gelichi, S., Librenti, M. (eds.) (2007) *Constructing Post-medieval Archaeology in Italy, Proceedings of the International Conference, Venice 2006*. Florence, All'Insegna del Giglio.

Giacobelli, M. (1997) I vetri del relitto di Grado. In AIASub (ed.) *Atti del convegno nazionale di archeologia subacquea, Anzio 1996*, 311–314. Bari, Edipuglia.

Gianfrotta, P. A, Pomey, P. (1981) *Archeologia subacquea: storia, tecniche, scoperte e relitti.* Milano, Mondadori.

Gluscević, S. 2006, Alcuni ritrovamenti medievali e postmedievali dagli abissi dell'Adriatico orientale croato. In M. Guštin, S. Gelichi and K. Spindler (eds.) *The Heritage of the Serenissima*, 73–76. Koper, Zalozba Annales.

Hall, M., Silliman, S. W. (eds.) (2006) *Historical Archaeology.* Oxford, Wiley-Blackwell.

Hicks, D., Beaudry, M. C. (eds.) (2006) *The Cambridge Companion to Historical Archaeology.* Cambridge, Cambridge University Press.

Johnson, M. (1990) *An Archaeology of Capitalism.* Oxford, Blackwell.

Panella, C. (1998) Anfore e archeologia subaquea. In G. Volpe (ed.) *Archeologia subacquea – Come opera l'archeologo sott'acqua. Storie dalle acque, VIII Ciclo di Lezioni sulla Ricerca applicata in Archeologia (Certosa di Pontignano 1996)*, 531–556. Firenze. All'Insegna del Giglio.

Parker, A. J. (1992) *Ancient Shipwrecks of the Mediterranean and the Roman Provinces* (BAR, In. Series 589). Oxford.

Radić Rossi, I. (2006) Il relitto di una nave mercantile presso l'isola di Kolocep. In M. Guštin, S. Gelichi and K. Spindler (eds.) *The Heritage of the Serenissima*, 85–90. Koper, Zalozba Annales.

Rodgers, B. A., Coble, W. M., Van Tilburg, H. K (1998) The Lost Flying Boat of Kaneohe Bay: Archaeology of the First U. S. Casualties of Pearl Harbor. *Historical Archaeology* 32/4, 8–18.

Romano, R. (1998) Prefazione. In S. Cavaciocchi (ed.) *Prodotti e tecniche d'Oltremare nelle economie europee, secc. 13.–18,* Istituto Internazionale di Storia Economica F. Datini, Prato, Atti delle Settimane di Studio e altri convegni, 14–19 aprile 1997, 29. Firenze, Le Monnier.

Sutton, J. (2000) *Lords of the East: the East India Company and its ships, 1600–1874.* London, Conway maritime company.

The Venetian Shipwreck at Gnalić (2004) *Annales Mediterranea.* Koper.

Volpe, G. (1998) Archeologia subacquea e commerci in età tardoantica. In G. Volpe (ed.) *Archeologia subacquea – Come opera l'archeologo sott'acqua. Storie dalle acque, VIII Ciclo di Lezioni sulla Ricerca applicata in Archeologia (Certosa di Pontignano 1996)*, 561–626. Firenze. All'Insegna del Giglio.

Volpe, G. (ed.) (1998) *Archeologia subacquea – Come opera l'archeologo sott'acqua. Storie dalle acque, VIII Ciclo di Lezioni sulla Ricerca applicata in Archeologia (Certosa di Pontignano 1996)*. Firenze. All'Insegna del Giglio.

Morphology and Constructive Techniques of Venetian Artilleries in the 16th and 17th Centuries: some notes

Marco Morin

VENETIAN ARTILLERY. – Early guns were of very rude construction. The successive improvements, so for as they can be traced, originated is the north of Italy, and Venice certainly had a large share in bringing them into the practice of war. The brothers Alberghetti, celebrated at first as artists in metal, to whose skill we owe those beautiful fountains in the court of the Ducal Palace which still delight the eye of the traveller, were induced to turn their attention to the casting of guns: and the introduction of boring machines is attributed to them. Leonardo da Vinci also, whose fame as an engineer is less than as a painter only in so far as his works were of a less popular nature, devised several improvements in the manufacture and management of artillery, which were easily reduced to practice by the Venetian workmen; and although he himself does not seem to have been in this immediate service of the Venetian Government still, as his plans became known, and his treatise on gunnery – probably the first scientific work on the subject – was published, he was really and effectively in the service of every Government whose officers had the brains into understand his teachings, or whose workmen had the hands to execute them; in which category the Venetians were pre-eminently included. Toward the end of the sixteenth century they introduced what must be considered as a primitive form of howitzer. for firing grape. It is described by Graziani as a sort of cask of very thick wood. barely a cubit in length, and of about the same bore as a mortar. It must thus have been, inside, about the size of a nine-gallon beer-barrel. This was loaded with leaden balls, and stones as large as an egg. And said to have done good service in into the battle of Lepanto; "on board those ships on which this horrible hail fell it made terrible havoc." (from *Fraser's Magazine* as quoted by *New York Times*, October 31, 1875.)

Introduction

This piece of newspaper writing of about 135 years ago, if, as far as accuracy is concerned, does not diverge a great deal from contemporary routine journalism, nevertheless shows how the importance of Venice in the field of guns and gunnery was, already in the past, widely and popularly perceived. Actually the Serenissima Repubblica, for centuries the most important Italian state and one of the major European countries, invested a huge amount of money and efforts in her heavy armaments and in the production of the necessary gunpowder. Moreover, this example contains a number of errors. In the court of the Ducal Palace there were two wells and not two fountains and the bronze well-heads were cast one by Alfonso Alberghetti and the other one by Niccolo di Conti. Leonardo da Vinci did not devise several improvements in the manufacture and management of artillery, and the primitive form of howitzer for firing grape was not used at Lepanto. We shall leave this catalogue of mistakes to military historians and get back to our main topic.

For the period discussed here, an investigation of the European artilleries reveals a generally notable morpho–logical similarity for which, in absence of writings and/or coats of arms, an origin is not always easily recog–nisable.

As far as the Venetian pieces are concerned, however, they disclose some distinctive peculiarities that can be of significant help to the underwater archaeologist, especially where bronze cast ordnance is concerned. However, first of all, we must analyze in some detail the various types of artillery in use from the second half the 15th century until the end of the 17th century. A first division can be appreciated between pieces made in iron and pieces made in bronze: the iron ones can be divided into those made by wrought iron and those realized by fusion cast.

Wrought iron is a two-component metal consisting of high purity iron and iron silicate – an inert, non-rusting slag similar to glass. These two materials are merely mixed and not chemically joined as in an alloy. Slag constitutes 1% to 3% and is in the form of small fibres up to 20,000 per inch of cross section. For hammer-welding wrought iron, the technique universally used for large and small pieces, see Smith and R. Rhynas Brown (1989).

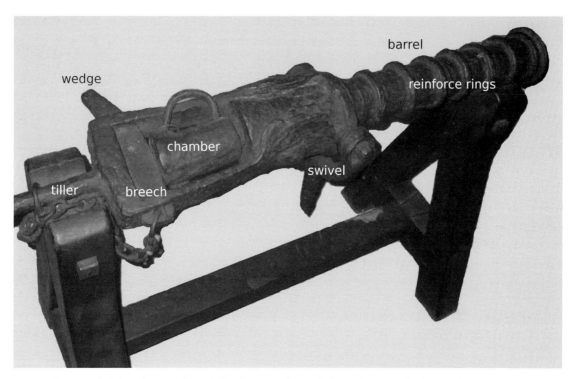

Figure 1.1. Wrought iron breech-loader swivel gun (Museo Nazionale di Artiglieria, Turin).

Wrought iron is an easy material to work by forging and the best results are obtained at temperatures in the range of 1150 to 1315°C. Wrought iron elements can be welded together without difficulty, always by forging. Structurally, wrought iron is a composite material as the base metal and fibres of slag are in physical association, in dissimilarity to the chemical or alloy relationship that generally exists between the constituents of other metals.

Wrought iron guns were made by the hoop-and-stave method: they were usually breech-loaders, using removable iron chambers with touchholes – containing the gunpowder and closed by wooden wadding. A stone cannonball or scattershot was placed in the barrel. The chamber was locked in place by a wooden wedge, in the bombards placed in wooden carriages or by an iron one in the full metallic pieces (Figure 1.1). These wedges had to be hammered in position in order to force the chamber against the barrel: each weapon was equipped with at least two chambers and so the firing rate was superior in comparison with similar calibre muzzle-loaders. Swivel pieces of this general type were used as railing pieces on large merchantmen and were the basic armament of smaller ones; without significant changes, they were in use for more than three centuries and so their presence alone is not sufficient to date a wreck.

On the main fighting ship of the Mediterranean – the galley – the first gunpowder ordnance mounted was probably a wrought iron breech-loader placed at the stern in wooden balks or in timber beds used to secure the cannon and prevent recoil while firing. Examples of these kinds of artilleries are the iron bombards of the *Mary Rose* wreck (sunk in 1545) and the ones now in the Tøjhusmuseet in Copenhagen (from the so-called Anholt wreck). Bernhard von Breydenbach, a wealthy canon of the cathedral at Mainz, who journeyed to the Holy Land in 1483–4, compiled the *Peregrinatio in Terram Sanctam,* a work that was printed in 1486. The book's map of Palestine includes an enlarged illustration of the galley in which he travelled, placed appropriately at the arrival point, the port of Jaffa. Breydenbach was accompanied by Erhard Reuwich, an artist from Utrecht, who is referred to in the text as the author of the map and the six views of Mediterranean towns: Iraklion, Modone, Rhodes and Venice – all of which are folding – as well as the single-page views of Corfu and Parenzo. In the Venice map, a galley with a hooped bombard on the stern can be seen, probably the oldest visual documentation known (Figure 1.2).

In the second half of the 14th century, wrought iron muzzle-loading large bombards were built and employed (in the War of Chioggia), but we do not have positive information on their possible naval utilization.

As far as casting is concerned we know that, in the whole Venetian Terra Ferma, especially in the Brescia (ASV, Senato, Deliberazioni Terra, reg. 4, 46v 28 Luglio 1457) and in the Vicenza territories, medium and small iron muzzle-loading bombards were being produced as early as the latter part of the 15th century (Awty 2007, 788). An extraordinary pattern is provided by a group of 4 practically identical pieces, owned by the Counts da Schio and preserved in their estate of Costozza (Vicenza). These can tentatively be date to 1450–1490 and due to their peculiar morphology that reminds us of the hoop-and-stave arrangement of a cask, only an accurate X-ray investigation has allowed us to establish that this had been realized by casting and not by forging (Figures 1.3–1.4).

To find Venetian cast iron artilleries of large calibre we have to wait until 1690, when in Sarezzo of Val Trompia (Brescia), Tiburzio Bailo began activity as a gunfounder

Figure 1.2. Iron bombard on a galley (from Bernhard von Breydenbach Peregrinatio in Terram Sanctam).

Figure 1.3. Four cast iron bombards (Counts da Schio estate, Vicenza).

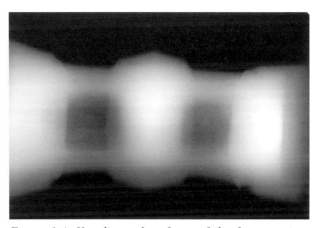

Figure 1.4. X-radiography of one of the four cast iron bombards.

with the help of Sigismondo III Alberghetti, member of the well-known bronze founder dynasty. Sigismondo III, by order of the Venetian Senate, travelled extensively in Europe to study the manufacture of cast iron artillery. In his opinion the best production was English and so, always by order of the Senate, he attended the casting of about 140 pieces of ordnance (cannons and mortars) manufactured in the Weald by Thomas Western for the Republic of Venice. These barrels can be recognised by the presence of St Mark's lion and the initials T W: among them three 18–inch surviving mortars are known in England (Blackmore 1976, 138).

The Bailo production, with the use of iron ore from the Brembana valley (the Val Trompia iron, very good for small arms barrels, was inappropriate for artillery), proved itself of an excellent quality and so, until the death of Bailo in 1708, Venice was able to supply her sail fleet with locally-produced iron artillery. After this, production was resumed by a Carlo Camozio in Clanezzo, north of Bergamo and nearer to the iron mines of the Brembana valley. Soon after

another iron cannon-foundry was established at Castro, in the north-west of the Iseo Lake, very near to the south end of the Brembana valley.

Venetian cannons of this period are similar in shape and calibres to the naval pieces casted in the rest of Europe but can be readily recognized by the lion of St. Mark and the name or initials of the gunfounders present in bas-relief on the barrels (Figure 1.5).

As far as bronze pieces are concerned they can also be divided into breech-loaders and muzzle-loaders, both obtained by fusion. As the material they were made of is both expensive and easily and infinitely recyclable, it is nearly impossible to find older specimens (14th–15th century) and our only hope is in underwater archaeology. We have information on both bronze naval and land bombards cast during the 15th century and we know that most of them

Figure 1.5. Venetian cast-iron naval gun of the 17th century from the "guns wreck" of Malamocco-Venice (photo by the author).

Figure 1.6. Cast bronze bombard (Tower of London, then Fort Nelson).

were of the two part class, probably comparable to the celebrated Great Bronze Gun, once at the Tower of London and now at Fort Nelson (Figure 1.6) (see, for example, Leonardo da Vinci's *Codex Atlanticus* 46br, 53r and 68r). Usually they were very large weapons made in two pieces, chase and breech, the two parts screwing together (ASV, Senato Terra, reg. 4, 65v, 21 febbraio 1457mv). The breech was shorter and of a somewhat inferior diameter than the chase: both parts were cast with prominent double mouldings at either end which were joined longitudinally by a number of crosspieces to form an equal quantity of sockets for the insertion of the levers used in screwing or unscrewing the two parts (Leonardo da Vinci's *Codex Atlanticus* 37r). It must be noted that, although made in two pieces, this kind of bombard was not of the breech-loading variety. Breech-loaders were of inferior size so that they could be opened without too much effort and were probably similar to iron ordnance of the same period. The same can be conjectured for muzzle-loaders at least until when, at the end of the century, trunnions were devised. Trunnions are the two projections on the side of the barrel which mount it in the carriage. As they allowed the barrel to be raised and lowered easily, and made it easier to fix it to a movable carriage, the integral casting of trunnions can be considered as one of the most important advances in early artillery.

Breech-loaders in Venice were usually of the swivel gun kind, the so-called *petriere da mascolo* and *petriere da braga*. In the former, where there would normally be the first reinforce, there was an open breech for a removable chamber; a slot on either side at the end of the breech was for the iron wedge which held the chamber in place, pressed sturdily against the bore. Another slot located in the base assured the draining of the breech during rainy weather. An iron swivel connected to the breech chamber made aiming easy (Figures 1.7 and 1.8). The name *petriera* (i.e. stone-thrower) was owed to the fact that this kind of

artillery originally shot stone balls, but later also grapeshot, firing a number of small lead balls at a short distance. It was a very effective short range weapon and, since the 16th century, Venetian galleys were armed with several 6- or 12-lb *petriere*, each one provided with 3 chambers.

The *petriera da braga* had a bronze barrel with trunnions and two symmetric ribs near the breech end: in those ribs was inserted a stout iron plate breech (the *braga*): for the rest it was similar to the *petriera da mascolo* (Figure 1.9).

The *moschetto da braga* was similar to the *petriera*, but of smaller calibre, usually a 1-pounder.

Before proceeding with our discussion it is important to note that the Venetian artillery denominations differed from those used outside its border. This is a problem since, as pointed out, for example, by Michael Lewis in his *Armada Guns* (1961), 15–16 "*.. nothing less than a full-dress monograph could deal ... with Elizabethan ordnance classification ...*". This is due principally to "*... the careless and erratic nomenclature employed by the contemporary writers, and, probably, by contemporary gunners, and even the gun-founders.*"

It must be remembered that terms like demi-cannon, whole cannon, demi-culverin, bastard culverin, etc. were never used in Venice. An English scholar, Brian G. Awty, of the Wealden Iron Research Group (2003), suggests that:

"*Another advantage of the Wealden guns was that they were made in the modern profile of the bronze guns cast at the Arsenal in Venice under the superintendence of Bernardo della Scuola. Scuola had commanded the magnificent French artillery train brought to Italy by Charles VIII in 1494, but was appointed Master of the artillery at Venice in 1496. The modern profile of gun is at once apparent in the two bronze culverins dated 1497 cast by Sigismondo Alberghetti, which now survive only in the form of Domenico Gasperoni's exquisite engraving*".

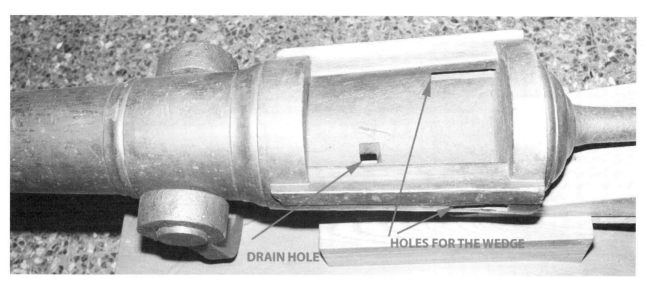

Figure 1.7. A bronze petriera da mascolo *(Museo Storico Navale, Venice).*

Figure 1.8 (left). Bronze petriera da mascolo *(Museo Storico Navale, Venice).*

Figure 1.9 (above). The iron "braga" of a 12 libbre petriera *(Museo Storico Navale, Venice).*

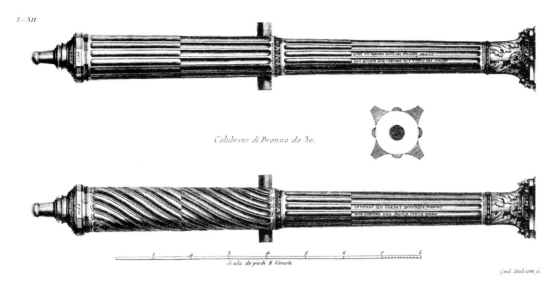

Figure 1.10. Two bronze culverins cast by Sigismondo Alberghetti (after Gasparoni 1779, table 13).

Indeed the two bronze culverins illustrated by the engraver Giuliano Zuliani (1730–1814) in table XII of the various copies of Domenico Gasperoni's manuscript *Artiglierie Venete*, were probably cast by Sigismondo Alberghetti II approximately one hundred years later: the date MCCCCLXXXXVII casted in the print on the central astragal is most likely an oversight of the artist (Figure 1.10). Furthermore Basilio della Scuola (and not Bernardo) was certainly not appointed "Master of the artillery", a rank that never existed in Venice. Basilio was a military engineer from Vicenza and commander of the French ordnance: banned from the Venetian Territory for reasons still unknown, in June 1495 he secretly offered the Council of Ten (ASV, Consiglio dei Dieci, Parti Miste, reg.26, 166r, June 28, 1495) to burn all King Charles VIII's gunpowder, thus destroying the French war materials. His offer was accepted and on the 9th December of the same year he was issued a one hundred years (!) safe-conduct (ASV, ibid., *ibid.*, 196v). He probably did not succeed in blowing up the French artillery train but he was employed to reorganize the Venetian land artillery (Mallet and Hale, 2006, Sanudo 1879).

> *"And it was started to make some artilleries to be used to attack places just as it is normally done with the huge bombards, artilleries that are carried on wagons the way the French are used to do.*
>
> *They are almost as long as passavolanti are, but bigger. They shoot balls weighting from 6 to 12 lbs and they remain always (also when they are fired) on said wagons.*
>
> *And it must be known that Basilio da la Scola from Vicenza was in this nation, he had been superintendent of the ordnance of the king of France, and so it was started to cast in Cannaregio (a zone of Venice) one hundred of said artilleries and Basilio was sent in our mainland with letters in order to fetch the lumber for the wagons that are being manufactured in Padua."*

Among the muzzle-loaders we find the following culverin-kind guns (the *artiglierie colubrinate* were one third longer and heavier than the corresponding calibre cannons):

– the *moschetto da 1 libbra* (robinet), a swivel gun with a calibre of approximately 45 mm and a length of 1 m;
– the *moschetto da zuogo,* a 1-pounder with a calibre between 42 and 45 mm and a length between 140 and 160 cm; it was also used to train the *scolari bombardieri* (new-enrolled artillerymen) and, when over-bored by use, the calibre was increased to that of a falconet and then used on board of galleys as such;
– the *falconetto* (falconet), a 3-pounder with a calibre of 50–55 mm and a length between 140 and 160 cm;
– the *falcone* (falcon), a 6-pounder with a calibre of 62–65 mm and a length between 150 and 170 cm;
– the *sacro* (saker), a 12-pounder with a calibre of 95–100 mm and a length between 210 and 270 cm;
  the *colubrina* (culverin), of 14 (107 mm), 16 (116 mm), 20 (124 mm), 30 (140 mm), 40 (153 mm), 50 (170,5 mm), 60 (179 mm), 90 (190 mm), 100 (207 mm) and 120 pounds (215 mm). The figures in brackets indicate the approximate diameter of the bores obtained from both direct measurements and printed or manuscript sources (Figures 1.11–1.14).

Cannons were roughly speaking one-third shorter and lighter than culverins of the same calibre: a 12–lb *aspide* had a length not far off from 170 cm and a weight on the order of 560 kg while the corresponding "*sacro*" could be long up to 250 cm (sometimes more) with a weight of 880 kg.

While the calibre of Venetian military artillery was carefully respected, weight and length could be dissimilar: the lighter pieces were set aside for naval service while the heavier were employed for land use in fortresses and walled towns.

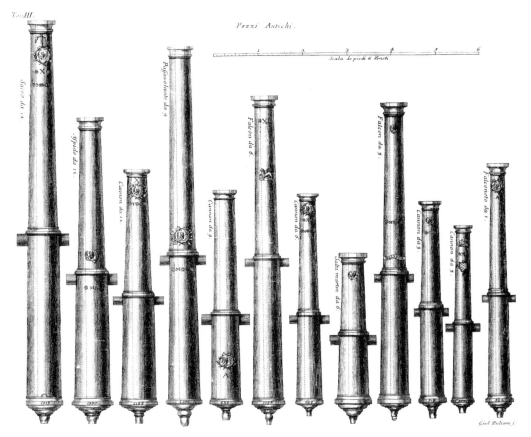

Figure 1.11. "Ancient" Venetian bronze pieces (after Gasparoni 1779, table 3).

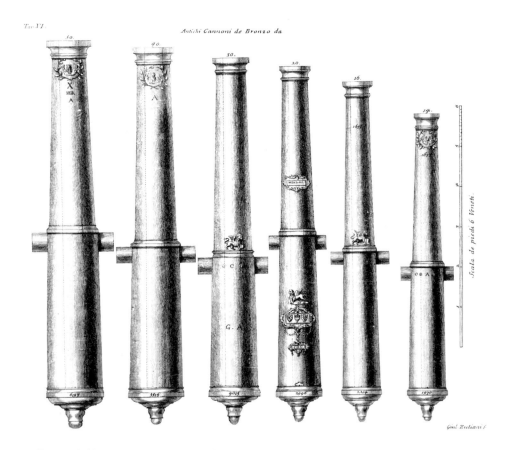

Figure 1.12. "Ancient" Venetian bronze cannons (after Gasparoni 1779, table 6).

Marco Morin

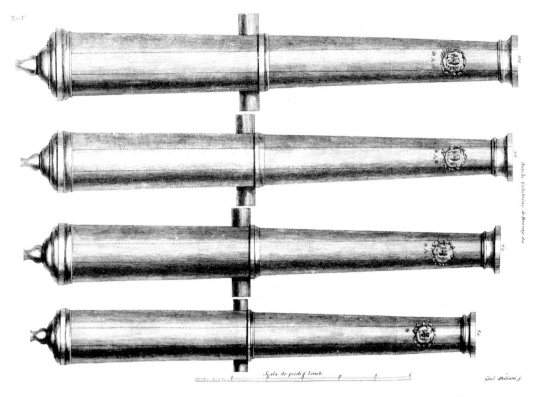

Figure 1.13. *"Ancient" Venetian bronze Culverins. (after Gasparoni 1779, table 5).*

Figure 1.14. *A 60 libbre Venetian cannon (Museo Storico Navale, Venice).*

For up to 12-lb pieces, the designation of the calibre was given by the weight of the lead ball that was shot in a forced test of the same piece: a sacro was submitted, for instance, to the test with lead balls of the weight of 12 thin or light Venetian pounds (1 pound = 301.2 g), while in practical use it shot balls of cast iron of equal diameter that, however, for the different specific weight of the two metals, actually weighed 9 lb.

For the artilleries of superior calibre, the test was carried out with the same iron balls that were to be normally used and, therefore, the designation denotes the weight in pounds of these last.

All these data refer to government-manufactured artilleries destined for naval and land military employment; the measures of those produced for civilians and destined to arm the merchant boats, on which we currently lack information, could vary in length and weight in relationship to the particular specifications supplied by the buyer.

Some documents testify to the existence of muzzle-loading perriers (*petrieri*) of middle to large calibre, but they deal with infrequent cases: in an important printed work (Ruscelli 1572) we find *petrieri* with calibres of 250, 200, 100 and 30 lb listed. In order to appreciate the dimensions and the main peculiarities let us consider the data, given at page 39r of the said work, regarding a 100–lb *petriere*.

"The weight of a 100–pound petriere should be 3920 lb, the length (must be) of 14 balls, that is 7 feet and 4.5 inches. At the breech (the diameter must be) 1 foot and half inch and the chamber (must have a calibre) of 20 pounds. It worth 316 ducats...."

From this same source we are informed that a 100 lb *colubrina* weighs 13,000 lb and measures in length 13½ feet in length (6,200 kg and 4.7 m); the proper value is of over 1227 ducats. A cannon of the same calibre had a weight of 11,000 lb and a length of 12 feet (5,250 kg and 4.18 m); the price was of over 1038 ducats. Even if the data related to the *colubrine* do not appear entirely acceptable, it easy to understand that the *petriere* was much shorter and lighter than the *colubrine* and cannon of equal calibre. The chase was thinner and the chamber, the inside portion where was housed the gunpowder charge, was of inferior diameter.

Venetian bronze artillery was considered to be the best of the Mediterranean world, second in Europe only to the German; and this merely, as has been suggested by contemporary authors, because the humidity of the Lagoon hindered the perfect desiccation of the moulds. The Republic was buying the best copper that could be found on the market, usually from Hungary where the local mines had a production of *"exceptionally good quality"* metal (Agoston 2005, 171). Copper of inferior characteristic from the Venetian mines of Agordo was used only in emergency when better material was not readily at hand, while tin was invariably delivered from the English mines of Cornwall.

Samples of metal obtained in 1974 from some pieces belonging to the Museo Storico Navale (Venice) and the National Museum of Artillery (Turin), were sent to Major John Guilmartin USAF, well known researcher of military history and now professor of Modern History at the Ohio University. Guilmartin submitted the samples for a semi-quantitative chemical analysis at the Frank J. Seiler Research Laboratory of the USAF Academy and very interesting results were obtained.

The bronze

The alloy used during the 19th century for the construction of the most recent bronze artilleries contained 80 fractions of copper, 10 of tin, 1 of silicon and 2 of zinc: this last element, according to some modern authors, makes for easier fusion and less porous alloy. The silicon, in varying percentages from 0.03 to 1.5%, acts as a reducer for the oxides present in the melt and permits the alloy to increase its hardness and resistance.

In the 16th century, the Venetian gunfounders, added 10% in weight of brass to the liquified copper and tin. The brass (*laton* in Venice) was produced by melting copper and calamine (*giallamina*, a hydrated hortosilicate of zinc: pure zinc was isolated only in 1746). In this way zinc and silicon was added to the alloy, resulting in a less porous, harder and more resistant metal. In a document of the 16th century we can actually read:

"If you want to cast artillery you need for every thousand pounds of copper eighty pounds of tin and one hundred pounds of brass .."

According to a manuscript (ASV Secreta, Materie Miste Notabili, busta 18bis) written by Giulio Savorgnan, a famous military leader of the Serenissima, bronze alloy was prepared with copper and 8–12% of tin, but *"In Venice they add 10% of brass to improve the melt as the copper, is not as perfect as the one used in Germany."*. The information is interesting as it confirms that the copper of Agordo, despite the refinement to which it was submitted, was of an inferior quality in comparison to that of the Tirol and Hungary.

It is interesting to note how the price of the copper raised from 40 ducats per 100 lb in 1510 to 70/80 ducats in 1521: this increase is tied in with the heavy politics of monopoly implemented by the Fuggers and the Hochstetters, international mercantile bankers and venture capitalists of the period, after the wars of the League of Cambrai. Other strategic products, such as saltpetre (the most important and most expensive component of gunpowder) did not increase in price. In 1504 it was 29 ducats per 1000 lb; in 1521 the saltpetre imported from Puglia was bought at 28 ducats. We can ascribe the doubling of copper prices mainly to the international success of bronze artilleries and the consequential increased requirement of necessary pieces to arm a rising number of fortresses and larger sized military fleets.

The results of the analysis were consistent with manuscript and printed sources: the presence of silicon and zinc was constant although with considerable differences in percentage due to the fact that the samples were taken from different parts of the barrels.

It disclosed a presence of tin at concentration between 3.9 and 11%: the quantitative analysis related to sampling of the mouth of a culverin cast by Sigismondo II Alberghetti can be seen in Table 1.1. As is evident from Table 1.1, there is the presence, in noticeable quantities, of zinc, lead, antimony, iron, nickel, antimony, silver, manganese and silicon.

Since the sampling of each single piece had been effected – for reasons for opportunity – in different areas of the gun, these results have to be take into account

Table 1.1.

piece	year	% Sn	% Zn	% Sb	% Pb	% Ni	% Ag	% Fe	% Si
P 221	<1571	5	0.2	0.2	0.1	0.1	< 0.1	0.02	0.01
P 222	<1571	4	0.8	**00.5**	0.2	**00.5**	<0.1	0.01	0.01

Figure 1.15. Initials of Venetian gunfounders and other marks.

with extreme caution. We have to keep in mind that, in a bronze article of great dimensions, obtained by fusion, it is not possible to determine the exact composition of the metal from the analysis of a superficial zone. Let us consider what happens during the fusion of a bronze containing 10% tin. Pure copper has a point of fusion of 1,083°C, or rather it is only at this temperature that solid copper directly turns into liquid copper. The presence of tin lowers the point of fusion bringing it, according to the concentration, to values ranging between 820°C and 1,030°C. In this way when, during the cooling process the temperature of the liquid alloy drops to 1,030°C, we have the separation of a solid. This will be a solid fraction (α) rich in copper because a bronze with a 2% concentration of tin begins to solidify at 1,030°C, while a solution richer in tin, with a inferior point of fusion, will remain in liquid state.

Thus, during the solidification process, the present elements (copper and tin) will separate and at last we shall have the solidification of liquid phases rich in tin: just about half of the bronze solidifies as phase (α), then the rest of the liquid alloy, risen to a tin concentration of the 18%, solidifies in a transitory phase (β) which, in turn decomposes in a mixture of phases (α) and (δ).

This is the reason why, in long objects cast in vertical position as artillery was, the composition is not homogeneous: the analysis of material recovered on the surface does not furnish valid information for the whole mass.

The Venetian muzzle-loading bronze gun

Large bronze muzzle-loading artillery cast in Venice for Government use is easily identifiable; what follows is a list of the main features that can be usefully employed to recognise this kind of ordnance.

– The constant lack of dolphins;
– The presence of only one reinforce;
– The lion of St Mark, both "*in moleca*" (head, torso and wings in a round or oval background) or "*andante*" (complete body with the Gospel) usually on the chase;
– The name or the initials of the gunfounder, sometimes on the chase, sometimes on the reinforce;
– The weight in Venetian heavy pounds (*libbre alla grossa*; 1 pound = 477 g) engraved on the base ring;
– The roman digit X, logo of the Council of Ten that, until 1586, was in charge of the state artillery (Figure 1.15).
– The presence or absence of this last feature permits us to date *ante quo* or *post quo* 1586 all the state owned bronze artillery. The presence of the coats of arms of the *Provveditori alle Artegliarie*, one until 1586, three afterwards, can be very useful.

The gunfounders

As it has been stated above, in all known Venetian artillery the name or the initials of the gunfounder is present, generally between small roses.

In 16th- to 17th-century Venice, the members of two families only, the *Alberghetti* and the *di Conti* (and their 17th-century relatives, the *Mazzaroli*) were active in this manufacturing domain. As far as the initials are concerned therefore, we are able, for instance, to find the following letters: * A * (family *Alberghetti*, certainly the work of one or more active members working in the same foundry), * S * A * (*Sigismondo Alberghetti*), * Z * A* (*Zuanne Alberghetti*), * N * C * (*Nicolò di Conti*), * T * C * (*Tomaso di Conti*), and so on.

With the help of the genealogies so far published (Morin

1983; Avery 2003) and using the above-mentioned general features it can be often possible to recognize the author.

Armament of the main warship, the Galley

To give an idea of what kind of artillery can be found on a military wreck of the period we are dealing with, we shall now examine briefly the normal armament of a standard warship.

During the 16th century, the principal military ship of the Mediterranean Sea, and therefore of the Serenissima, was the galley. Named in Venice *galea sottile* (thin or light galley) to distinguish it from merchantmen, heavier and higher at boards – we remember that *galee grosse* regularly faced the Atlantic to reach the Flanders and England – this had two masts equipped with Latin sails. During battles, in the manoeuvres of entrance and exit from the harbours and in cases of absolute calm and windless weather, she was propelled by 160–200 rowers (*galeotti*) and could reach a speed of 7/8 knots for brief time periods. The length of the hull varied between 40 and 45 m; its width fluctuated between the 5 and 6.7 metres.

Between 1290 and 1540 the standard Venetian galleys were triremes with 25 or 30 benches on each side, and three oarsmen to a bench, each man pulling a separate oar. The galley had but one deck. That was divided into three parts, a fighting platform in the bow, a larger and higher stern castle and, in between, the rowing space running almost the whole length of the galley. This last sector was divided, lengthwise, by a gangway (*corsia*) down to the centre. The deck space available for oars and rowers extended out beyond the sides of the live work of the hull, for the timbers on which the oars rested, the outriggers frames (*postizo*), were placed out over the water supported by brackets which rose from the beam ends (Lane 1934, 93).

Due to the long and thin form of the hull, the galley could carry heavy artillery only at the bow. The largest piece, a cannon or a culverin, was placed in the *corsia* mounted on a particular type of gun carriage similar to a sleigh, entirely deprived of wheels. On firing the piece recoiled and skidded along the *corsia* until it come to stop slightly and not always, against the main mast, protected at its base by a special pad of cordage (*stramazeto*).

Close to the *corsiero* two sakers or two *aspidi* and two falcons were positioned on swivel mounts while two *falconetti* were similarly positioned at the stern; a certain number of muskets and *petriere* was placed in the various side zones of the *postizo*. All these pieces were fixed to the

bulwarks or, as far as the larger bow ones are concerned, to a thick structure probably connected to the hull.

A galley's armament could vary depending the size of the ship, its employment and the availability of the various pieces. For instance in 1540, the galley of the provveditore Bondumier, probably a very large one, was armed with a 50-lb culverin, two 12-lb sakers, six 12-lb *aspidi*, one *moschetto da zuogo* and 36 1-lb robinets (ASV – CX, parti comuni, reg. 13, 216r, 1 Ottobre 1540). In 1543 (ASV – CX, parti comuni, reg. 15, 130R, 28 Marzo 1543) the galley of the provveditore Giustinian was armed with a 100-lb cannon, two 12-lb *aspidi*, two 6-lb falcons, seven 3-lb falconets, four *moschetti da zuogo* and 29 breech loader robinets (*moschetti da braga*). In 1568 (ASV – CX, parti comuni, reg. 28, 133r, 31 Agosto 1568) the galley of Giacomo Celsi was armed with a 60-lb culverin, two 16 lb cannons, three 6-lb falcons, two 3-lb falconets, two *moschetti da zuogo*, two 6-lb *petriera*, fourteen 3-lb *perriers*, eight breech-loader robinets (*moschetti da braga*).

Abbreviations

ASV: Archivio di Stato di Venezia

References

Agoston, G. (2005) *Guns for the Sultan*. Cambridge.

Avery, V. (2003) State and Private Bronze Foundries in Cinque-cento Venice: New Light on the Alberghetti and di Conti Workshops. In P. Motture (ed.) *Large Bronzes in the Renaissance*, proceedings – Washington, 15–16 October 1999 (*Studies in the History of Art*, 64), 241–275. Washington.

Awty, B. G. (2003) The breakthrough of the 1540s in the casting of iron ordnance. *Journal of the Ordnance Society* 15, 19–27.

Awty, B. G. (2007) The Development And Dissemination of the Walloon Method of Ironworking. *Technology and Culture*, vol. 48, October, 783–803.

Blackmore, H. L. (1976) *The Armouries of the Tower of London*, I *Ordnance*. London.

Gasperoni, D. (1779) *Artiglieria veneta*. Venice.

Lane. F. C. (1934) *Venetian Ships and Shipbuilders of the Renaissance*. Baltimore.

Lewis, M. (1961) *Armada Guns*. London.

Mallet, M. E. and Hale J. R. (2006) *The Military Organisation of a Renaissance State*. Cambridge.

Morin, M. (1983) Entry Alberghetti. In *Algemeines Kunsterlexicon*, vol I, 779–784. Leipzig.

Ruscelli, G. (1572) *Precetti della Militia Moderna*. Venice.

Sanudo, M. (1879) *I diari*, I. Venice.

Smith, R. D., Brown. R. R. (1989) *Bombards Mons Meg and her sisters*. London.

2

Venetian Ordnance in the Shipwrecks of the Mediterranean and Atlantic Seas

Carlo Beltrame

Introduction

An investigation of the evidence of Venetian wrecks, both from publications and from unpublished new discoveries, has allowed us to identify about thirteen wrecks containing ordnance, as well as some isolated guns. This work has received great help from Marco Morin and Renato Ridella who have introduced the author to the world of the historic artillery.

The wrecks are distributed right along the routes of the Serenissima Republic (Figure 2.1). Starting from Venice, where we find the so called "Glass wreck" and "Guns wreck" in the harbour entrance of Malamocco, we move to the Dalmatian coast where we find the Gnalic wreck. Continuing along the Croatian coast there are the Kolocep and the Palagruza islands wrecks which are the subject of a Unesco Research Project between the University Ca' Foscari and the University of Zara, in collaboration with the Croatian Conservation Institute of Zagreb. In the Eastern Mediterranean we have recorded only the isolated finds from Haifa in Israel, but if we go back along the Italian coast we have to take account of the guns found near Crotone and the wreck of Torre Faro of Messina. In Sicily there is evidence of a ship sunk at Filicudi island and the written and iconographical records of guns being found at a shipwreck in Castellammare di Trapani.

Along the Lybic coast of the Cirenaica, an Italian team has recently documented the wreck of the Venetian vessel *Tigre*, sunk in 1705.

It is curious how many wrecks of Venetian ships are present in the Atlantic sea, along the coasts of Great Britain and Ireland. In the South of England we can mention the Teignmouth and the presumed Isle of Wight wrecks while further North we have the ships wrecked during the expedition of the *Spanish Armada*. These are the *Balancera* or *Balanzera* ship, better known as *Trinidad Valencera*, wrecked in Kinnagoe Bay and the *Labia* or *Lavia* ship sunk in the Sligo bay, both in Ireland.

Not all these wrecks can be identified with certainty as being Venetian and not all the findings of isolated guns can be definitely linked to wrecks.

This study can confirm that guns are the most important indicators of modern age wrecks. If indeed we exclude the *fusta* of Lazise where it is possible that there was contemporary salvage of the artillery in the 1509, and the medieval galley of Venice which probably predates the arrival of shipboard guns, all the wrecks of Venetian ships have ordnance on them.

The wrecks

The so-called "Glass wreck" was found off the entrance to the harbour of Malamocco by amateur divers. The site has been excavated by Marco D'Agostino and Idra company who recovered many blocks of raw glass and other objects, which could be attributed to a Roman wreck contaminating a more recent wreck (D'Agostino 2008). Other objects indeed would date the second wreck to, more or less, the beginning of the seventeenth century.

Two very similar iron swivel breech-loading guns (*petriere da mascolo*) have been found. A swivel mount and two removable chambers (*mascoli*), which could be used on these weapons, have been found near them. Some stone shot and two wedges are other artefacts related to artillery. It is interesting to note that while the wedge of the elongated shape can be associated with this type of *petriera da mascolo*, the wedge with a merlon shape had to be used with a *petriera da braga*; as well documented by Moretti (1672, figs. 8, 9) and also by other archaeological findings.

The so called "Guns wreck" was found in the opposite side of the harbour entrance of Malamocco. The shipwreck can be dated to between the end of the XVII and the beginning of the XVIII century (D'Agostino, Galletta, Medas 2010). It contained four cast-iron guns of both Venetian and English production, but the finding of a breech chamber gives testimony to the ship being armed with swivel guns, too.

The site excavated near the small island of Gnalic, south of Biograd, is one of the most impressive wrecks of the Mediterranean both for the number and for the quality of the objects and for their condition and preservation. Although

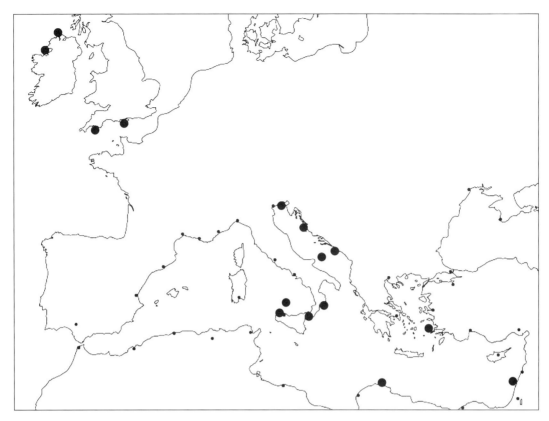

Figure 2.1. Map of distribution of Venetian wrecks.

it has been interpreted as a Venetian galley, we have demonstrated that it must have been a round ship, about 40 m long. The type of anchors, the cargo, the thickness of the frames, together with the types of artillery recovered, is proof of this assertion (Beltrame 2006).

The cargo was composed mainly of thousands of beautiful glass vessels perhaps from Murano, windowpanes, mirrors and semifinished metals (Lazar and Willmott 2006). Indeed, the ship carried brass leafs and wire and lead ingots in wooden barrels (Kelez 1970). Hundreds of spectacles, shaving razors and parts of chandeliers, perhaps made in Lübeck, were also part of the cargo (Stadler 2006). Damask and linen shirts were contained in a chest (Davanzo Poli 2006). Various objects relating to the commercial activities and the life aboard complete the diverse list of artefacts recovered (Petricioli S. 1970).

The artillery, studied by Ivo Petricioli (1970) and Marco Morin (2006), is composed of eight guns. There are two bronze *12 libre* sakers, 350 cm long and with a calibre of 9 cm (Tab. 1.1); at the breech, the numbers 2360 and 2380 respectively have been engraved to indicate the weight in Venetian *libre grosse*. The Roman numbers and the Z and A initials indicate that they were cast by *Zuane Alberghetti* II in 1582 (Figure 2.2).

The ship also carried three bronze *12 libre petriere da braga*, where the *braga* is in very corroded iron or absent. An empty coat of arms and the shape of one swivel gun are very similar to pieces in the Naval museum in Istanbul. The C which is present on another piece could have been cast by a member of the famous *di Conti* family of Venetian

Figure 2.2. Detail of a bronze saker cast by Zuane Alberghetti found in the Gnalic wrecks (photo by the author).

Figure 2.3. Detail of a bronze petriera da braga *cast by a member of the Di Conti family found in the Gnalic wrecks (photo by the author).*

founders (Figure 2.3). The fourth small piece is a bronze one *libra moschetto* with a curious coat of arms – perhaps of French origin. The same coat of arms is on a big gun signed with an A of the Alberghetti in the Askeri museum of Istanbul.

The last two pieces are two bronze minions (heavy falcons), called in Venetian terminology *9 libre passavolanti*, about 260 cm long with a calibre of 8 cm and of possible French origin (Morin 2006; Ridella 2007).

All the pieces had to be for private customers because of the absence of the winged lion and X symbol of the *Consiglio dei Dieci* magistracy, usually found on guns cast for the state until 1587.

The wreck also contained a wooden stopper from a breech chamber, slow match, two stone and one iron shot and a bronze gunner's rule very similar to other artefacts found on the wreck of the *Trinidad Valencera*, that is the Venetian *Balancera*.

The ordnance of the wreck would suggest that the ship sunk at the end of the 16th century.

In the waters of the island of Palagruza (ancient Pelagosa) two bronze guns and a bell have been recovered from a wreck. One gun is 260 cm long and bears a coat of arms with a cross, which belongs to the *Gritti* family of Venice, and the initials AL and G (Table 2.1: 2). The rich decoration, which, because is very similar to that one on a piece signed by CAMILLI ALBERGETI and made for a member of the *Gradenigo* family exhibited outside the Askeri museum of Istanbul (reg. n. 266), seam, in our opinion, a style typical of this member of the family of founders, who worked in Venice between 1517 and 1528 (Morin 1992, 781), and the other initials C and A on the gun allow us to attribute this object to this artist.

The second gun is about 2 m long and bears the same coat of arms of the *Gritti* family except for the T and C

initials of *Tomaso di Conti* who was active, according Avery (2003, 249), in the 1520s–1530s (Table 2.1: 3). The same s-faceted surface is visible on a big piece decorated with a lion and signed with a T and a C and on an other big piece decorated with a lion and the coat of arm of a member (A...) of the *Gradenigo* family and signed with a T and a C in the Askeri museum of Istanbul (reg. n. 405, 408). This manifacturing seams typical of this founder.

Given the working dates of the two founders, the likeliest candidate for the initials AL-G is *Alvise Gritti* (better known as *Ludovico*), son of the doge *Andrea*, a famous and wealthy merchant and politician in his own right. In the 1520s he lived in Constantinople as a trader and in the 1530s he was involved in the politics in Hungary where he was murdered in 1534 (Nemeth Papo and Papo 2002). In the 1520s he was involved in the export of tin for the Turkish gun foundries (Nemeth Papo and Papo 2002, 30–31).

Since Alvise was an illegitimate son of the doge and so he was not a *patrizio*, it may seem strange that he was able to mark his guns, cast in Venice, with his father's coat of arms and initials. Because a brief research in the Archivio di Stato di Venezia (for example: ASV, M. Barbaro, *Arbori de patritii veneti*, VI, c. 473) has allowed many other members of the Gritti family candidates to be recognised from the initials AL-G, some as *Alessandro* and some *Alvise Gritti*, the problem of the identification is still open and would need a long and complex investigation.

The ship that was wrecked near the island of Kolocep was probably trying to enter the harbour of Ragusa, that is, the ancient Dubrovnick. It carried hundreds of bottles and vessels (Radic Rossi 2006) and some pottery dating the wreck to the beginning of the 17th century but generically not of Venetian production (S. Gelichi, pers. comm.).

Together with some metal objects, three bronze *petriere da mascolo* have been recovered by amateur divers (Table 2.3: 1). The only one the author has been able to document belongs to a type which is found over a wide geographical spread and that, thanks to a comparison with two pieces on display in the Naval Museum of Venice, suggests they could have been produced in Venice. Indeed, both these two *petriere* show the Lion *in moeca* of Venice; the gun on the left has got the monogram of the *Alberghetti* family while that on the right bears the initials of *Marcantonio di Niccolò di Conti*. The latter, since it was recovered by a fisherman off Chioggia, must have been on a ship (Avery 2005, 442).

The F and M initials engraved on the coat of arm on the chase of both the Kolocep piece and of an artefact from the Naval museum of Istanbul, belong to the owner of the ship.

At least three iron guns are still on the seabed of Kolocep but because of the concretion covering their surface we have been not able to identify them.

In 1973, off Haifa or Athlit, a fisherman recovered a bronze saker 340 cm long and with a calibre of 9 cm (Roth 1989). The initials Z and A and the style of the decorations, similar to those present on the pieces from the wrecks of Gnalic and the *Balancera*, allow us to attribute it to *Zuane*

Table 2.1: 1. Bronze culverin-saker from the Gnalic wreck (Croatia) cast by Zuane Alberghetti (after Petricioli, I, 1970, fig. 11), 2. Bronze gun from the wreck of Palagruza (Croatia) cast by Camillo Alberghetti (courtesy Irena Radic) 3. Bronze gun from the wreck of Palagruza (Croatia) cast by Tomaso di Conti (courtesy Irena Radic), 4. Bronze saker from Haifa (Israel) cast by Zuane Alberghetti (after Roth 1989, fig. 1).

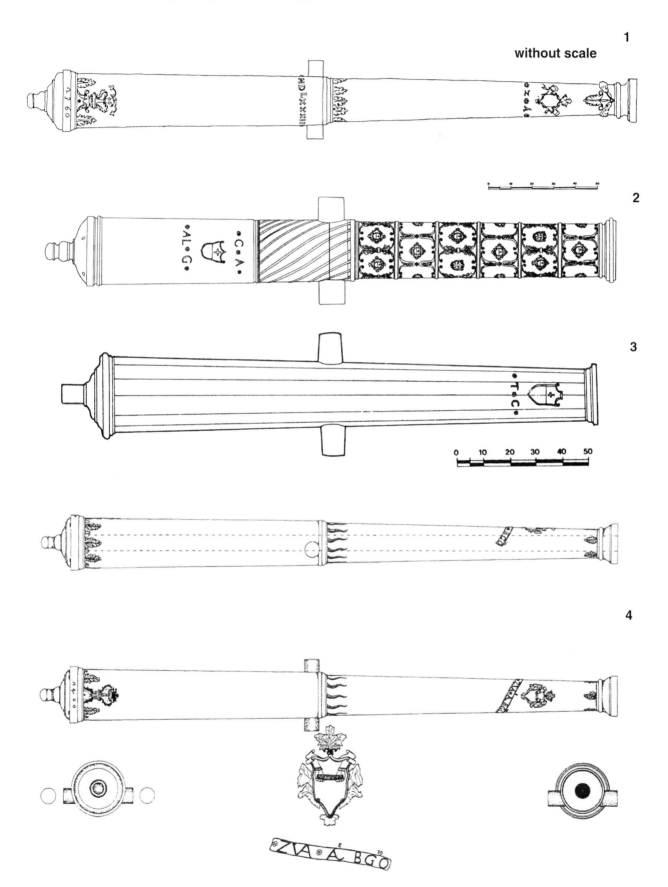

Table 2.2: 1. A bronze falconetto *found off the Isle of Wight (England) made by Zuane Alberghetti (after Tomalin, Cross and Motkin 1988, fig. 2), 2. Bronze saker from the wreck of Teignmought (England) made by Sigismondo Alberghetti (after Dudley 1989, fig. 1), 3. Bronze* falconetto *from the wreck of Teignmought (England) made by Sigismondo Alberghetti (after Preece and Burton 1993, fig. 13), 4. Bronze culverin from the wreck of the* Trinidad Valencera *(Balancera) cast by Niccolò di Conti (after Martin and Parker 1999, 272) 5. Bronze saker from the wreck of the* Trinidad Valencera *(Balancera) cast by Zuane Alberghetti (after Martin and Parker 1999, 272).*

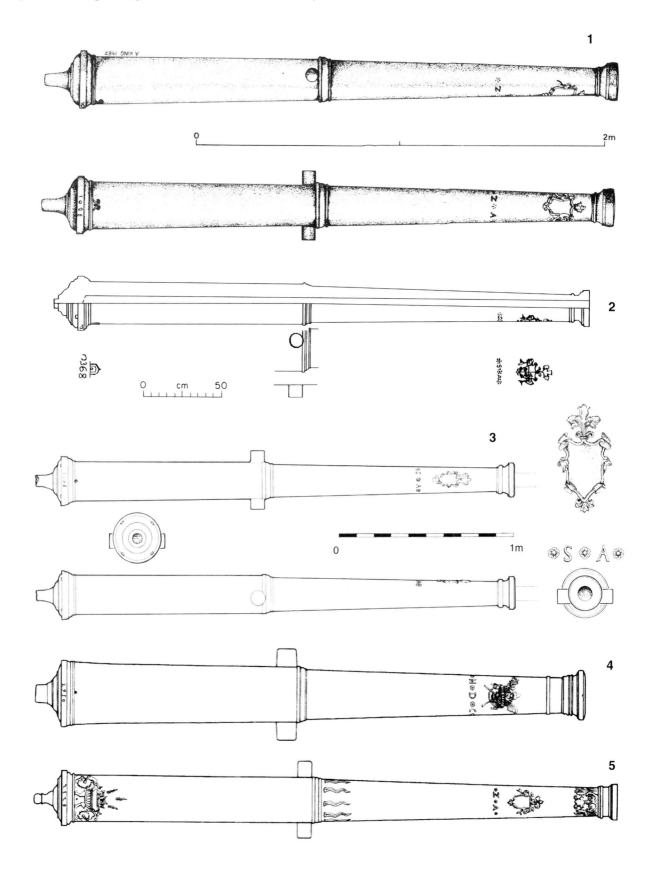

Table 2.3: 1. Bronze petriera da mascolo *from the wreck of Kolocep (Croatia) (drawing by Elisa Costa), 2. Bronze and iron* petriera da braga *from the wreck of the* Trinidad Valencera *(Balancera) (after Martin and Parker 1999, 273), 3. Bronze and iron* petriera da braga *from the wreck of the* Labia *(after McElvogue 2002, 41), 4. Bronze and iron* petriera da braga *from the wreck of Teignmouth (England) (after Preece and Burton 1993, fig. 14).*

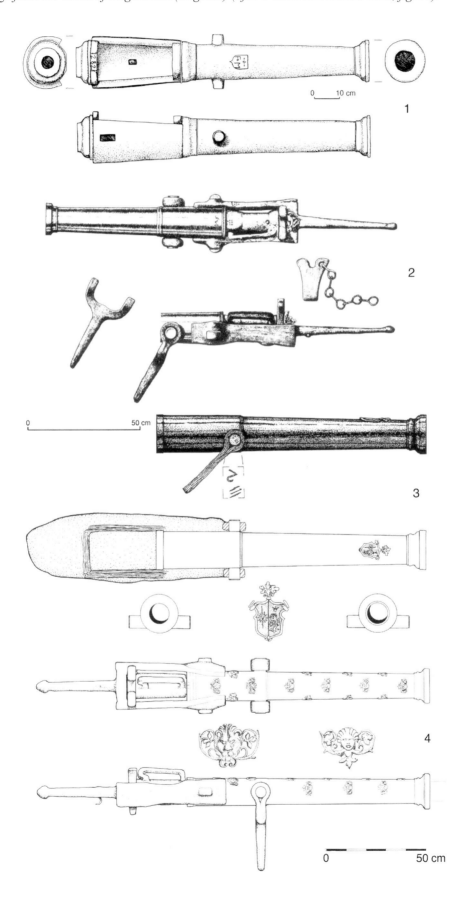

Figure 2.4. (Left), Two bronze falconetti *or* falconi *found near Crotone (photo by the author with the permission of the Civic Musem of Crotone). (Right), Detail of one of the falconetti from Crotone cast by Marco di Conti. The X of the Consiglio dei Dieci is present.*

Alberghetti the second, active, according to Morin (1992, 782) between 1573 and 1586 (Table 2.1: 4).

In the sixties of the 19th century, sponge-divers saw about forty bronze guns off the Isle of Symi in Greece. Nine of them had been raised; at the artillery museum of Woolwich, in England, there are five of these objects: three guns, with a calibre of 9.5 cm and 202 cm long and two *petriere da mascolo,* with a calibre of 7.6 cm and 102 cm long. All the pieces showed the Lion *in moeca* which indicates that they probably belonged to a state, and to quite a big, vessel (Hewitt 1871).

In the civic museum of Crotone two bronze *falconetti* or *falconi* 154 cm long are on display (Figure 2.4). On the chase they show the Lion *in moeca*, the X belonging to the Council of Ten and the monograms M and C of *Marco di Conti I*, active in the Arsenal – according to Avery (2003, 249) – between 1526 and 1567. Seven bronze pieces signed with M and C are on display in the Askeri museum of Istanbul (reg n. 255, 256, 280, 284, 286, 287, 297).

The long *petriera da mascolo* with the *mascolo* in the holder cannot be Venetian. The Turkish bronze gun with an Islamic Arab inscription could be evidence of a fight between a Christian and a Turkish ship west of Capo Colonna (Figure 2.5). The Lion and the X suggest that the two *falconetti* could have belonged to a galley.

Two bronze and iron *petriere da braga*, one bronze *mascolo* and fifteen stone and iron shot come from the sea of Torre Faro near Messina. The presence of other finds of probable Venetian origin suggest the existence of a wreck of a Venetian ship (Scordato in this volume).

The presence off Castellammare del Golfo di Trapani, at Magazzinazzi, of a shipwreck of a vessel carrying Venetian ordnance can also be documented from written and iconographic sources. A manuscript from Palermo dating to 1703 (Palazzolo 2007, 72), (brought to my attention by Renato Ridella), records the recovery of a bronze gun, probably belonging to a wreck, with two coats of arms and the image of Santa Caterina in correspondence with the trunnions (Figure 2.6). The dolphin, on one of the coat of arms, would indicate that the owner of the piece was a member of the Venetian family *Dolfin* while the Roman numerals and the inscription OPUS ALBERGETI tell us that it was cast by one of the *Alberghetti* family in 1547.

The ordnance on display at the archaeological museum of Lipari has been officially attributed to the wreck of an 18th-century Spanish vessel at Capo Graziano on Filicudi Island (Kapitaen 1985). Thanks to Ridella's communication and the kind collaboration of the archaeologists at the museum, we have been able to make a preliminary study of the pieces. These are a bronze *falconetto* (Figure 2.7), 2 m long with a calibre of 6.5 cm, and two bronze *petriere da braga*. An empty shield and the monogram N and C on the *falconetto* suggests it was cast by the founder *Niccolò di Conti II* who, according to Avery (2003, 249), was active between 1559 and 1601 (Figure 2.8). Three pieces of artillery signed by this founder are in the Askeri museum of Istanbul (reg. n. 132, 275, 397).

The two bronze *petriere da braga*, which are lacking the *braghe*, are 150 cm long and have calibres of 9 and 9.5 cm. Some common pottery, a copper cauldron, some bricks

Figure 2.5. Turkish bronze gun with Arab inscription found near Crotone.

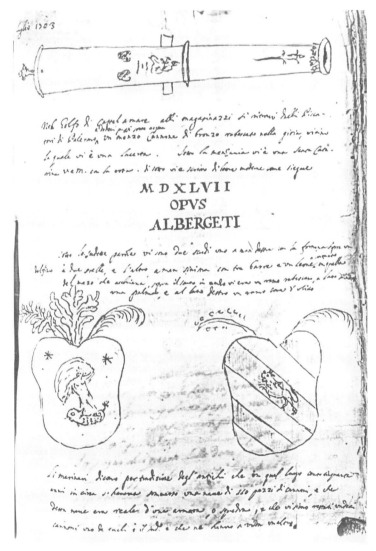

Figure 2.6. Manuscript from the Archivio di Stato di Palermo, dating in the 1703, which records the recovery of a bronze gun at Castellammare di Trapani. The dolphin, on one of the coat of arms, indicates the Venetian family Dolfin while the inscription tells that it was cast by an Alberghetti in 1547 (courtesy Antonino Palazzolo and Gianni Ridella).

Figure 2.7 (above). A bronze falconetto *and two bronze* petriere da braga *in the Archaeological Museum of Lipari (photo: Marcello Consiglio, with the permission of the Direction of the museum).*

Figure 2.8 (left). An empty shield and the monograms N and C, on the falconetto *made by Niccolò di Conti the second (photo: Marcello Consiglio, with the permission of the Direction of the museum).*

the written sources (ASV, Senato, Dispacci, Provveditori di terra e da mar, filza 1341) it carried 48 bronze guns, 12 swivel guns and 22 iron guns but only the last have been found on the site (Tusa in this volume).

Exiting beyond the Pillars of Hercules, there are three or four wrecks of Venetian ships.

In the South of England, at Teignmouth, from 1975 to 1995, a group of sport divers excavated a site and recovered hundreds of artefacts relating to life aboard ship and its equipment, as well as items for the defence of the ship. These included 120 pieces of iron and stone shot and two *mascoli* for the various pieces of artillery recovered. These include a bronze saker with the monogram S and A and a shield showing a lion rampant and a wheel (Dudley 1989; Preece and Burton 1993; Wilson 1993; Preece 2004) (Table 2.2: 2). While of course the wheel has to belong to the Venetian family *Molin*, we can only suppose that the lion belonged to the *Badoer* family.

The same monogram S and A (belonging to the founder *Sigismondo Alberghetti*) is on two bronze *falconetti* one of which was still attached to a fragment of the carriage (Table 2.2: 3). It is probable that the guns, which are decorated with a mute coat of arm, were made by *Sigismondo II*, active perhaps from 1566 to 1610 (Morin 1992, 783), although we cannot exclude completely *Sigismondo I* or *Sigismondo III*. In the Askeri museum of Istanbul there are ten pieces signed with S and A (reg. n. 260, 268, 269, 274,

and a millstone come from the site where it appears that anchors and iron guns have also been seen in the past.

The *Tigre* vessel was intentionally sunk by its captain on 7 April 1705 to avoid it being captured by enemies along the coast of the Cirenaica at Ras al-Hilal. According to

276, 290, 298, 299, 301, 378) and the piece number 276 shows the same mute coat of arm visibile on the *falconetti* from Teignmouth.

The three *petriere da braga* are beautifully decorated with heads of cherubins and heads of lions and at least one is complete with its *mascolo* and its *cuneo* to stop it (Table 2.3: 4). We do not know who produced these pieces, but we can notice that the cherubins are a motif also used by *Marcantonio di Conti* – who worked from the end of the 16th century to 1638 (Avery 2005) – on some of his productions.

Another bronze *falconetto*, also with a fragment of its carriage, has been found off the Isle of Wight (Tomalin, Cross and Motkin 1988) (Table 2.2: 1).

The monograms Z and A and the style, which is very similar to that one of the pieces of Gnalic and of the *Balancera*, suggests it was more likely to have been cast by *Zuane Alberghetti II*, active from 1573 to 1586 when he was put in jail (Morin 1992, 782), rather than *Zuane Alberghetti I*. The gun could be associated to a wreck under preliminary investigation containing North Italian pottery as well (Watson and Gale 1990; Advisory Committee on Historic Wrecks Sites 2005).

We want to conclude our *excursus* on the Venetian wrecks with the evidence of the two ships that took part at the expedition of the Spanish Armada in the Levant Squadron after they had been commandeered, at Lisbon, by Phillip II. With the *Ragazzona*, which sunk off Corunna in December 1588 (Martin and Parker 1999, 244; ASV, Archivio notarile Catti, reg. 3360, fol. 86 (21 March 1589)), the Venetian ships in the fleet were reduced to three. In addition to the *Ragazzona,* which was the flag ship of the Levant Squadron, there was the *Balancera*, possibly owned by *Alvise Balancer,* a merchant active at the end of the 16th century (Tenenti 1959, 113). This *Balancera* was renamed *Trinidad Valencera* by the Spaniards and was rated at 1100 tons (Martin and Parker 1999, 23–24). Furthermore, there was the *Lavia* or *Labia*, rating at 728 tons (Martin and Parker 1999, 263; AGS CS 2a leg. 280: f. 12), which took the name of the family of the wealthy merchant *Paolo Antonio Labia* (Birch 2004, 15; AGS CS 2a leg. 280: f. 12; ASV, archivio notarile Catti reg. 3360, fol. 34, 1 February 1589). Although these ships had been armed with additional guns and munitions in Lisbon, the equipment and the original artillery aboard were Venetian.

The *Balancera,* which was wrecked in Kinnagoe bay in Ireland, has been excavated by Colin Martin (1979) who recovered, together with elements of the equipment and objects for the life aboard, a gunner's rule (Rodrìguez-Salgado 1988, 180; Martin 1997, 5–13) – very similar to the one from Gnalic but made of wood rather than bronze – and also four pieces of ordnance. These were a bronze saker, 345 cm long with a calibre of 9 cm, made by *Zuane Alberghetti II* (Table 2.2: 5), a bronze culverin, 325 cm long with a calibre of 11.8 cm (Table 2.2: 4), a bronze falcon, 292 cm long with a calibre of 7.2 cm, made by *Niccolò di Conti II* and then a bronze *petriera da braga* with the iron *braga* (Rodrìguez-Salgado 1988, 177–178; Martin and Parker 1999, 272–274; Martin in this volume)

(Table 2.3: 2). The falcon presents a decoration similar to that one on a piece signed with ND and C and dated 1539 in the Askeri museum of Istanbul (reg. n. 132).

The *Labia*, sunk in the Sligo Bay in Ireland, has been the object of a non-disturbance survey by an English team (Birch and McElvogue 1999; Birch 2004). From the site, a bronze *petriera da braga* with a calibre of 9 cm has been recovered. The eagle on its coat of arms is the symbol of the *Labia* family (Table 2.3: 3).

Two guns (probably bronze), with their perfectly-preserved carriages, have been left *in situ* and are waiting for the continuation of the research on this very promising site (Birch and McElvogue 1999; McElvogue 2002; Birch 2004, 183–212).

Conclusions

As a conclusion to this brief overview of the Venetian wrecks, we can say that it is impressive how many they are when compared to those of other states

Thus we also have many more Venetian guns to study, in comparison with guns from other states especially in the Mediterranean area. This result can be only partially explained by the attention that the Venetian wrecks have received in comparison with those of other states. The Venetian ships are well attested in the Adriatic, in the central Mediterranean and in the Atlantic in a quite limited period, between the latter half of the 16th century and the first twenty years of the 17th century. The *Tigre* ship and the "Guns wreck" of Malamocco, sunk in the beginning of the 18th century, are the only exceptions. This result itself is interesting but perhaps need to be verified through the collection of more data.

Considering that most of the ordnance does not bear the image of the lion, symbol of the government ownership, it seems that many Venetian wrecks belong to private, round ships; the only evidence of guns made for the State, that is with the image of the lion, come from Croton, Symi, Cirenaica and the "Guns wreck" of Malamocco.

In conclusion, the archaeological evidence confirms what we know from the written sources – that in this period, the monopoly of bronze artillery production belongs to the *di Conti* and *Alberghetti* families. From the sea, eight pieces made by the *di Conti* have been recovered and ten made by the *Alberghetti* family of which the largest single number are those cast by *Zuane* the second. This evidence would confirm the impression that the *Alberghetti* family was little more productive than the *di Conti* one that we have had registering 35 pieces, signed with the typical A, and only 21, signed with the typical C, in the Askeri museum of Istanbul.

Nautical archaeology also allows us to state that, curiously, as the wrecks of the *Balancera*, of Palagruza and perhaps of Gnalic indicate, it was quite common for a ship to carry guns cast by both the families, that is to say that the quality of their production had to be very similar. But only further marine discoveries of guns will be able to confirm this and the other preliminary considerations.

References

Advisory Committee on Historic Wrecks Sites (2005) *Annual Report 2005*. Department of Culture, Media and Sport. London.

Avery, V. J. (2003) State and Private Bronze Foundries in Cinquecento Venice: New Light on the Alberghetti and di Conti Workshops. In P. Motture (ed.) *Large Bronzes in the Renaissance*, Symposium Papers XLI (Studies in the History of Art, 64), 241–276, New Haven-London.

Avery, V. (2005) >>giovene di spirito e d'ingegno<<: New Light on the Life and Work of the Venetian Renaissance Bronze Caster Marcantonio di Niccolò di Conti (1576–1638). In M. Gaier, B. Nicolai, T. Weddigen (eds.) *Der unbestechliche Blick. Festschrift zu Ehren von Wolfgang Wolters zu seinem siebzigstein Geburtstag*, 438–463. Trier.

Beltrame, C. (2006) Osservazioni preliminari sullo scafo e l'equipaggiamento della nave di Gnalic. In Gustin, M., Gelichi, S., Spindler, K. (eds.) *The heritage of the Serenissima. The presentation of the architectural and archaeological remains of the Venetian Republic, proceedings of the international conference, Izola-Venezia 2005*, 93–95. Koper.

Birch, S. (2004) *The Streedagh Armada Wrecks. Historical background and site report for the Spanish Armada wrecks of la* Lavia, *la* Juliana *and* Santa Maria de Vison *1982–2002*. Unpublished report.

Birch, S., McElvogue, D. M. (1999) *La Lavia, La Juliana* and the *Santa Maria de Vison*: three Spanish Armada transports lost off Streedagh Strand, *The International Journal of Nautical Archaeology*, 28.3, 265–276.

D'Agostino, M. (2008) Il relitto del Vetro di Venezia. Alcune considerazioni per una rilettura cronologica. In L. Fozzati, C. Pizzinato (eds.) Malamocco. Studi di Archeologia Lagunare e Navale, 145–153.Venezia.

D'Agostino, M., Galletta, G., Medas, S. (2010), Il relitto "dei cannoni" di Malamocco, Venezia. In S. Medas, M. D'Agostino, G. Caniato (eds.) Navis, Archeologia, Storia, Etnologia, Atti del I Convegno Nazionale, Cesenatico 2008, Bari, 63–70.

Davanzo Poli, D. (2006) I reperti tessili di Gnalic. In Gustin, M., Gelichi, S., Spindler, K. (eds.) *The heritage of the Serenissima. The presentation of the architectural and archaeological remains of the Venetian Republic, proceedings of the international conference, Izola-Venezia 2005*, 98–99. Koper.

Dudley, E. R. (1989) Alberghetti Guns, *The International Journal of Nautical Archaeology*, 18.3, 268.

Hewitt, J. (1871) Venetian bronze guns recovered by divers in the Mediterranean, *Archaeological Journal*, 28, 305–308.

Kapitaen, C. (1985) Capo Graziano. Relitto E: nave da guerra del XVIII secolo. In L. Bernabò Brea, M., Cavalier (eds.) Archeologia subacquea nelle Isole Eolie. *Archeologia Subacquea 2* (Bollettino d'Arte 29 Suppl.), 98–99.

Kelez, I. (1970) O sirovinama, *Vrulje*, 1, 40–45.

Lazar, I., Willmott, H. (2006) *The glass from the Gnalic wreck*. Koper.

Martin, C. J. M. (1979) *La Trinidad Valencera*: an Armada invasion transport lost off Donegal, *The International Journal of Nautical Archaeology*, 8, 13–38.

Martin, C. J. M. (1997) *Ships as integrated artefacts: the archaeological potential*. In M. Redknap (ed.) *Artefacts from Wrecks*, 1–13. Oxford, Oxbow.

Martin, C., Parker, G. (1999) *The Spanish Armada* (revised edition). Third edition, Manchester, Mandolin.

McElvogue, D. M. (2002) A description and appraisal of ordnance from three Spanish Armada transports c. 1588, *Journal of the Ordnance Society*, 14, 31–50.

Moretti, T. (1672) *Trattato dell'artiglieria*. Brescia.

Morin, M. (1992) Alberghetti. In K. G. Saur (ed*.) Allgemeines Kuenstlerlexicon. Die bildenden Kuenstler aller Zeiten und Voelker*, 2, 779–784. Muenchen-Leipzig.

Morin, M. (2006) Le artiglierie del relitto di Gnalic. In Gustin, M., Gelichi, S., Spindler, K. (eds.) *The heritage of the Serenissima. The presentation of the architectural and archaeological remains of the Venetian Republic, proceedings of the international conference, Izola-Venezia 2005*, 95–97. Koper.

Nemeth Papo, G., Papo, A., 2002, *Ludovico Gritti. Un principe-mercante del rinascimento tra Venezia, i turchi e la corona d'Ungheria*. Venezia.

Palazzolo, A. (2007) *Le torri di deputazione nel Regno di Sicilia (1579–1813)*. Istituto Siciliano Studi Politici ed Economici, Palermo.

Petricioli, I. (1970) Sidra i topovi. *Vrulje*, 1, 9–15.

Petricioli, S. (1970) Vaga i utezi. *Vrulje*, 1, 37–39.

Preece, C. (2004) Evidence for high status at sea: the Church Rocks wreck, *Proceedings of the Devon Archaeological Society*, 62, 99–119.

Preece, C., Burton, G. (1993) Church Rocks, 1975–83: a reassessment, *The International Journal of Nautical Archaeology*, 22.3, 257–265.

Radic Rossi, I. (2006) Il relitto di una nave mercantile presso l'isola di Kolocep. In Gustin, M., Gelichi, S., Spindler, K. (eds.) *The heritage of the Serenissima. The presentation of the architectural and archaeological remains of the Venetian Republic, proceedings of the international conference, Izola-Venezia 2005*, 85–90. Koper.

Ridella, R. G. (2007) Two 16th century Papal esmerils in the Cleveland Museum of Art, Ohio, and some notes on bronze pieces of ordnance with a polygonal section. *Journal of the Ordnance Society*, 19, 5–38.

Rodriguez-Salgado, M. J. (ed.) (1988) *Armada 1588–1988. An international exhibition to commemorate the Spanish Armada*. London, National Maritime Museum.

Roth, R. (1989) Two sakers from Israel, *The International Journal of Nautical Archaeology*, 18.1, 61–66.

Stadler, H. (2006) The brass candlesticks, sconces and chandeliers from Gnalic wreck. In Gustin, M., Gelichi, S., Spindler, K. (eds.) *The heritage of the Serenissima. The presentation of the architectural and archaeological remains of the Venetian Republic, proceedings of the international conference, Izola-Venezia 2005*, 107–109. Koper.

Tenenti, A. (1959) *Naufrages, Corsaires et Assurances maritimes à Venise 1592–1609*. Paris, S.e.v.p.e.n.

Tomalin, D., Cross, J, Motkin, D. (1988) An Alberghetti bronze minion and carriage from the Yarmouth Roads, Isle of Wight, *The International Journal of Nautical Archaeology*, 17.1, 75–86.

Watson, K., Gale, A. (1990) Site evaluation for maritime sites and monuments records: the Yarmouth Roads Wrecks investigations, *The International Journal of Nautical Archaeology*, 19.3, 183–192.

Wilson, V. (1993*) The Story of Teignmouth's mysterious wreck* (Teignmouth collector series, book 1). Teignmouth.

Archival sources

M. Barbaro, *Arbori de patritii veneti*, VI, c. 473, Archivio di Stato di Venezia.

The Race to Big Calibres During the First War of Morea and Sigismondo Alberghetti's Guns of New Invention

Guido Candiani

Between 1684 and 1699 the Republic of Venice and the Ottoman Empire fought their sixth and penultimate military conflict: the first War of Morea. Following the Venetians' initial capture of the Peloponnese – thanks to a series of spectacular amphibious assaults led by the Capitano Generale Francesco Morosini – the war was fought almost entirely at sea. In an attempt to break the equilibrium between the two evenly matched fleets, both sides launched efforts to deploy guns of ever larger calibre. It was in this context that the Venetians adopted a new type of cannon, capable of launching explosive projectiles. Gradually deployed throughout the Venetian fleet during the final phase of the war, the newly invented guns were also employed during the final conflict between the Venetians and the Turks (the second War of Morea, 1714–1718). However, in neither case did the new guns offer the Venetian fleet the decisive advantage the Republic had hoped for.

In its final phase, the first War of Morea witnessed an intense series of naval battles. Between 1695 and 1698, both the Republic of Venice and the Ottoman Empire sought a decisive victory through the widespread deployment of battle fleets composed of ships of the line. Over the course of four campaigns, the two fleets fought nine major engagements, transforming the Eastern Mediterranean into the most active site of naval conflict on the globe. Nevertheless, it was immediately clear that neither side was capable of scoring a decisive victory over the other – both on account of the intrinsic defensive strength of their respective lines, and because of the inability of the existing guns to breach the thick hulls of the vessels. This stalemate drove the Ottomans and then the Venetians to seek new artillery technologies to tilt the equilibrium in their favour.

The Ottomans dusted off the great stone cannons the Sultan's forces had employed with great success in the fifteenth and sixteenth centuries. Thanks to the lower specific weight of stone compared to that of iron, these older pieces were capable of launching much larger projectiles than ordinary guns, while still maintaining an acceptable

weight. In 1697 the Ottomans launched their first three-decker, which boasted three batteries of ordinary cannons of 16, 12, and 7 *okka* – the first two calibres were slightly greater than the English 40 and 32 pounder, while the third was equivalent to an English 20 pounder. In addition, the ship carried four to six stone cannons rated at 44 *okka*, and capable of launching a ball with a diameter of perhaps 230 mm (equivalent to a hypothetical English 124 pounder). Other Ottoman ships of the line carried similar pieces, which promised to inflict serious damage to enemy ships, even with only a limited number of direct hits. (Archivio di Stato di Venezia=ASV, *PTM*, filza 1336, 12.7.1697).

The need to match the Turkish stone cannon, drove the Venetians to introduce a gun capable of shooting an explosive projectile on a straight trajectory – in contrast to mortars, which employed a very steep trajectory – and therefore capable of striking a moving target such as an enemy ship. The principal figure in the development of the new guns was Sigismondo Alberghetti, *fonditore pubblico* (public gunfounder) in the Venetian Arsenal. Alberghetti belonged to a veritable dynasty of artillery casters: his ancestors had been employed in the same capacity by the Republic for nearly two centuries (Morin 1992). With his new invention, Alberghetti assumed a preeminent and highly original place in the world of artillery design and manufacture. The late seventeenth century witnessed a great deal of experimental activity aimed at overcoming the ever-more evident limits of naval guns in the face of stouter hulls. While in the past, the close-quarter nature of most naval engagements had favoured boarding tactics aimed at capturing and burning enemy vessels, the introduction of line tactics had reduced the opportunities for boarding, thereby transforming naval warfare into artillery duels in which traditional guns proved incapable of creating a decisive advantage. To restore power to naval artillery, the Venetians tried several new solutions involving explosive projectiles. Beginning in the 1670s, mortar techniques and technology made significant progress (the Venetians used the new technologies to conquer the Peloponnese). The English and French fleets had also experimented with these technologies, but had abandoned them due to the fear of storing explosive projectiles on board ships at sea (Paixans 1822, 83–84, 88).

Alberghetti had first encountered the issue during a journey to England in the early 1680s. He had been sent there to purchase iron guns and to investigate the possibility of learning the techniques necessary to produce them in the Venetian Arsenal. In July 1684 he wrote a letter from London in which he first broached the possibility of employing an iron cannon loaded with a hollow projectile filled with explosives (ASV, Senato Mar, filza 653, 9.8.1684). The French bombardment of Genoa in May of the same year had amply demonstrated the terrible destructive power of such projectiles in coastal bombardments when launched from mortars mounted on *galiotes a bombes*. The French successes inspired the Venetian founder to consider the possibilities of employing bombs in ship-to-ship combat as well. He proposed building a gun with a Venetian calibre of *120 libbre* (equivalent to 212 mm) that could fire a hollow projectile of the same weight as the solid shot from a Venetian 20 *libbre*, which was roughly equivalent to an English 15 pounder (the Venetians measured the weight of solid balls in *libbre sottili* instead of *grosse*). Alberghetti also intended to use a spherical powder chamber, a technology drawn directly from recent advances in mortar design: the spherical chamber allowed the use of a greater charge without the need to increase the thickness of the gun. The more powerful charge together with the lighter projectile would, in Alberghetti's opinion, allow the construction of a very light and short gun in spite of the large calibre. The new gun would, he claimed, demolish the flanks of enemy ships and provoked explosions and fires below decks. It is the very same concept that would lead to the introduction of the French designer Paixans' *canon-obusier* in the 1830s, which would in turn lead to the development of iron hulls to replace traditional wooden ships.

Alberghetti's concept for the projectile called for a cylindrical design: two iron hemispheres joined by a central cylindrical body. The main goal that the Venetian caster had set for the design was that of facilitating the production of the projectile on the lathe, so as to obtain accurately turned projectiles that would reduce the gap between the round and the barrel – the so-called windage – thereby increasing the initial velocity of the projectile and augmenting its accuracy and penetrating power. The cost of turning traditional round balls on the lathe would have been excessive – a perfect round ball was considered one of the masterpieces of lathework – while a cylindrical form could be turned with relative ease and at great savings. The cylindrical design also had the distinct advantage of preventing the projectile from turning about during loading, thus bringing the lit fuse on the round into contact with the propellant charge, with resulting misfires or worse (Alberghetti 1703, 3–4). In this respect Alberghetti's cylindrical bombs were superior to Paixans' traditional round balls, which had to be fitted with a wooden *sabot* (shoe) to prevent their turning about during loading (Paixans 1822, 209). The

sabot arrangement scored the barrels of Paixans' guns, reducing their effective life. Another characteristic that distinguished Alberghetti's design from Paixans' was the much greater effective range expected by the Venetian guns, thanks in part to an innovative sighting mechanism. Thus Alberghetti's innovations were twofold: large calibre pieces capable of firing explosive projectiles and at a far greater effective range with respect to traditional guns. Not only would the enemy suffer from the explosions, but he would not even be in a position to return fire. In this sense, Alberghetti anticipated the British Admiral "Jack" Fisher's motto *"hit first and hit hard"* by two centuries.

The Venetian Senate – which was always alert to innovations in artillery technology – accepted the proposal and ordered two specially built iron *120 libbre* calibre guns from England. Six calibres long and weighing 3,500 Venetian *libbre grosse* (1670 kg) (far less than ordinary Venetian *20 libbre* calibre gun), the new guns were cast under Alberghetti's supervision in Sussex at the Thomas Western foundry in Ashburnham. Tested in early 1685, they proved to have a range of over five kilometres – confirming the best hopes of their inventor (ASV, *Senato Mar*, filza 657, 24.3.1685). Alberghetti planned to mount four such guns on every Venetian ship of the line, and an equal number on every great galley, still the pride of the Republic's battle fleet. Unfortunately for him – and as he himself would often admit – he lacked the essential "talents" for convincing his interlocutors (and his financers for that matter) of the quality of his ideas. Once the guns reached Venice, they lay forgotten in the Arsenal. In large measure, this neglect was due to recent Venetian successes at sea. The Venetian fleet enjoyed an easy supremacy in the early phases of the war, which *"put to sleep the industry and art of arms with which one studied how to prevail against enemies."* Moreover, on his return from London, Sigismondo became embroiled in a dispute over how to fuse mortars with a *protegé* of the influential Capitano Generale Francesco Morosini. Alberghetti came out the loser in the dispute, and more importantly was damaged politically by the encounter. The *"cannons of new invention"* as they would later be called, lay abandoned in the warehouses, while the Senate shifted its attention to the production of traditional iron guns in the Republic's mainland territories.

The recovery of Ottoman naval power after 1693, the Venetian defeat at Chios in 1695, and most of all the adoption by the Turkish fleet of the great stone cannons, brought the "cannons of new invention" back to mind. In late 1696 – following the limitations shown by the great galleys in the recent battle of Andro – the commander of the galleys requested permission to employ Alberghetti's guns for the purpose of matching "the fury" of the enemy ships of the line (ASV, PTM, filza 1386, 2.12.1696). In June 1697, the Senate decided to take up the project once again. In the meantime the public founder had conceived of two distinct models of the gun. The first, destined for the great galleys, was a Venetian *200 libbre* calibre gun (265 mm), weighing 5,000 *libbre grosse* (2385 kgs); the second, designed for ships of the line, was the same as the ones

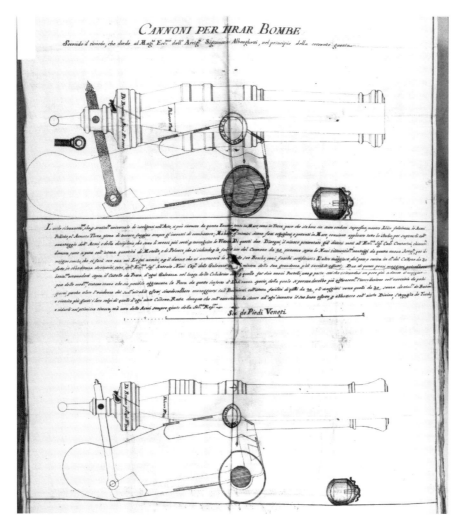

Figure 3.1. Drawing of the guns of new invention (above calibre 200, under calibre 120). It can be noticed the cylindrical shells, the two-wheels carriage and the elevating/sighting mechanism (permission Archivio di Stato di Venezia).

cast in England a decade earlier (Venetian *120 libbre*/212 mm calibre, 3,500 *libbre grosse*). Both models were to be cast in bronze in the Arsenal itself, and equipped with two-wheel carriages – perhaps to facilitate repositioning them to achieve superior sweep. In the notes attached to the design, Sigismondo expressly indicated that the guns were intended to contain the Turks who had become "proud and powerful" on the sea (ASV, Senato Mar, filza 735, 14.6.1697).

In October 1697, after another inconclusive naval campaign, the Senate approved the casting of the new pieces, and by November a *120 libbre* calibre gun was ready for trials. The tests were delayed by bad weather, but were eventually undertaken with great success on 6 December. The noteworthy performance in terms of both range and accuracy was due in large part to the reduction of the windage between projectile and bore. The cannons of new invention had a windage of one tenth of an *oncia* (2.9 mm) while English guns of the same period achieved no better than a 7.5 mm one. Even the *carronades*, introduced at the end of the 1770s achieved no better than a 3.7 mm windage (Biblioteca Nazionale Marciana=BNM, ms. it., cl. VII,

1542 (8889), *Obiezioni e risoluzioni sulla nuova artiglieria*, n. 7; Padfield 1973, 105). The new guns also proved easy to aim, thanks to a novel sighting mechanism mounted over the trunnions that was far easier to use than a traditional artillery quadrant. The results of the trials persuaded the *Provveditori alle Artiglierie* (the magistracy in charge of the Republic's entire artillery park) to requisition six of the new guns for every two-deck first-rate ship of 70–80 guns (the largest then in service). After debating the issue, the Senate opted to mount four per ship on a trial basis, and ordered the Arsenal to cast 48 guns for twelve first-rates (ASV, Senato Mar, filza 739, 14.12.1697).

Alberghetti, despite the fact that he now enjoyed the support of important members of the patriciate, once again found someone ready to block his path. This time his opposition came from the Englishman Jacob Richards, who had recently been appointed *Sergente Generale dell'Artiglieria* of the Republic. Richards came from the nation that was proving itself the most dynamic naval power in the world, and yet he still contested Alberghetti's project. However, it is worth remembering that following the Glorious Revolution, England had entered a conservative period in naval policy that would last until 1740 – and that this political climate influenced Richards' thinking. He recorded his doubts on paper immediately on his arrival in Venice in June of 1697 and later reiterated them in March of 1698, after the casting of the first forty-eight cannons. Richards stressed the danger of handling explosive projectiles at sea – which had placed an English ship at grave risk during analogous trials – thereby raising similar fears in Venice because several vessels had recently been lost due to unexplained explosions. In addition, the Englishman judged Alberghetti's cannon too light, and doubted the efficacy of the cylindrical projectiles. He proposed instead spherical shot filled with inert clay instead of dangerous gunpowder (ASV, Senato Mar, filza 735, 14.6.1697; filza 741, 8.3.1698). The Senate decided to hold a trial comparing the traditional spherical loads with the new cylindrical projectiles. The tests were held on 26 March and 12 April, 1698. Once again, the Alberghetti's munitions emerged as clearly superior. The cylindrical projectiles showed greater range and precision, as well as far lesser barrel scoring that Richards' spherical shot (ASV, Senato Mar, filza 741, 16.4.1698).

Despite the fact that thirty-three "*cannons of new invention*" were immediately dispatched to the Levant, the intervention of the Englishman had delayed not only the availability of the guns, but also of the new munitions. These delays had serious repercussions in terms of the deployment in battle of the new technology. At Nauplion, the Venetians' most important forward base, they were only able to mount two 120 guns on the topdeck of every first-rate, while the great galleys carried a single 200 on the quarterdeck. Along with the new guns, Venice shipped 600 cylindrical projectiles for the 120s. However, to save time, 289 of them had been manufactured out of stone, and were consequently inert. Stone could be shaped in the Arsenal itself, while the iron projectiles had to be cast in mainland foundries (ASV, Senato Mar, filza 742, 15.5.1698). The delay caused by Richards' trials also set back the training of crews for the new guns. This last task was assigned to one of Sigismondo's brothers, Carlo Alberghetti, who would also command the new artillery once it was fully deployed with the fleet. At any event, thanks to the ease of aim and accuracy of the new pieces, the results of the training exceeded even the most optimistic projections. In the general trials undertaken on the Lido on 24 August, almost all the gunners achieved "*a success [of aim] unheard of with any sort of artillery tried up until now*" (ASV, Senato Mar, filza 767, 16.9.1702; BNM, ms. it., cl. VII, 1542 (8889), *Informatione circa li cannoni di nuova invenzione*). The Venetian fleet appeared to have found a weapon capable of altering the balance of power on the high seas.

The true test arrived at the battle of Mitilenos, fought on 20 September, when twenty Venetian ships of the line – twelve armed with "*cannons of new invention*"– faced twenty-five Ottoman ships supported by about half-a-dozen corsair vessels. The new weapons performed well, but their impact was not what Sigismondo Alberghetti had hoped.

On the flagship *Rizzo d'Oro*, Sigismondo's brother Carlo directed the guns with great courage and skill under the watchful eyes of the squadron commander, Daniele (4°) Dolfin, who issued him a certificate of merit. The two other admirals present at the scene, Pietro Duodo and Fabio Bonvicini, declared themselves particularly satisfied with Alberghetti's cannons. Nevertheless, they also downplayed the innovative nature of the new guns. Dolfin appreciated, above all, the rate of fire, while Duodo noted that the gunners were able to fire very few explosive projectiles because no more than 54 had arrived from Venice due to the delays caused by Richards' objections. In any case, both Duodo and Bonvicini were contrary to the use of explosive projectiles, because they feared that they could do as much damage to friendly ships as to the enemy (ASV, PTM, filza 1341, 22.9.1698; filza 1337, 26.9.1698; filza 1133, 4.10.1698). Above all, none of the three admirals thought to use the "cannons of new invention" at the great ranges imagined by Sigismondo Alberghetti. Thanks to the sighting system and the consequent ease of aiming the guns, Alberghetti maintained that his guns could hit a ship to a range of two miles (nearly 3,500 m). He placed particular emphasis on the long interval between the aiming of traditional guns and the actual shot – a result of the rigid firing sequence. By contrast he argued, his "*cannons of new invention*" could actually be manoeuvred and aimed "*like muskets*" by a mere three-man crew and without any interruption in aiming, thus greatly reducing the time between sighting and firing (Alberghetti 1703, 8). In many ways, the technology anticipated the constant aim system introduced in 1898 by the Englishman Percy Scott, which initiated the most important revolution in shipboard gunnery since the first deployment of guns on ships in the second half of the fifteenth century (Padfield 1973, 211). During the battle of Mitilenos, the limited availability of projectiles and the lack of Alberghetti's range tables meant that the guns were only employed in traditional close-quarter combat. The eye-witness testimony – including Turkish accounts – record several instances of ships withdrawing with enormous holes above the waterline that had been caused by the new guns of the *Rizzo d'Oro*. Indeed, the new cylindrical projectiles had penetrated both flanks of the enemy ships. Nevertheless, the close range meant that the projectiles had not entered the near flank at a sufficient angle to penetrate below the waterline of the opposite flank, which would have, in all probability, sunk the target. The straight trajectory, combined with the low resistance offered by the superstructure on both sides of the Turkish hulls also meant that the charged rounds did not detonate inside the ship – an analogous issue to the problem faced by gunners two centuries later when firing piercing munitions against unarmoured targets.

Mitilenos ended up being the last battle of the war, which ended in early 1699. The Venetians judged the "*cannons of new invention*" to be of little use in peacetime and opted to remove them from the fleet and deploy them as shore batteries at home – a direct consequence of the tensions in the Adriatic caused by the War of Spanish Succession

(1701–1714). Later, they were warehoused, and once again forgotten. Alberghetti himself died in 1702, which also put an end to a series of trials he had planned for more thorough testing of the guns' capabilities. The weapons were rediscovered only with the onset of the second War of Morea (1714–1718). Caught unprepared by the Ottoman assault, the Venetians quickly resolved to redeploy the *"cannons of new invention"* aboard first-rates, and to arm them with both explosive and inert iron projectiles, as well as stone munitions. New trials were conducted with one of the 120 guns, all of which confirmed the ease of loading and the high degree of accuracy even at significant ranges. Moreover, the trials included three explosive rounds whose fuse was lit when the gun was lit. Two of these detonated as expected. The first penetrated the mock hull and set fire to the gun carriages stacked behind it. The second shot set fire to the mock hull itself, a demonstration that particularly impressed the observers. (ASV, Senato Mar, filza 833, 23.2.1715). This time, ships in service also received the *200 libbre* calibre guns that had originally been intended for the great galleys. Eight *"cannons of new invention"* (two 200s and six 120s) became the standard equipment for Venetian first-rates.

The guns were put into use on 8 July, 1716 in the Corfù channel during the very first naval engagement of the new war. The battle followed an Ottoman assault on the island by infantry supported by ships. The Venetians had the better of the encounter and successfully relieved the island's beleaguered fortress. Much of the credit was given to the *"cannons of new invention,"* even though they only fired inert rounds (ASV, PTM, filza 1339, 13.7.1716). Explosive projectiles were employed in the three major battles fought the following year. Nearly 1,300 cylindrical rounds – both explosive and inert – were expended in these battles, but there was no evidence that the explosive rounds caused particular damage to the enemy fleet. By this time, all agreed that the new guns were too short and too light. The short barrels posed a fire risk when fired against the wind due to sparks from the muzzle blast; while the light weight reduced the firing rate because the guns was not stable on the carriage and had to be manoeuvred back into position between each shot (ASV, PTM, filza 1342, 22.9.1717). It remains an open question – especially in light of the positive reports concerning rate of fire in the earlier war – to what degree these problems were a function of the guns, and to what degree they were due to the lack of experience of the crews firing them. Indeed, a manpower crisis had forced the Venetians to hurriedly recruit inexperienced seamen for the war. The criticisms did not prevent the new guns from being deployed on the new second-rate ships that entered service in 1718. These were 60 gun ships that the

Venetians hoped would be capable of serving in the line in wartime and replacing the role of first-rates in peacetime. These new ships carried ten *"cannons of new invention"* (four 200s and six 120s), as compared to the eight mounted on 70–80 gun first-rates (ASV, Senato Rettori, filza 182, 9.12.1717; Senato Mar, filza 859, 10.2.1718).

The new guns were last used in the course of the three day battle of the coast of Cape Matapan between 20 and 22 July, 1718. However, the sources make no specific reference to their performance. After the war the Venetian Senate confirmed the importance of the guns in the eyes of the authorities when it mentioned their utility in a 1725 decree that listed the lessons learned in the war (ASV, Archivio Gradenigo Rio Marin, busta 317, 22.9.1725). The guns continued to be part of the standard armament of Venetian ships of the line until at least the middle of the 18th century. In any case, the Venetian navy did not square off against another fleet for the remainder of the Republic's existence, and the guns invented by Sigismondo Alberghetti were never used in anger again.

In conclusion, it could be argued that the *"cannons of new invention"* offered the Venetian battle fleet a potentially revolutionary weapon, but that due to conservatism (typical of turn of the 17th-century navies) they did not have the impact that their inventor had predicted and hoped for. Venetian commanders hesitated to use them with explosive munitions and did not fire them at the extended ranges that Alberghetti had designed them for. Consequently, the guns were only fired at the close ranges typical of the day, and mostly with inert projectiles. Under such conditions, the guns were capable of inflicting serious damage to enemy ships, but could not destroy the solid structure of ships of the line. More than a century would pass before explosive rounds would become a mainstay of European fleets. At that time, thanks to the first industrial revolution, explosive munitions will meet a response in the widespread adoption of ironclads, thus initiating a struggle between gun and armour that would last until the definitive abandonment of battleships following the Second World War.

Translation by Karl Appuhn, whom the author sincerely thanks.

References

Alberghetti, S. (1703) *Artiglieria Moderna Veneta.* Venezia.
Morin, M. (1992) Alberghetti. In K. G. Saur (ed*.) Allgemeines Kuenstlerlexicon. Die bildenden Kuenstler aller Zeiten und Voelker,* 2, 779–784. Muenchen-Leipzig.
Padfield, P. (1973) *Guns at Sea.* London, Evelyn.
Paixans, H. J. (1822) *Nouvelle Force Maritime.* Paris.

4

Two Venetian Swivel Guns from the Messina Strait, Italy

Rossella Scordato

Introduction

Messina Strait has been a busy seaway since the Bronze Age (Bacci 2001, 271–301) and the frequency of shipwrecks is connected to its geomorphologic structure. There have been difficulties sailing here throughout history, as evidenced by the many archaeological finds found underwater. A group of artefacts related to a post-medieval wreck comes from this area which includes two swivel guns. The site is located along the Sicilian coast, 13 km from the main city of Messina, exactly between the villages of Torre Faro and Ganzirri.

The process of rescuing the artefacts started in 1982 and was completed within 10 years. It can be divided into three distinct periods. First, in 1982, one of the two swivel guns was fortuitously found at a depth of 25 m and 100 m from the seashore. On this occasion, local police divers identified the site and raised the two ordnance pieces lying on the seabed. After salvage they were preserved in a municipal storehouse, then later they were finally moved to Soprintendecy in Messina. Some years later a group of objects from the same area was recovered by two fishermen and in 1991, finally, the archaeological section of Messina Soprintendecy allowed a scientific survey. Recoveries, then, were not just the consequence of archaeological actions but there were also accidental discoveries. Unfortunately none of the documentation produced at the time by the Aquarius Company is available. The absence of scientific records and of a site plan obscures the exact distribution of objects on the seabed. Contexts are therefore hypothetic, based on scuba divers' descriptions.

The finds

Artillery

The two swivel guns are *petriere da braga* (Figure 4.1). This is the Venetian term used in 16th-century manuscripts writings where these types of guns are described (Collado 1586; Sardi 1621; Moretti 1672).

This type of gun is defined as a short-barrelled breech-loading piece throwing stone projectiles, from which is derived the name *petriere*. Later, such guns fired cast-iron shot as well as stone. They consist of a cast bronze barrel and two iron components: the yoke by which the guns were fixed on the bulwark of a ship and the *braga,* a wrought-iron holder where the *mascolo* (removable chamber) was lodged (Morin 2006).

Due to the effect of sea water, the iron parts are not well preserved, and for this reason the *braga* is often incomplete or missing. In the Torre Faro examples they are broken and included in a mass of concretion. One is completely separated from the barrel. When swivel guns were produced, the *mascolo* holder was assembled and fixed to the barrel by two lateral lugs cast with the barrel itself. These peculiar features are well described in some drawings in 16th- and 17th-century printed texts (Sardi 1621; Moretti 1672).

An important characteristic was the separate casting of the *braga* from the barrel; other swivel guns, cast in a single piece, had the *mascolo* holders cast integrally with the rest of the gun. In this case they are defined as *petriere da mascolo* (Morin 2006) and are made exclusively of bronze.

It is necessary to note the distinction that, while in Northern Europe, swivel guns were completely cast or forged of iron (*sling*) (Smith 1995, 109), in the Mediterranean area, most states able to produce artillery made and used bronze breech-loading swivel guns. Following Pietro Sardi (1621), it is known that both swivel guns – iron and bronze ones – coexisted and their use was still common in the17th century:

"In Ollanda, in Amsterdam & altre sue città marittime, & in Zelanda se ne fanno di ferro battuto in numero grande, di varie portate di palle di pietra, come io ne ho vedute battere, & in Marseglia ne ho veduto gettare un gran numero di bronzo e servono per i Vasselli, come si vede tutto il giorno, sopra quelle barche provenzali, e di ferro sopra quelle navi, e Vasselli dei Paesi Bassi"

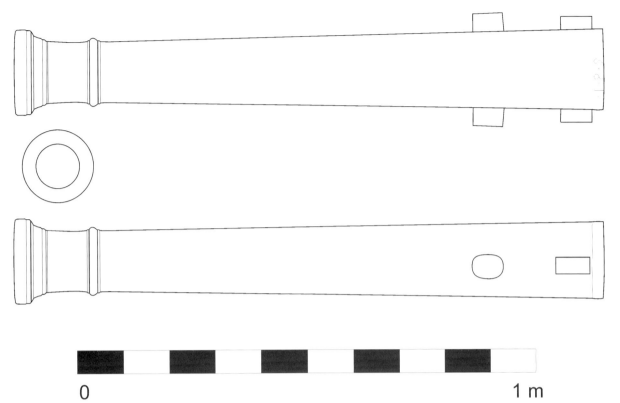

Figure 4.1. Bronze breech-loading swivel gun (petriere da braga) *(drawing by the author).*

Figure 4.2. The ordnance and the marked weight on the breech (photo by the author).

Collado – in 1586 – states that *petriere da braga* are rare and used especially on ships, towers and fortresses. Those are places where the limited space made muzzle-loading a problem. Breech-loading guns were then favoured for their ease in loading and firing. Aiming was managed by the *tiller,* which rotated the piece on the swivel.

Only Venezia and Genoa cast *petriere da braga* (called by the Genoese *smerigli petrieri alla veneziana).* Genoese founders expressed the barrel weight in *cantari* rather than *libre;* this information is important, making it possible to identify *petriere da braga* as Venetian if combined with its marked weight in *libre.* At this moment we know of only one surviving Genoese *petriera da mascolo:* exhibited in the Museo della Guerra at Rovereto (Ridella 2008, 293–294, fig. 4, b). The inventor of the iron/bronze swivel gun could have been "*M. Matthio Beccalua, il quale è uomo di molto giudicio nell'Arsenale"* in Venice (Capobianco 1598, 7r).

Apart from a few differences, the pieces from Torre Faro are quite alike, though they are not in good condition: iron parts are very corroded or missing. The barrel length (without the *braga)* is 118 cm (46.45 inches), the diameter at the bore is 95 mm (3.75 inches), they threw a 9 Venetian *libre sottili* shot with a bore/length ratio of 12.42. Capobianco (1598, 7r) and Moretti (1672, f. 18), in their handbooks, suggest a barrel length of 10–12 diameters for this sort of guns. These guns are undecorated pieces without any founders' initials, artistic features or *arme* (coats-of-arms). Just one of the *petriere* shows a marked weight on the base ring: 185 (*libre* not *cantari).* The estimated weight is 215 *libre* corresponding to 102.55 kg (using for the conversion the Venetian *libra grossa:* 477 g) not too far from the 88.25 kg engraved weight of the barrel (Figure 4.2). This value was the closer one in comparison with other European weight system units.

We can compare these guns with other surviving *petriere*

da braga, which confirm their main use aboard ship, since most come from wreck sites. Other comparative guns are preserved in European museums: Venice Naval Museum (Morin 2006), Istanbul Naval Museum (Bishop Smith 1997) and Varna Naval Museum (Smith 2000, 6).

For a methodological approach to the study of historic ordnance, a study of the mouldings can be rewarding, especially when the gun is unmarked (Ridella 2004, 29–30). Each gun's typology has its own structural standards and proportions, but casting allows the founder to create the piece with a personal design. The foundry created a peculiar profile, especially at the breech and the muzzle mouldings of the barrel. In the case of a swivel gun we can examine the muzzle design closely (*gioie della bocca)* (Sardi 1621, 26).

Torre Faro's guns show a slight similarity with a *petriera* now preserved in Lipari's Museum (Eolian Islands) and raised from the sea off the Filicudi Island in association with a *falconetto* (Beltrame in this volume) bearing the initials N C (*Nicolò di Conti,* a Venetian gun founder) (Figure 4.3).

Comparisons may be made with *Di Conti*'s other gun productions (Figure 4.4). The ordnance cast by this Venetian family has a very plain profile which accords to sober Venetian style. The muzzle mouldings are comparable to a Doric capital, with a larger first band and the profile gradually shrinking towards the muzzle neck.

The pieces considered for comparison were:

A *Media colubrina* recovered from *La Trinidad Valencera* with initials * N * D * C * (Martin and Parker 1999)
B *Falconetto* off Crotone with initials * M * C *
C Gun from Venice Naval Museum with initials * I * C *
D *Falconetto* recovered off Filicudi with initials * N * C *

Figure 4.3. Muzzle mouldings comparison. Petriera *from Torre Faro (on the left),* petriera *from Filicudi (on the right) (photos by the author and M. Consiglio).*

Figure 4.4. Di Conti muzzle mouldings comparison (image A after Martin and Parker 1999, 272, photo B: S. Medaglia, C: M. Morin, D: M. Consiglio)

The absence of any mark of state ownership on the pieces suggests they were cast for a private individual and formed the defence of a private ship, rather than a state naval or commercial galley. Artillery cast for the Venetian Republic's use bore the lion of St. Mark, *Provveditori alle Artiglierie*'s coat of arms, the initials of gun founders and – until 1588 – the roman number "X" of the *Consiglio dei Dieci* (Morin 2006).

In addition to the guns two bronze *mascoli* were found. They do not fit either of Torre Faro's swivel guns because the diameter of the gunpowder muzzle bore is smaller than that of the breech of the guns. They are very alike, measuring 20.5 cm in length and with a base diameter of 7 cm; one has a smaller muzzle bore of 2.7 cm with a maximum diameter of 5.5 cm for one of them and 2.5 × 5.7 cm for the other. The latter *mascolo* still has its own wooden bung (*coccone*) measuring 2.5 × 2.7 cm which preserved the gunpowder inside. On each bronze cylinder a touch-hole and two square-holes (rounded-holes in the tapered one) can be recognised. The holes were for attaching the *mascolo*'s handle, which has disappeared because it was made of iron.

A group of sixteen iron and stone shot was recovered. Some of them were incorporated into a mass of concretion composed of pebbles from the sea floor. The eight iron balls have a diameter of *c.* 7 cm; the stone ones range from 12–19.5 cm. None of them, like the powder chambers, fits the swivel guns.

Ship's equipment

No wooden trace of the hull remains, but some items related to the ship were discovered.

A group of fourteen nails has been found on the site. They are made of copper and copper alloy and show a wide range of shank-lengths from 2.3 to 19 cm. Only five nail heads exist and their diameters range from 1.3 to 2 cm, the others are broken on the top so just the shanks remain. They are all square-sectioned spikes: three of them are curved and three of the straight ones have some grooves on their surface to fit better in wood timbers.

Four coaks in copper alloy, fixed in the centre of hardwood sheaves belonging to the sail rigging, have similar but not identical measurements: A. 3.2 cm × 2.9 cm, 1.2 cm thick and 1.9 cm diameter hole; B. 3.2 cm × 3.1 cm, 1.3 cm th. and 2.0 cm d.; C. 3.5 cm × 3.4 cm, 1.8 cm th. and 2.0 cm d.; D. 3.9 cm × 3.8 cm, 1.9 cm t. and 2.0 cm d. Other elements of this type are known from Gnalić and *La Trinidad Valencera* wrecks (Martin 1979, 32–33).

A sounding lead of truncated cone shape measuring 7.3 cm in height, with a lower base of 7.3 cm diameter and a smaller base of 6 cm, is made of lead covered with a bronze laminate, the edges of which are fixed to the base by some small triangle-shaped bronze cuttings. On the top base there is a small hole for a line. The anomaly in comparison with known sounding leads is that it lacks a concave bottom.

A steelyard has been recorded, composed of a beam, broken and missing of its initial part, with a length of 17.6 cm and 0.6 cm thick, and its bronze counter weight, measuring 7.4 × 5.4 cm. The counter weight has a globular shape like the steelyard weights found on the Spanish Armada wrecks (Flanagan 1985, 119–120; Flanagan 1987) and the *Church Rocks* wreck (Preece and Burton 1993).

A morion was found, broken in several pieces of which the largest fragment is 22 cm and identifiable as a typical

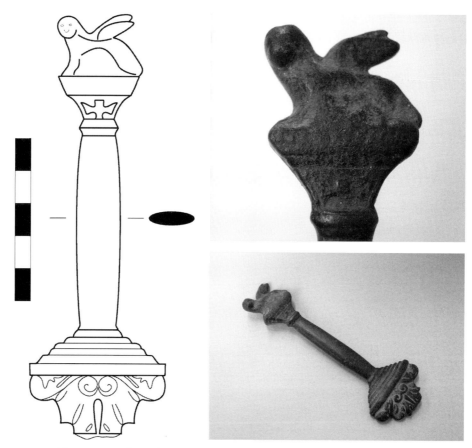

Figure 4.5. The stiletto's handle (drawing and photos by the author).

16th-century military helmet. Its material is very fragile having been underwater, which has caused the loss of part of its metallic alloy.

The hilt of a *stiletto* has the shape of San Marco's column in Venice with the lion on the top (Figure 4.5). It bears a Greek cross on the capital and six steps at the base, decorated with spirals. It is broken at the top of the blade join. It has a flat section, so is unlikely to be a *bombardieri*'s rule, because they normally had a triangular shape (Blair 1979, 473–474). The connection with Venice is very evident but this kind of artefact is, until now, an *unicum*.

Finally there was a very corroded, very small copper coin with a diameter of 12 mm and a thickness of 1.2 mm. It has been suggested (Musolino 1994, 36) that it is probably an Ottoman coin since is possible to see a turkish type on its surface (Pamuk 1999). In measurements and material it is identified as a *mangır* issue of the period of Süleyman the Magnificent (1520–1566) (Kabaklarlı 1999, plate 30).

Conclusion

Analysis and identification of ordnance pieces in a modern wreck site should be useful tool for finding and understanding some characteristics of the ship which carried them. When provenance and national features can easily be identified, the study of morphological and structural details may further help the interpretation.

In the case of the finds from Torre Faro, the lack of any archaeological documentation, objects removed from their context and a missing plan of the location of objects on the seabed created some difficulties. However it was possible to formulate some conjectures including pertinence to one or more shipwrecks. It seems likely they belong to just one wreck because they come from the same area but this is not proof positive. Some artefacts found were in use over a long period of time (from ancient to modern) – the steelyard, the sounding lead and the nails – while others confirm dating to the end of the 16th century – the coin, the morion and the artillery. Cast bronze guns started to be widely used during the 16th century around the Mediterranean area, although this kind of swivel gun was still in use in the 17th century. The association of the guns with the hilt of the knife suggested, at first sight, a Venetian product; this was confirmed later by the comparison of particular characteristic of pieces produced by Venetian gunfounders.

There are no timber remains of the hull so it is difficult to pinpoint exactly what kind of ship it was. Torre Faro's swivel guns were probably mounted on a private vessel because they have no sign of ownership of the Serenissima Republic. In this case, the merchant ship was the so-called *"nave tonda"* (round-ship), travelling along this maritime route from Venice or that in any case carried Venetian artillery. Torre Faro's swivel guns were, presumably, carried onboard a private commercial ship following a similar route

Table 4.1. Other petriere da braga from shipwrecks.

Wreck	Bore	Length	Weight	Marked Weight	References
Church Rocks (Teignmouth)	97 mm	192.8 cm	168 kg		Preece and Burton 1993, 263.
Filicudi: Relitto E	89 mm	101.5 cm			Beltrame in this volume.
Gnalic	91 mm	107 cm			Beltrame and Morin 2003, 10–14.
Gnalic	45 mm	87 cm		87	Ibid.
Gnalic (2 pieces)	91 mm	112 cm			Ibid.
Labia	87 mm	132 cm			Birch and McElvogue 1999, 273; McElvogue 2002, 35, 42.
Trinidad Valencera	86 mm	172.7 cm	136.08 kg	125	Martin 1975, 200.

of Venetian trades journeys of the *muda* (Doumerc 1991, 357–358). Even if it was not controlled by the Senate, the round-ships navigated the same harbours with their cargos (Lane 1983, 5–6).

At the end of the 16th century, Messina was the meeting port for different maritime itineraries and the goods yard of commercial trades from East and Atlantic Sea (Hocquet 1991, 404; Hocquet 1999, 174). Messina was the port of call where wares were stocked, sorted and redistributed. From the mid-16th century, it became an entrepot for merchandise coming from England or Flanders to reach the northern Adriatic Sea (Cancila 1978, 124): English ships left their products in Messina going to, or coming from, the East; in the same way, Venetian merchantmen sold and bought goods there. Venetian traders had consulates in the Sicilian city from a couple of centuries before as well as Genoese, Catalan end French ones (Cancila 1978, 130).

Acknowledgments

This text is the result of a thesis dissertation for which I would like to express my gratitude to people who followed me in that work. First of all Professor Carlo Beltrame who first proposed I attend a study on Venetian artillery and made me interested in it and who supported me in a remarkable way. Dr Marco Morin and Dr Renato G. Ridella who helped me out with any doubts and queries. Finally I want to thank Dr Grazia Musolino who allowed me to study the archaeological remains preserved in Soprintendecy of Messina.

References

Bacci, G. (2001) Archeologia subacquea sul versante Siciliano dello Stretto di Messina. In G. N. Bacci, G. Tigano (eds.) *Da Zancle a Messina un Percorso archeologico attraverso gli scavi II*, 271–301, Messina.

Beltrame C., Morin M. (2003) Una testimonianza dei traffici veneziani alla fine del Cinquecento, *L'archeologo subacqueo*, IX.3, 10–14.

Birch S., McElvogue D. M. (1999) La Lavia, La Juliana and the Santa Maria de Vison: three Spanish Armada transports lost off Streedagh Strand, *The International Journal of Nautical Archaeology*, 28.3, 265–276.

Smith R. Bishop (1997) *Two 16th Century Venetian Cannon in the Turkish Naval Museum*. Lisbon, Silvas.

Blair C. (1979) *Enciclopedia ragionata delle armi*. Milano, CDE.

Cancila O. (1978) Commercio estero, in *Storia della Sicilia*, vol. VIII, 121–161. Napoli – Palermo.

Capobianco A. (1598), *Corona e palma militare di artiglieria*, Venezia.

Collado L. (1586) *Pratica manuale di arteglieria*, Venezia.

Doumerc B. (1991) Le galere da mercato, in *Storia di Venezia, Temi, Il Mare*, 357–395. Roma, Treccani.

Flanagan L. N. W. *et al.* (1985) *Tresors de l'Armada*. Bruxelles.

Flanagan L. N. W. (1987), Steelyards and steelyard weights, *The International Journal of Nautical Archaeology*, 16. 3: 249–265.

Hocquet J.-C. (1991) L'armamento privato, in *Storia di Venezia, Temi, Il Mare*, 397–434. Rome, Treccani.

Hocquet J.-C. (1999) *Denaro, Navi e Mercanti a Venezia 1200–1600*. Rome.

Kabaklarlı N. (1999) *"MANGIR" Copper Coins of Ottoman Empire 1299–1808*. Istanbul, Uşaklılar Eğıtim Ye Kültür Vakfı.

Lane F. C. (1983) *Le navi di Venezia: fra i secoli XIII e XVI*. Torino, Einaudi.

Martin C. (1975) *Full Fathom Five: Wrecks of the Spanish Armada*. New York, The Viking Press.

Martin C. (1979) La Trinidad Valencera: an Armada invasion transport lost off Donegal, *The International Journal of Nautical Archaeology*, 8, 13–38.

Martin C., Parker G. (1999) *The Spanish Armada*, (rev. ed.) Manchester, Manchester University Press.

McElvogue D. M. (2002) A description and appraisal of ordnance from three Spanish Armada transports c. 1588, *Journal of the Ordnance Society*, 14, 31–50.

Moretti T. (1672) *Trattato dell'artiglieria*. Brescia.

Morin M. (2006) Artiglierie navali in ambito veneziano: tipologia e tecniche di realizzazione, *Quaderni di Oplologia*, 23, 3–28.

Musolino G. (1994) Testimonianze di relitti del XVI secolo nello Stretto di Messina. In *Atti VI Rassegna di Archeologia Subacquea. Giardini Naxos 25–27 ottobre 1991*, 129–142. Messina.

Pamuk Ş. (1999) *A Monetary History of the Ottoman Empire*. Cambridge, Cambridge University Press.

Preece C., Burton G. (1993) Church Rocks, 1975–83: a reassessment, *The International Journal of Nautical Archaeology*, 22, 257–265.

Ridella R. G. (2004) Dorino II Gioardi: a 16th -century Genovese gunfounder, *Journal of Ordnance Society*, vol. 16, 27–41.

Ridella R. G. (2008) «General descritione del'artiglieria che si ritrova nel Regno di Corsica e Isola di Capraia». Bocche da fuoco nelle fortificazioni costiere genovesi di Corsica tra Cinque e Seicento. In M. G. Mele, G. Serreli (eds.) *"Contra Moros y Turcos". Politiche e sistemi di difesa degli Stati mediterranei della Corona di Spagna in Età Moderna, Atti del convegno Villasimius-Baunei, 20–24 settembre 2005*, 289–314. Cagliari.

Sardi P. (1621) *L'artiglieria,* Venezia.

Smith R. Bishop (2000) *16th century swivel guns in Spain, Greece, Bulgaria and Cyprus*. Lisbon, Silvas.

Smith, R. D. (1995) Wrought-iron swivel gun in Mensun Bound (ed.), *The Archaeology of Ships of War: based on papers presented at an international conference held at Greenwich, London on 31 October – 1 November 1992*, 104–113. Oswestry, A. Nelson.

5

A Venetian Ship Sunk in Cyrenaica at the Beginning of the 18th Century

Sebastiano Tusa

For some time now, the Soprintendenza del Mare of Sicily has had a fruitful collaboration with the Department of Antiquity of Libya. The area in which this collaboration has had good results is the sea of Cyrenaica. Among some important discoveries that have been made within the frame of this joint expedition was the finding of a wreck in the gulf of Ras al-Hilal, not far from the eponymous cape that is the northernmost point of Cyrenaica (Figure 5.1). An extensive and careful survey of the area which contains the remains of the wreck was carried out at a depth of about 20 m. The complete mapping of the remains and objects was completed along with a wide and careful photographic documentation. Unfortunately almost nothing of the wooden parts of the sunken ship were found apart from some scattered pieces of wood whose limited dimensions and lack of diagnostic features did not give us any chance of identification. The only part of the ship that we identified was the galley (kitchen) because of the many baked bricks lying all in one place without any significant order. The main bulk of the

wreck's remains were the 31 iron cannons so far identified and which can be divided into two different sizes. Few objects were recovered and among those worth recording are scissors (Figure 5.2), some pewter dishes (Figure 5.3), a teapot, candle stands, some objects connected with the sailing system and fragments of at least two bronze bells with Christian iconography (Figure 5.4).

It was due to the analysis of the objects and the presence of the cannons with the St Mark Lion that we had no doubt about the Venetian origin of the ship (Figure 5.5). Using such data we started an extensive research in the Venetian archives with the help of Giovanni Caniato. But, by chance, we received a letter from an amateur (Giuseppe Alecci) who visited our website after reading of the our activities in the press. He was kind enough to give us a possible identification and name of the ship: *Tigre* (Tiger). After reading the documents concerning the ship *Tigre* we had no doubt that the sunken ship of Ras al-Hilal was indeed the *Tigre*.

Figure 5.1. General view of sunken cannons.

Sebastiano Tusa

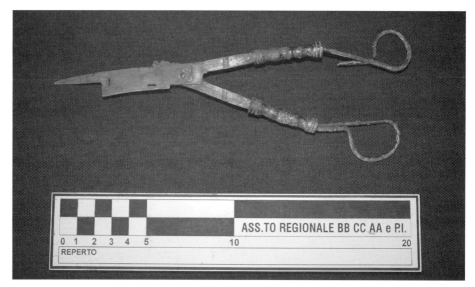

Figure 5.2. Scissors.

Figure 5.3. Pewter Dish.

Figure 5.4. Bronze Bell.

It was a first class ship, built by Iseppo di Zuanne de Pieri and launched in the Arsenale on 5 March 1696. It was well armed (*Colubrine di bronzo da 30: n 2; Colubrine di bronzo da 20: n 4; Colubrine di bronzo da 14: n 2; Cannoni di bronzo da 30: n 24; Cannoni di bronzo da 14: n 2; Cannoni di bronzo da 12: n 12; Sacri di bronzo da 12: n 2; Cannoni di ferro da 20: n 22; Mascoli di bronzo da 6: n 24; Petriere di bronzo da 6: n 12*) (Levi 1896, 27).

The ship had a very short life, but a glorious end. It was one of the strongest Venetian warships although from later original documents we understand that there was something wrong in the quality of some equipment and important parts of the ship as well as in some repairs done after a storm. A good source about such problems is the dispatch sent by Marc'Antonio Diedo, Capitano delle Navi (*Archivio di Stato, Venezia. Senato, Dispacci, Provveditori di terra e da mar, filza 1341;* Trapani 6 Aprile 1705) which can also be seen as the beginning of the tragic history of the final days of our ship. It was in Trapani for repairs after a heavy storm that occurred not far from Spinalonga (north-east Crete) at the entrance of Mirabello Gulf where there was a Venetian fort on the small island of Kalidon captured by the Turks in 1715.

The *Tigre* sailed from Trapani under the command of Michiel Cosadino, bound for Napoli in Romania (modern Nauplia in Peloponnese). Nauplia had been recently retaken by the Venetians under the command of Francesco Morosini in 1686. Nauplia had always been a very important strategic port along Mediterranean ancient sea routes especially for ships bound for Constantinople and the Holy Land. In Nauplia the *Tigre* was loaded with wheat and took aboard passengers, sailing on 26 February in the waters of Saronic Gulf. At the entrance of this gulf, not far from the small island of Spetses (Porto delle Spezie), she dropped anchor to collect wood from the shore.

This was the last stop before she sailed towards Crete on 28 February 1705, taking advantage of a good wind blowing from the East and North. But the wind strengthened, becoming a heavy storm, causing the captain great difficulties. Probably due to the poor quality of the repairs as well as of the original construction, the ship lost its mainmast as well as a great deal of other equipment. In addition, the rudder? was broken and the captain tried to hold the ship using two long ropes tied to the stern. Beside the severe damage to vital equipment of the ship, holes appeared in the hull. The crew showed great courage working tirelessly to try and close up the holes and pump out the sea water from the hull. The situation was turning into tragedy since it was impossible to stop her sailing fast to the South. She was driven past *Cerigo* and *Cerigotto* (Kithyra and Antikithyra), two islands between the southernmost part of the Peloponnese and Crete, Venetian bases controlling the sea routes between the Ionian and Aegean seas until 1797, without being able to reach land.

The *Tigre* was helpless, at the mercy of strong winds with only the foremast still standing. But the situation grew worse as it became almost impossible for the

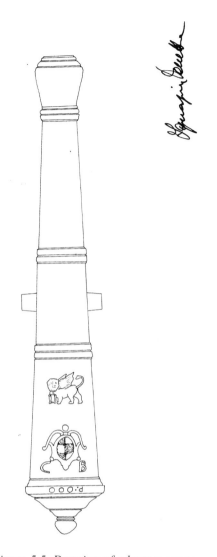

Figure 5.5. Drawing of a bronze cannon.

ship to maintain its course; moreover the crew were so exhausted they were losing the battle against sea water increasingly swamping the ship since the damage to the stern worsened.

After three days of increasingly difficult sailing and having bypassed Crete on the East side the *Tigre* reached the African coast near Cape Sant'Andrew, today called Ras al-Hilal, on the northernmost part of Cyrenaica. Suddenly the *Tigre* was intercepted by local patrols belonging to the Caramallis. In order to avoid the ship being taken by enemies, since it had a full complement of artillery, the captain, Michiel Cosadino, tried to blow her with gunpowder. But this proved impossible due the powder having become damp. Instead he decided to anchor not far from the coast in order to let the crew and passengers reach land easily, leaving the ship to sink in about *"quindeci passa d'acqua"* (about 8 m depth). Only two sailors and ten soldiers were lost when the ship sank without warning on the 7 April 1705!

The crew, the passengers and the captain were captured by enemy forces (about 3000 soldiers) and taken to the

Figure 5.6. Ship's equipment in situ.

port of Derna, a few miles East of Ras al-Hilal. The local chief decided to send the prisoners as a gift to the Bey of Tripoli. Tripoli was quite far from Derna, but a French tartan was at his disposal to bring this poor human cargo to the final destination. But the weather was still so bad that the French ship was forced east instead of taking the westward route and had to land at Bomba, 60 miles east of Derna! In Bomba the enemy landed to recover from the grueling journey. The Venetian commander, claiming to be ill, remained on board and used this opportunity to arrange a surprise attack with his crew. Thanks to his courage, Cosadino succeeded in seizing the French tartan and, cutting the anchor's ropes, took command of the ship and sailed towards freedom. Destiny changed and the Venetians reached Nauplia by passing Crete (Archivio di Stato di Venezia, Senato, Dispacci. Provveditori di Terra e da Mar. Filza 951. Dispaccio 89).

This is the synthesis of the real story of a Venetian warship which met a tragic destiny, a forgotten story that only thanks to the archaeological research in the sea of Cyrenaica became known. There is no doubt that the sunken relics of a huge warship in the waters of Ras al-Hilal belong to the *Tigre*. Although there are no traces of the wooden hull due to the absence of sandy soil which could have protected the wood from worms and other destroying factors, the numerous and rich amount of metal, clay and stone objects scattered on the bottom of sea over a very large area give us the assurance that this is what remains of the *Tigre* (see Figure 5.6).

It is a story that reveals the difficult period in Venice's history when she was losing her power in the Mediterranean. Cyprus and Crete had been lost. Only a few isolated ports still remained in the hands of the *Serenissima*. Moreover her prestige was decaying. In another glorious period *Tigre* would not have been seized and the crew captured. Since Venice was losing power many local rulers of North Africa were increasing or imposing heavy tolls for the simple transit of ships that Venice refused to pay. This was, along with the heavy damage by storm, the cause of the tragic end of *Tigre*.

That it was a period of crisis is shown also by the poor quality of the workmanship and the repairs to the ship. But it is also proved by the presence of fragments of at least two different bronze bells. These were not the ship's bells, but objects removed from different churches and monasteries in Greece due to the imminent Turkish invasion.

The finds represent sad days for Venice and an illustration of her people's courage which we have tried to honour through our research; it has given us the opportunity to bring back a forgotten story from Venice's past.

References

Archivio di Stato di Venezia, Senato, Dispacci. Provveditori di Terra e da Mar. Filza 951. (Dispaccio 89).

Archivio di Stato di Venezia. Senato, Dispacci, Provveditori di terra e da mar, filza 1341.

Levi, C. A. (1896), *Navi da guerra costruite nell'Arsenale di Venezia dal 1664 al 1896*. Venice.

6

Genoese Ordnance Aboard Galleys and Merchantmen in the 16th Century

Renato Gianni Ridella

Introduction

It is common knowledge that at the dawn of the modern era, Genoese ships, like those of the other Mediterranean powers, were divided into two categories: sailing freighters and the oared galleys. These both derived their peculiarities, structural and operational, from the Roman *naves onerarie* and *trireme* respectively, via the Byzantines. I repeat this truism only to introduce a subject, in contrast comparatively unknown, concerning the ownership and the management of these two types of vessels in Genoa. Her Republic, born in the 10th century more like a trade company than a true State was, throughout its whole life (ending in 1797), a political body with a rather light touch where the private interests of its merchant and financial oligarchy had a prevalent role (see Grendi 1987).

For these reasons during its epic development in the Middle Ages the Republic never had its own public fleet. The participation in the Crusades, the colonization in the eastern Mediterranean and the Black Sea and the wars against Pisa and Venice, were always carried out with ships placed at its disposal by private citizens remunerated by hire or profit sharing.

Then, when Genoa's eastern colonies fell into Turkish hands in the second half of the 15th century, the Genoese oared ships lost their function of transport and served only as warships. As a consequence, and also because of their high operating costs, the Genoese galleys were reduced in number from more than a hundred to a few dozen.

In contrast, the sailing ships maintained their prevalent civilian function even if, when required, they could be armed for war (*armate in guerra*) and employed as troop and supply carriers or used as floating strongholds.

In 1559, however, the Republic did fit out a little squadron of state galleys (at first four ships) in order to oppose the North African piracy along the Ligurian and Corsican coasts and to escort the silver shipments coming from Spain as reimbursements for the loans of the Genoese financiers to the Spanish Crown (Lo Basso 2003, 206–207).

The modernization of Genoese sea ordnance from the end of the 15th century, and the previous situation

Examining the archival documentation we can affirm that in Genoa modern sea ordnance was born from a decree of July 1498. Actually, on 29th of that month the *Officium Maris* (Office of the Sea), a magistracy of the Republic, had enacted this provision (D'Albertis 1893, 232–233):

> "... that every ship which rates more than 10,000 Cantara *(480 tons)* has to have two bronze cannons: one weighing 27 Cantara *(1,286 kg)* and the other one 23 *(1,096 kg)*, both firing a 50 Libre *shot (roughly 16 kilos)*. As well as four falcons each weighing 7 Cantara *(334 kg)*. This in addition to the ordinary equipment composed of 35 iron bombards and 15 archibuxi *(in this case corresponding to the French arquebuses-à-croc as the individual shoulder weapons were still represented by crossbows)*, these last made of iron or bronze".

That resolution answered a submission from the *Consiglio degli Anziani* (Council of the Elders), dated 4th July, that said (Gatti 1978, 18):

> "... we think it has been known for some time that the foreign nations, especially the French, have introduced heavy bronze ordnance aboard their ships. So, although this ordnance is placed in small vessels, shooting from a long range, it is enough to defeat every big ship. For this reason, nowadays, our sailing is dangerous even if our ships are of a large size, which everyone knows and they are very well equipped with iron bombards".

From these words we can understand that in this period the Genoese merchantmen, though very large and carrying a lot of bombards, had become an easy prey for smaller piratical or corsair ships that had, in contrast, the new bronze ordnance. With these long-range weapons they were able to hit the Genoese vessels, while keeping themselves out of the range of fire of the latter.

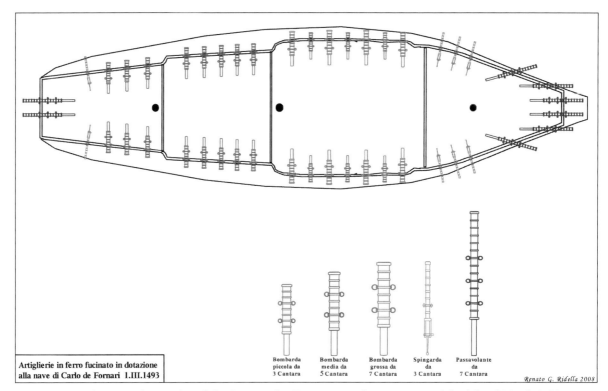

a) *Wrought iron ordnance aboard the Genoese ship* Fornara *according to a notarial deed dated March 1493.*

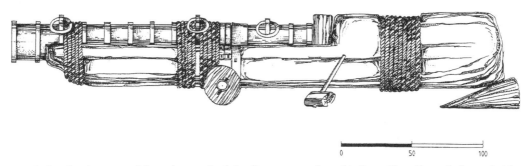

b) *Medium weight bombard recovered from the wreck of the Genoese merchantship* Lomellina *(from Guérout, Reith and Gassend 1989).*

c) *The barrel (tromba) of a passavolante (from Gasperoni 1779).*

d) *Lead coated wrought iron shots for the* passavolanti, *re-employed in a bronze demi culverin found in the Sciacca wreck (Photo: Soprintendenza di Agrigento).*

Figure 6.1. Wrought iron ordnance aboard Genoese merchant ships and galleys in the second half of the 15th century.

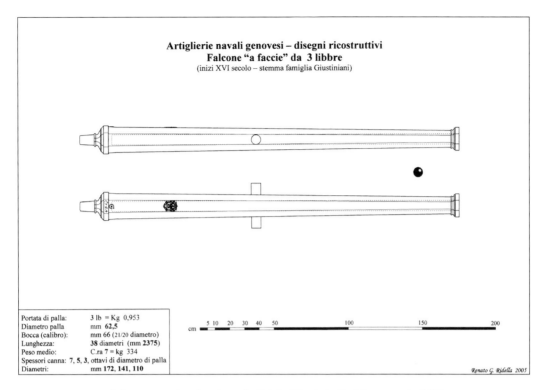

Artiglierie navali genovesi – disegni ricostruttivi
Falcone "a faccie" da 3 libbre
(inizi XVI secolo – stemma famiglia Giustiniani)

Portata di palla:	3 lb = Kg 0,953
Diametro palla	mm **62,5**
Bocca (calibro):	mm 66 (21/20 diametro)
Lunghezza:	**38** diametri (mm **2375**)
Peso medio:	C.ra 7 = kg 334
Spessori canna:	**7, 5, 3**, ottavi di diametro di palla
Diametri:	mm **172, 141, 110**

Renato G. Ridella 2005

a) *Reconstructive drawing of a Brizio Giustiniani's falcon cast in 1498.*

b) *Early 16th century Genoese falconet found off Lido Burrone, Favignana (Egadi Islands, Sicily). The weight mark Cantara 6 – Rotoli 74 corresponds to 321 kg (Photo: Antonino Palazzolo).*

Figure 6.2. Early Genoese bronze ordnance: falcons and falconets.

A notarial deed (ASG, NA, f. 1296, 1.II I.1493) informs us that in 1493 the ship *Fornara* (Figure 6.1a) was equipped with 30 wrought iron bombards of various sizes and weights (Figure 6.1b), 8 light *spingarde* and 8 heavy *spingarde*. I think that the first could represent the early swivel guns as can also be gathered, in another case, from one on them being placed in a crow's nest (*gabbia*) (Gatti 1978, 19). While the latter should correspond to the long barrel *Passavolanti* (Figure 6.1c) that then already fired lead shot – diameter about 100 millimetres (Promis 1841, 175–177) – containing an iron dice or rough spherical iron shot covered with a thin coating of lead (Figure 6.1d). However, their fire could not reach satisfactory distances, possibly owing to their weak structure, which was not able to withstand strong charges of powder, and also to the loss of pressure between their barrel and the removable chamber. That is confirmed by the adoption, after the 1498 decree, of the bronze falcons (Figure 6.2) which then also employed lead shot (D'Albertis 1893, 234).

From the archives (see also Ciciliot in these volume) we know that various types of Genoese bombards then existed. The light one weighing 3 *Cantara* (140 kg), the medium at 5 *Cantara* (240 kg) and the heavy at 7 and 9.5 *Cantara* (330 and 450 kg). For this last type we also know the length: 8 *Palmi* (*c.* 2.00 m), and the weight of its stone shot: 25 *Libre* (8 kg, with a diameter of roughly 190 mm).

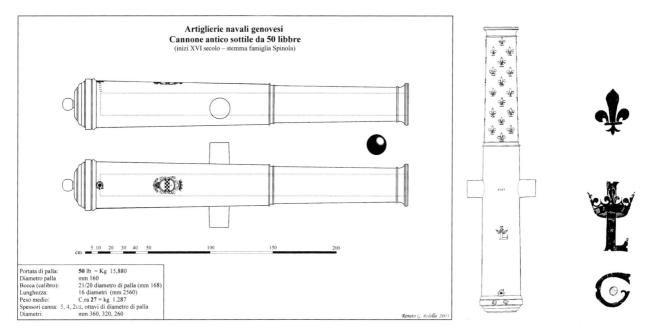

Figure 6.3. Reconstructive drawing of a lightweight Genoese cannon (left) made by comparison with an exemplar (right) cast for Louis XII of France (1498–1515), now preserved in the Musée de l'Armée, Paris (inventory N. 73 – From Guérout & Liou 2001).)

The bronze cannons cited, weighing from 23 to 27 *Cantara*, that had to supplement the fire of the bombards, succeeded in this function only because of the higher destructive power of their cast iron shot – 50 *Libre* in comparison with the 15–25 of the stone shot. But their range of fire would not be very much longer than that reached by the bombards because their weight shows that they had thin walls and a short length (possibly 15–16 bore diameters). We do not know their true appearance as none of them have survived (to the present) but I think they may resemble the coeval French light cannons (Figure 6.3) since, in this period, there was evidently a correlation between the French (Provençal) and Genoese gunfounding (Ridella 2006, 167). Maybe they were chambered pieces and could enter into the Italian category of the *Cannoni sottili* (cannons having thin walls). Owing to their unsatisfactory performance, their production would already have stopped in the first years of the 16th century, but we can still find some of them in the 1540 inventories of Genoese merchant ships.

Returning to the 1498 decree, the Genoese ship-owners did not have to go abroad to stock up with bronze pieces in order to provide equipment conforming to the decree of the *Officium Maris*. Indeed, two skilful gunfounders were then working in Genoa, Gregorio I Gioardi and his almost contemporary nephew Andrea Merello. In another archival record of the same year (ASG, NA, f. 1037, 3.IX.1498, 19.XI.1498) we read that the latter cast two cannons and four falcons for the ship *Santa Maria*, owned by the nobleman Bartolomeo Roisecco. A note specifies that the four falcons '*have to be of the same type as those aboard captain Brizio Giustiniani's galleys*' cast by Gregorio I Gioardi (Figure 6.2a). From this record we know that a similar evolution regarding the ordnance had already started

in the oared Genoese warships that up to this period were equipped with bombards and *passavolanti*, too. The number and typology of the wrought iron ordnance aboard the Genoese galleys toward the end of the 15th century could be gathered, till now, only from a more recent source dating to 1513 when the Republic gave Andrea Doria the command of two such ships hired from private owners (Figure 6.11a). As the equipment set for these galleys consisted of only six bombards each, Doria asked that they also be strengthened with bronze falcons but that was denied him. At that time the Genoese State was rather poor though populated by a number of very wealthy persons and, in order to increase his fire power, he was eventually obliged to purchase two falcons out of his own pocket from his cousin Nicolò Doria (Pandiani 1935, 10, 15).

The development in the 16th century – composition of the equipment

Anyhow, aboard the public and private Genoese galleys, the wrought iron pieces should have been entirely replaced with bronze ordnance before 1540 (ASG, Mar, f. 1666) while they continued to be employed on the merchant ships for a large part of the 16th century. Actually, they could still be useful in close range fire, with stone or canister shot, against the piratical North African foists just before the boarding. An example of that are the bombards (Figure 6.1b) found in the wreck of the Genoese merchant ship *La Lomellina*, sunk on Sept 1516 in the bay of Villefranche, Provençal coast (Guérout, Rieth and Gassend 1989, 99–111). Her bronze ordnance, possibly the two cannons and the four falcons set in the 1498 decree, was surely recovered soon after the wreck, together with the field pieces she was carrying.

Coming back to the galleys, we can see that in the

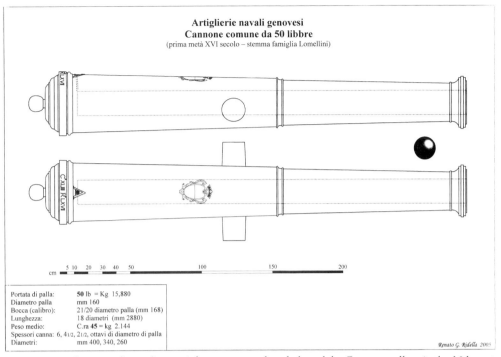

a) *Reconstructive drawing of a medium weight cannon employed aboard the Genoese galleys in the 16th century.*

b) *Genoese heavy battery cannon cast, possibly by Gregorio II Gioardi, around 1560. Now in the Royal Artillery Museum, Woolwich (Photo: Robert Smith & Ruth Brown).*

Figure 6.4. Genoese bronze cannons in the 16th century.

early 1540s the bronze ordnance equipping the *Galea Patrona* (vice-flagship) of the Republic was composed of a *Canone de la corsia* (centreline cannon), two *Sagri* (sakers) and two *Smerigli* (breech-loading esmerils) (ASG, Mar, f. 1666). From archives we can understand that the main piece was no longer the light-weight cannon of the 1498 decree but a medium-weight one that we can label as a *Cannone comune* (Figure 6.4 a), the weight of which ranged from 40 to 45 *Cantara* (1,906–2,144 kg). Like the previous one it should be quite similar to the contemporary French cannon, some exemplars of which are displayed in

the Musée de l'Armée, Paris (inventory numbers: N. 72, N. 75, N. 76, N. 78, N. 80). The earliest information about this type dates back to 1507 when Gregorio I Gioardi was obliged to move his foundry to Lerici, a country near La Spezia, as the French garrison from the stronghold of the *Castelletto* bombarded the Genoese harbour zone where he usually worked (Ridella 2006, 172). This happened during the revolt of the commoners which was quickly stifled by the Genoese aristocrats with the help of Louis XII of France. At first these cannon were also intended to be employed as battery pieces but it soon became evident that,

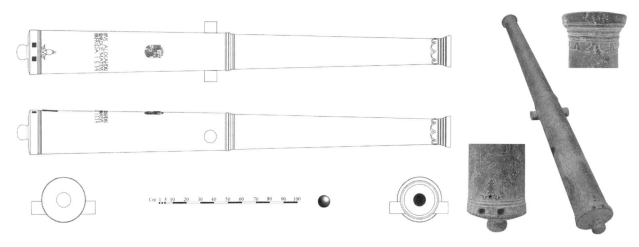

a) *Heavy piece cast by Alessandro Gioardi in 1534, now at Famagusta (from Ridella 2004a).*

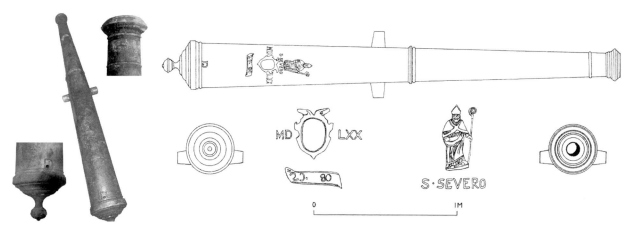

b) *Heavy piece cast by Dorino II Gioardi in 1570, in the National Museum of Ireland, Dublin (Drawing from McElvogue 2002).*

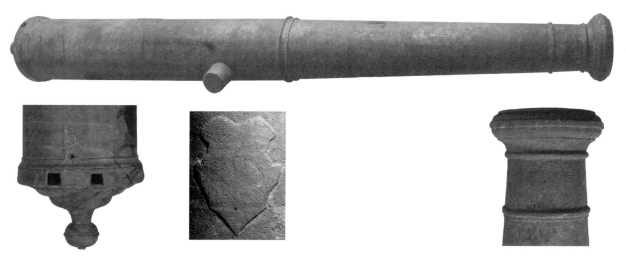

c) *Medium weight piece cast by Gio. Battista Gandolfo (1580s-1590s), found off Brsecine, Croatia (Photo: Renata Andjus).*

Figure 6.5. Bronze sakers from Genoese manufacture.

because of their rather thin walls, they could not sustain the continuous fire needed in a siege operation. For this purpose heavier cannons, the *Cannoni rinforzati*, began to be produced (Figure 6.4b). In Genoa the first report about this type dates to 1514 when the same Gregorio I Gioardi cast a cannon weighing 53.15 *Cantara* (2,532 kg) by the re-melting of an old bombard named *La Cagnassa* (The Bad Bitch) (ASG, AS, f. 3098, 29.III.1514). But until 1547 only a few of these heavy cannon were produced and none of them could be drawn up when, in the same year, the Republic had to form a battery to besiege the castle of Montoggio where the survivors from Gio. Luigi Fieschi's failed plot had been entrenched (ASG, CGF, f. 621). The ten cannon deployed there were only of the medium-weight type and some of them, too overheated by the continuous fire, burst, killing or wounding their gunners (Oliva 2001, 40). So, from this time, the employment of the medium-weight cannon was limited to the galleys, where they had to fire only a few shots before the boarding and remained in this function for almost the entire 16th century.

Looking again at the *Galea Patrona* we can observe that the firepower of the Genoese galleys should have been increased, in the first decades of the 16th century, with the adoption of heavier pieces than the falcons – the sakers. From the inventories of the Genoese strongholds and of the merchant ships, during the 1530s–1540s, we learn that these first medium-weight types fired a 6 *Libre* (1.9 kg) shot, had a bore diameter of 83–85 mm, a length of 28–30 diameters and weighed roughly 12 *Cantara* (572 kg). In 1535 Luchino II Gioardi, Gregorio's half-brother, cast two sakers of this weight for the Spanish ship *Santa Maria de Bisogno* (from Majorca – captain: Pedro Gilet (ASG, NA, f. 1739, 22.V.1535)). However, in general, the Spaniards requested from the Genoese gunfounders longer (35 diameters) and heavier sakers than these last, like the one cast by Alessandro Gioardi in Messina, Sicily, in 1534 (now displayed at Famagusta, Cyprus (Figure 6.5a)) or that produced more recently (1570) by his cousin Dorino II Gioardi (Figure 6.5b) for the Catalan ship *La Juliana*, (sunk off Streedagh Strand, Sligo (Ireland), in 1588 when she was serving in the Armada (McElvogue 2002, 35–40; Ridella, 2004b)). At this wreck site a bronze piece from amongst the 24 taken aboard the Levanter ships from the walls and the fortress of Palermo in April 1587 was also found, photographed but left *in situ*. It is a demi cannon, not a saker as has been written, mistaking the Sicilian *Cantaro* (79 kg) with the Spanish *Quintal* (46 kg). Thanks to its Sicilian weight mark *Cantara 20 – Rotoli 82* (1,654 kg) and with the help of Prof. Antonino Palazzolo (2007, 71–72), I was able to identify it as that cast by the Sicilian gunfounder Federico Musarra in 1549, bearing the figure of San Calogero, patron saint of Palermo (ASPa, TRP, NP, 2036, 8.V.1587). Only one exemplar of the medium-weight Genoese sakers seems to survive, that mentioned in this volume by Irena Radic Rossi , recently found off Brsecine near Dubrovnik, Croatia (Figure 6.5c). It lay close to the coast together with other broken bronze pieces that could have been scraps intended for re-melting or it

perhaps belonged to the equipment of a ship burnt down and sunk in that place. From the evidence of the pictures I received from its restorer, Renata Andjus, I think it may have been cast during the last two decades of the 16th century by Gio. Battista Gandolfo (Genoa *c.* 1535–1601). Indeed, the same monogram IB (for *Iohannes Baptista*) it has on the touchhole appears in a piece, dated 1591, where his whole name and surname written in Latin, *Io. Baptista Gandulphus*, are engraved on the base-ring, too (see Figure 6.10c).

Amongst ordnance aboard the *Galea Patrona* from the 1540s, two *Smerigli* also appear. In Genoa, this term then denoted both the smallest pieces that shoot stone balls or canisters and those that fired iron and, more frequently, lead shot weighing less than a *Libra* down to six *Once*. They could be either muzzle or breech-loaders as we learn from those two supplied by Dorino II Gioardi to the Genoese ship-owner Tomaso Bestagno in 1564 (ASG, NA, f. 1795, 15.V.1564): *... smerigios duos metali et unum de uno pecio et alium a masculo de rubis novem singulo* ('... two bronze esmerils one made in a single piece and the other with a removable chamber, each one weighing nine *rubbi*', i.e 71.5 kg). It is possible to match such a description, looking at

a

b

Figure 6.6. Genoese Smerigli petrieri (esmerils).

a) *Muzzle-loading type possibly cast by Battista Merello in the 1550s, recovered from the Sciacca wreck (Photo: author).*
b) *Breech-loading type (16th century), maybe found off Carloforte, SW Sardinia, it is now kept in the War Museum at Rovereto, Trento (Photo: Museo della Guerra di Rovereto).*

the images of two exemplars. One (Figure 6.6a), muzzle-loading, raised from the Sciacca wreck which I would date to the early 1550s, and another (Figure 6.6b) displayed in the Museo della Guerra at Rovereto.

Turning to the merchant ships, we have a certain number of archival records referring only to the early 1540s as the previous records and the later 16th-century state records seem to be lost. They deal with the *Revisiones* (inventories) of Genoese ships, in the *Maritimarum* collection of the Genoa State Archives (ASG, Mar, f. 1665–1666), in which we can observe a rather chequered situation. In order to make clear the lack of uniformity in the ordnance equipment, I show here some examples:

Navis Rubea (1540)
>   2 bronze cannons (of the old light-weight type weighing 27 *Cantara* each one)
>   2 bronze sakers (weight 14 *Cantara*)
>   3 bronze esmerils
>   28 iron bombards
>   12 iron esmerils

Navis Lercara (1540, captain Francesco Cibo Costa)
>   2 bronze demi culverins (weight 25 *Cantara*)
>   2 bronze demi cannons (weight 32? *Cantara*)
>   8 iron bombards
>   18 iron esmerils

Navis Angeli de Flisco (1541, owner Angelo Fieschi)
>   3 bronze demi cannons (no weight)
>   1 bronze saker (no weight)
>   12 iron bombards
>   1 iron *passavolante*
>   16 iron esmerils

Navis Doria (1541, owner Ambrogio Doria)
>   2 bronze demi cannons (no weight)
>   2 bronze sakers (no weight)
>   2 bronze falcons (no weight)
>   14 iron bombards
>   12 iron esmerils

Navis Ruisecha (1544, owner and captain Leonardo Roisecco)
>   2 bronze pieces (weight 30 *Cantara*, maybe demi cannons)
>   2 bronze pieces (weight 22 *Cantara*, maybe demi culverins)
>   2 sakers (weight 12 Cantara)
>   8 iron bombards
>   8 iron esmerils

Navis Spinola (1544, owner and captain Luigi Spinola)
>   2 bronze pieces (weight 35 *Cantara*, maybe demi cannons)
>   10 iron bombards
>   3 iron *passavolanti*
>   33 iron esmerils

We do not know the tonnage rating of these vessels but, as they had bronze pieces according to the 1498 decree; it should have been larger than 480 tons and indeed in the

same papers we can find ships carrying only wrought iron ordnance which should have been smaller.

In 1546, trying to resolve such a confusion, the magistracy of the *Conservatores Navium* (Keepers of the ships) enacted a regulation that fixed number and total weight of the bronze pieces with which a merchantman had to be armed in proportion to its rating, at this time expressed in *Salme*. The *Salma* was a unit of dry volume (275 litres) used in Sicily to measure cereal [loads] and, as the Genoese ships freighted Sicilian corn above all else at the time, this system of rating had been adopted – fixing the rough equivalence 1 *Salma* = 4 Genoese *Cantara* (190.6 kg) (Gatti 1999, 86). Here are *Conservatores*' provisions (Calegari 1970, 91):

– More than 2500 *Salme* (over 475 tons): 5–6 pieces weighing 100 *Cantara* (4,765 kg)
– from 2000 to 2500 *Salme* (380–475 tons): 4 pieces weighing 80 *Cantara* (3,812 kg)
– from 1600 to 2000 *Salme* (300–380 tons): 3 pieces weighing 60 *Cantara* (2,856 kg)
– from 1400 to 1600 *Salme* (270–300 tons): 2 pieces weighing 40 *Cantara* (1,906 kg)

The ships rating less than 1400 *Salme* had to carry no bronze pieces as '*they have not a crew sufficient to handle ordnance ... and for this reason this ordnance could serve better to give weapons to the enemies than to defend these ships*'.

As we can note, the average weight of those pieces amounted to 20 *Cantara*, which is intermediate between a saker (13 C.) and a demi culverin bastard (27 C.). This last type of gun from that period, with the removal of the old thin wall ordnance, became the heaviest bronze piece aboard the Genoese merchant ships. The Genoese *Bastarda* fired a 12–15 *Libre* (3.8 – 4.8 kg) iron shot, had a calibre of about 110 mm and was long 25–27 calibres. Its form and size were quite similar to those of the French *couleuvrine batârde*, an exemplar of which was recovered from the Sciacca wreck. This piece, bearing a Genoese weight mark, shows Francis I's salamander and should have been cast in the last years of his reign (1546–47). According to my researches it belonged to the equipment of the ship *San Juan* from San Sebastian, Biscay, and was purchased by the Genoese ship-owner Nicolò Zerbino in 1580 (Ridella 2005, 98). A fine exemplar of a Genoese demi culverin bastard is that raised off San Leone, Agrigento – Sicily in 2006 and now displayed in the archaeological park of the Valle dei Templi (Figure 6.7a). The monogram BS on its touchhole means that it should have been produced by Bartolomeo Sommariva (possibly around 1565), when he was about 25. Here I would briefly mention this gunfounder, who moved to Spain in the first 1580s, worked in Lisbon for the Armada in 1587 and then in Malaga from where in 1592 he went back to Lisbon. He was very much blamed by his contemporaries and by recent authors as a bad gunfounder, but the latter never ask themselves why he was not thrown out, and how he continued his career, taking up the prestigious direction of the foundry in Seville before 1608 from where, in the

a) *Naval piece cast by Bartolomeo Sommariva, found off San Leone, Agrigento (Photo: Alessandra Nobili).*

b) *Naval piece found off Fornells, Minorca, now at the San Felipe Fort (Photo: Museo Militar de Menorca).*

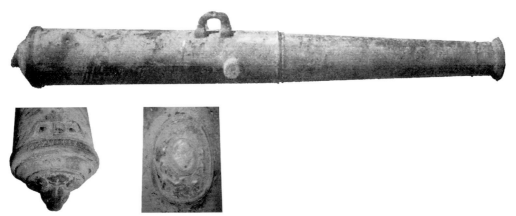

c) *Fortress piece found off Fornells too, cast by Dorino II Gioardi (Photo: Museo Militar de Menorca).*

d) *Naval piece displayed in the Turkish Military Museum, Istanbul (Photo: Robert Smith & Ruth Brown).*

Figure 6.7. Genoese demi culverins bastard.

a) *Comparison between French and Genoese muzzle mouldings in medium/heavy pieces.*

b) *Comparison between Genoese and Venetian muzzle mouldings in light/medium pieces.*

c) *Evolution of the Genoese muzzle mouldings shape through the 1560s.*

Figure 6.8. The Genoese muzzle mouldings in the 16th century.

following year, he addressed his *Memorial* to the king Philip III (Ridella 2009, 33–40).

In Bartolomeo's demi culverin we can note that the muzzle-mouldings show the archaic French-Genoese form shaped like a simple capital enriched with a square fillet (Figure 6.8a), while in the lighter pieces (sakers, falcons, etc.) the simple capital very similar to that present in the Venetian bronze guns till the 1670s (Figure 6.8b) appears to be prevalent. Now, in the Genoese ordnance that angled shape seems to be replaced, possibly after 1565, with a new rounded form (Figure 6.8c) and remained virtually unchanged until the mid-18th century together with the single reinforcement structure. So this difference can be used as a means of dating.

Two other Genoese demi culverins bastard were found off Fornells, Minorca, and are now kept in the San Felipe Fort, Mahon. They are a little spoiled but, looking at their muzzle mouldings, I think they could both have been cast before 1570. One of them (Figure 6.7b) shows the Genoese weight mark *Cantara 27 – Rotoli 62* (1,316 kg) in Arab numerals carved between the touchhole and the smooth coat-of-arms typical of the merchant sea ordnance. The other (Figure 6.7c) bears on the touchhole the D of Dorino II Gioardi and its cascable is moulded into the head of a lion. It has an illegible weight mark in Roman numerals on the base ring and is fitted out with dolphins (handles). Such evidence means that it represented a fortress piece taken aboard the ship wrecked off Fornells as sea ordnance

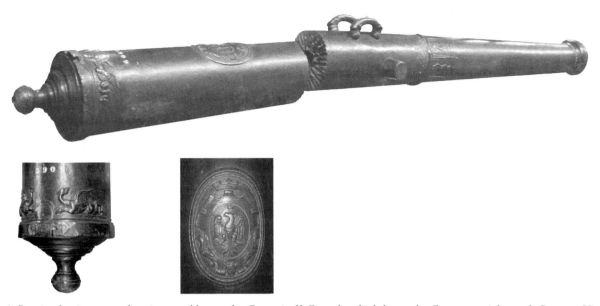

a) *Demi culverin extraordinaria, possibly cast by Gregorio II Gioardi, which bears the Genoese weight mark Cantara 50 – Rotoli 65 (2413 kg). The eagle is the heraldic symbol of Palermo. Now in the Museo del Ejercito, Madrid (Photo: Museo del Ejercito, Madrid).*

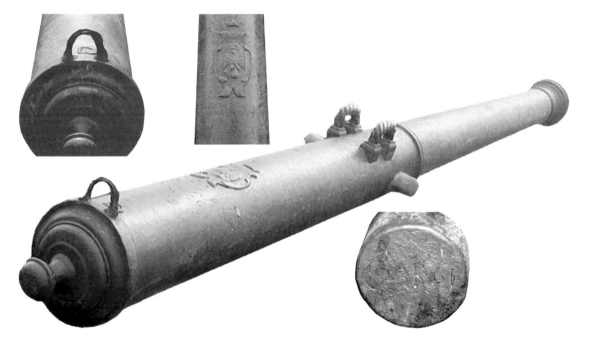

b) *Saker cast by Dorino II Gioardi as the 'D' on the touchhole states. Its weight mark on the trunnion says Cantara 23 – Rotoli 61 (1125 kg). Now in the Castillo de la Mota, San Sebastian (Spain) (Photo: José Manuel Matés Luque).*

Figure 6.9. Two Armada surviving cannon produced in Genoese foundries for the city walls of Palermo, Sicily, in 1575–76.

(Ridella 2005, 113, f. 13). This difference between these two demi culverins means that, at least in the second half of the 16th century, it is possible to distinguish a Genoese sea piece from a Genoese field piece and now I think we can properly discuss a Genoese naval ordnance. Other examples of field artillery taken aboard some ships are represented by two pieces that I found in Spain. They are a demi culverin *extrordinaria* (very long) cast, possibly, by Gregorio II Gioardi in 1575 displayed in the Museo del Ejercito, Madrid (Figure 6.9a) and a saker produced the

following year by his cousin Dorino now in the Castillo de la Mota at San Sebastian/Donostia (Figure 6.9b). They belonged to a supply of at least 50 pieces (battery cannon, demi cannon, demi culverins, sakers and *Petrieri*) made by some Genoese gunfounders (Dorino II and Gregorio II Gioardi, Gio. Battista Gandolfo and the brothers Sommariva) for the city walls of Palermo and its Spanish fortress, the *Castel a Mare*. Thanks to their Genoese weight marks engraved on the right trunnion, and with the help of Prof. Palazzolo, I was able to understand that they were taken aboard the six ships embargoed by the Spaniards in Sicily to form the Armada Levanter Squadron. Possibly they were the only pieces of the 24 (11 of Genoese manufacture), which were taken from Palermo in 1587 (ASPa, TRP, NP, 2036, 8.V.1587), to go back to Spain after the failed expedition against England. One, perhaps the only one, of those Levanter ships to survive from the expedition was the Genoese *Santissima Trinità di Scala* (Giacomo Scala was her former captain, who died in Gibraltar and was replaced by Francesco Isola, and the owner was the Genoese nobleman Nicolò Lomellini), which entered the port of Santander, northern Spain, very badly battered. She was dismasted and lacking the boat and four anchors of the six she had when she sailed; possibly she had lost them at Gravelines when the Armada was attacked by the English fire ships (I found the report of her purser Battista Gabrielli in ASG, NA, f. 3167, 10.VI.1606).

Another Genoese naval demi culverin is kept in the Turkish Military Museum (Askeri Muze), Istanbul. In its picture (Figure 6.7 d), provided to me by Ruth Brown, we can read the weight mark *Cantara 26 – Rotoli 75* (1,275 kg). Its shape is quite similar to that of the contemporaneous Venetian pieces save for the iron handle – possibly an extension of a crown-piece holding the bore mould still during the casting and used also as a rear sight – the remains of which are recognizable in the two rusty square bulges present in the base ring peculiar to the French-Genoese system (see Figure 6.9b).

During the same period (1550s–1570s), on the Genoese merchant ships, the obsolete iron bombard began to be replaced with a particular type of bronze guns. They were muzzle-loading chambered pieces deriving from the old *Cannoni petrieri* (end 15th–early 16th century) and then called simply *Petrieri* in the inventories. This category had a large diffusion in the Genoese ordnance also through the whole 17th century mainly on the city walls and strongholds as, owing to their small dimensions, they could easily be worked into the narrow casemates placed in the sides of the bulwarks. From this position they could fire stone or canister shot, sweeping the walls and enfilading the enemy infantry in attack. Three category of *Petrieri* were produced:

– the heavy ones firing a 15–18 *Libre* (4.8–5.7 kg) stone shot, weighing 14–20 *Cantara* (670–860 kg) and having a bore diameter that can be estimated as 160–170 mm.
– the medium, 9–12 *Libre* (2.9–3.8 kg), weight 7–10 *Cantara* (330–480 kg), bore diameter 135–155 mm
– the light, 6 *Libre* (1.9 kg), weight 4–5 *Cantara* (190–240 kg), bore diameter 120 mm.

Aboard the merchantmen vessels, the medium *Petrieri* were mainly employed, like the two (Figure 6.10 a), dated *c.* 1570, recovered from the *Juliana* wreck (McElvogue 2002, 38–40) and the couple recently found near the Grebeni islet, Vis island – Croatia (Radic Rossi, pers. comm.). These last (Figure 6.10b), considering a particular piece of evidence about them, could have been cast by Francesco Sommariva, Bartolomeo's brother, maybe in the

1590s and one of them shows the weight mark *Cantara 9 – Rotoli 53* (454 kg). The light *Petrieri* were placed mostly in the smaller boats like, for example, a single piece in the oared *Fregate coralline* engaged in the coral fishing along the coasts of Corsica and Sardinia (Gatti 1999, 211). Off this last island, possibly near Calasetta or Porto Torres, was found an exemplar of this kind was found (Figure 6.10c) cast by Gio. Battista Gandolfo in 1591 (Ridella 2008, 300, f. 11) and marked *Cantara 4 – Rotoli 84* (231 kg). Another two light pieces (Figure 6.10 d) found in 1907 near the *Molo Vecchio*, the Genoese old jetty, at present displayed in the Museo del Mare "Galata", Genoa, should belong to the same period. Their weight marks are *Cantara 4 – Rotoli 96* (236 kg) and *Cantara 5 – Rotoli 6* (241 kg).

We can find two medium/heavy *Petrieri* in the inventory of the ship *La Trinità* rating 4,500 *Salme*, dated 9th July 1579 (ASG, NA, f. 3014, 9.VII.1579):

– 2 *Mogiane* (heavy sakers), weighing 16 *Cantara* each.
– 2 *Bastarde* (demi culverins bastard), 21 *Cantara* each
– 2 *Pedrieri*, 14 *Cantara* each
– 1 *Sagro* (really a heavy falcon), *Cantara 10 – Rotoli 25*
– 2 *Sagri* (really heavy falcons), 8–9 *Cantara* each
– 2 *Falconetti* (falconets), 4 *Cantara* each
– 2 *Pedreri alla veniciana* (breech-loading swivel guns with bronze barrels and iron *braghe* (chamber holders), 4 *Cantara* each
– 1 *Sagro di ferro coratto* (cast iron short saker) 9 *Cantara*
– 2 *Bombarde* (wrought iron bombards)

Here we can see that the old wrought iron ordnance has almost entirely disappeared while the first cast iron pieces begin to appear. The total weight of the bronze ordnance (13 pieces) exceeds 145 *Cantara* (6,900 kg) and is compatible with the rating of the ship. It is also evident that the falcons (here improperly called sakers), had become heavier than the first types, as is verifiable in the exemplar from the Sciacca wreck that I dated to the 1550s and ascribed to Battista Merello and his brother-in-low Dorino II Gioardi (Ridella 2005, 104).

In the same period a smaller ship, the *Santa Maria della Grazia* (2,600 *Salme*), had a heavier and more uniform equipment (Gatti 1999, 333) composed of 6 *Bastarde* (22–23 *Cantara* each), 4 *Pedrieri* (9–10 *Cantara* each), 3 *Smerigli* (swivel guns firing lead/iron shot, 3.5 *Cantara* each), 2 *Bombarde* (7 *Cantara* each).

The maximum in bronze ordnance equipment had to be that reached aboard the *Nostra Signora Incoronata* (alias *La Coltellera* – 820 tons) which in 1594 carried 6 demi culverins, 4 heavy *Petrieri*, 4 medium *Petrieri*, 2 heavy sakers, 9 swivel guns, with a total weight of 18,500 kg (ASG, NA, f. 3860, 1.III.1594).

The situation of the Genoese galley ordnance from the eve of Lepanto to the 1590s

From an archival record dated 18th July 1560 we can consider the ordnance then equipping the galley *Capitana*

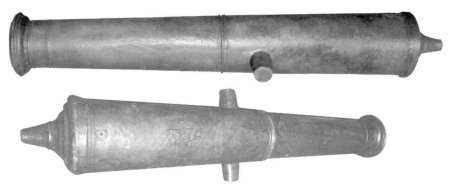

a) *Medium weight pieces from the* Juliana *wreck, the lower showing the 'D' of Dorino II Gioardi (Photos: Robert Smith and Jim Stapleton).*

b) *Couple of medium weight pieces found off Grebeni, Island of Vis, Croatia (Photo: Danijel Frka).*

c) *Light piece, cast by Gio Battista Gandolfo in 1591, found in the sea of Sardinia (Photo: Mario Galasso).*

d) *Couple of light pieces found off the port of Genoa in 1907 (Photo: author).*

Figure 6.10. Genoese naval Petrieri.

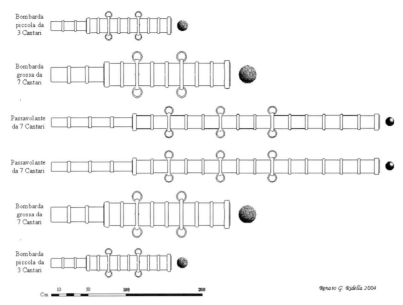

a) *Hypothesis about the wrought iron equipment toward the end of the 15th century.*

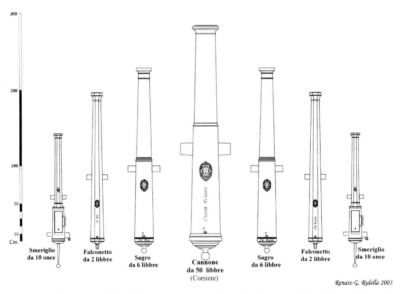

b) *Reconstructive drawing of the ordnance equipping the galley* Capitana *(flagship) of Genoa in 1560. The ordinary galleys, like the vice-flagship (*Patrona*) in the 1540s, lacked the two falconets.*

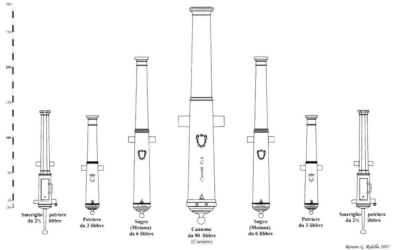

c) *Reconstructive drawing of the ordnance of Gio. Andrea Doria's galley* Donzella *in 1582.*

Figure 6.11. Development of the ordnance aboard the Genoese galleys from the end of the 15th century to the 1580s.

(flagship) of Genoa (Figure 6.11b), when she was sold to the Duke of Tuscany and given to his commissioner Antonio Martelli on the shore of Castagneto, Leghorn (ASG, MG, f. 1, 18.VII.1560). This inventory, though presenting an incorrect terminology as it was possibly written by an unskilled clerk, shows that she carried 5 main pieces. As we know that the *Capitane* were more heavily armed in comparison with the ordinary galleys, we can deduce that these last lacked the two falcons and were in the same situation as in the early 1540s (supra 43). Niccolò Capponi (2006, 185–190), in his analysis of the ordnance of the Christian galleys fighting in the battle of Lepanto (1571), underlines this lighter equipment peculiar to the *Ponentine* ones (Western: Spanish, Genoese, Tuscan and Papal) in comparison with that of the *Levantine*, or Venetian ones,

on which the pieces, particularly the swivel guns, were more numerous. The inventories of the *Capitana* and the *Patrona* of Genoa in 1570–71 (ASG, MG, f. 1, 31.VIII.1570, 9.III.1571) and those of the four galleys sold to the Spanish Crown by the Lomellini in 1575 (evidence that I first reported to Capponi: ASG, NA, f. 3150, 23.IV.1575), confirm his assertion. But it is evident that a little after this period, the Genoese galleys began to strengthen their equipment, as we learn from the sale contract for ten of Gio. Andrea Doria's galleys purchased from him by the Spaniards in 1582 (ASG, NA, f. 3156, 3.I.1582). Nine of them, like for example the *Donzella* had actually increased their armament to five main pieces. Part of the inventory, written in Spanish and referring to this galley, says:

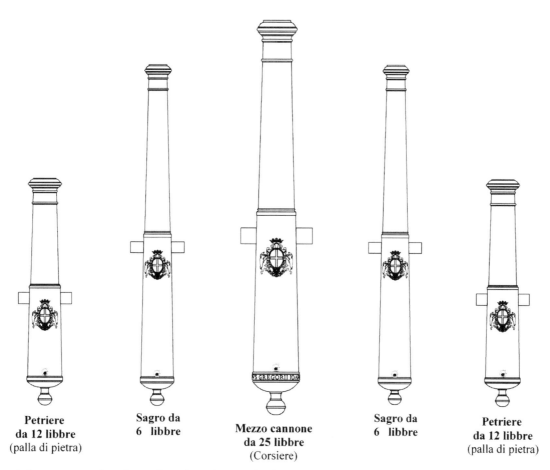

| Petriere da 12 libbre (palla di pietra) | Sagro da 6 libbre | Mezzo cannone da 25 libbre (Corsiere) | Sagro da 6 libbre | Petriere da 12 libbre (palla di pietra) |

a) *Reconstructive hypothesis about the ordnance of a Genoese public galley in the 1590s (after Ridella 2004b).*

b) *Naval demi cannon cast by Francesco Sommariva around 1590, weighing Cantara 42.90 (Kgs 2044). At present it is displayed in the Museo del Ejercito, Madrid (Photo: Museo del Ejercito, Madrid).*

Figure 6.12. Evolution of the ordnance aboard Genoese galleys toward the end of the 16th century.

Artilleria

–   *Un cañon de cruxia, con una A sobre el fogon sin otra
    ninguna señal, que peso qaurenta y qautro quintales*
    (Cantara) *y cinquenta y tres rotulos ...*
–   *Una moyana* (saker), *con el mismo señal que el cañon,
    y escrito en guarismo onze quintales* (Cantara) *y veinte
    y seis* [rotulos] *...*
–   *Otra moyana* (saker), *con la propria señal que el
    cañon, escrito en guarismo onze quintales* (Cantara)
    y setenta y dos [rotulos] *...*
–   *Dos pedreros, con una señal de B sobre el fogon en
    entrambos, y con las armas Doria, que pesaron siete
    quintales* (Cantara) *y setenta y seis rotulos* (both) *...*
–   *Dos esmeriles, sin ninguna señal octabados, con sus
    mangos de hierro, y quatro masculos, pesaron, el metal*
    (bronze) *siete quintales* (Cantara) *y quarenta rotulos
    y el hierro cinquenta rotulos* (both) *...*

From this data I propose this reconstruction (Figure 6.11c).

It must also be remembered that the Republic and the
most important Genoese galley owners, like the Lomellini
and Doria, had at their disposal sizeable spare equipments
that could serve not only to arm new ships but also to
increase the ordnance of those already at sea. Indeed,
when we learn that in 1570, Bartolomeo Sommariva cast
more than 261 *Cantara* (12,440 kg) of bronze pieces (we
do not know how many pieces: Merli, Belgrano 1874, 50),
nominally for Gio. Andrea Doria's *Capitana nuova* (new
flag galley); we can then calculate that with such a weight
of ordnance, another Capitana or two ordinary galleys could
easily be equipped, too. Besides we know that the same
Gio. Andrea, at his great-uncle Andrea Doria's death on
25th November 1560, had also inherited 15 spare pieces
weighing in total 386 *Cantara*, sufficient to equip five new
galleys (Borghesi 1996, 193, 211).

In the 1590s a rather substantial change, that I had
wrongly attributed to the 1570s (Ridella 2004b, 28, f. 1),
had to happen (Figure 6.12a). Actually, up to now, we could
understand that change only by comparing more recent
(early 17th century) records (ASG, MG, f. 4, 9.VII.1608)
with surviving pieces of ordnance. It consisted, above all,
in the replacement of the old 50 *Libre* centreline cannon
with a modern 25 *Libre* reinforced demi cannon (Figure
6.12b). As this last piece – with its thicker walls and
greater length – weighed only a little less than the previous
piece (certainly more than 40 *Cantara*) the frame of the
galley did not need to be modified. We can make some
simple suppositions about the reasons for this measure.
The new centreline piece had a longer range, could stand
a higher rate of fire and be reloaded more quickly than
the 50 *Libre*. These performances allowed a galley to hit
a sailing warship, over and over again, while holding itself
out of range from the ship's much more numerous, but less
powerful, guns. Of the complementary pieces the two 6
Libre medium sakers remained in use accompanied with
two 12 *Libre* medium *Petrieri*. Except for the centreline
piece, this arrangement seems to mirror that, of almost
forty years earlier, reported in 1552 to the Duke of Florence
by an emissary of his sent to Genoa in order to gather

information about Andrea Doria's galleys (Borghesi 1970,
159). The respective ordnance equipment – 1 *cannone*, 2
sagri, 2 *cannoni petrei* and 4 *smerigli piccoli* – could have
been simply theoretical as I never found a similar one in
the actual inventories of the following years.

Coming back to the 1590s, surprisingly in this case,
the public galleys were the first to be refitted with
this combination of ordnance that remained practically
unchanged through the following two centuries. Then the
private ship-owners followed this example. In 1629, in an
estimated budget to equip four galleys that had to be fitted
out for the King of Spain, the Pallavicini expected to have
to purchase for each of them (AADG, AP, f 19, n 31):

–   One centreline demi cannon, weighing 40 *Cantara*
    and firing a 25 *Libre* shot;
–   two sakers, weighing 12 *Cantara* and firing a 6 *Libre*
    shot;
–   two *Pedreri*, weighing 8 *Cantara* and firing a 10 *Libre*
    (stone) shot.'

And now there is another little known fact. When the
English established a naval base in Tangier, Morocco,
which they had received in 1662 from the Portuguese,
they not only asked the help of Genoese technicians for
the building of the outer breakwater (Mannoni 1991, 37)
but to also form a little squadron of galleys in order to
patrol the neighbouring coasts. They actually purchased
two hulls, one in Leghorn and the other in Genoa
(Giacomone Piana 1997), and for the respective ordnance
turned to Domenico Ramone, then serving the Republic
as a public gunfounder. Indeed, they did not have at their
disposal brass naval pieces with the performance of the
Mediterranean galley ordnance. Besides, we know that
on 31 July 1682 the Genoese *Magistrato d'Artiglieria*
(Magistracy of the Ordnance) asked for the return of two
heavy falcons (*Cantara* 9.56 and 9.52) and two medium
Petrieri (*Cantara* 10.50 and 10.30) lent in 1674 to His
Majesty's galley commander, the French Jean Baptiste du
Teil, pieces that then were still in Tangier (ASG, FF, MA,
f. 361, 31.VII.1582).

Fortune and decline in the Genoese manufacture of bronze naval ordnance

Analyzing archival and bibliographic data in order to
reconstruct the productive activity of the 16th-century
Genoese gunfounders I was able to establish that they were
very busy in the first three decades of the second half of
this century. That has to be imputed mainly to some large
state orders like that from the Republic, engaged in the
reconquest of Corsica in the years 1553–1559, and then
in the equipping of the regained towns and fortress (see
Ridella 2006). Besides, in the period cited there were also
sizeable Spanish orders: in 1557–59, 142 pieces for the
city walls and fortress of Milan (Ridella 2005, 105–106);
in 1571–72, an undefined number of pieces for the Spanish
strongholds in the *Stato dei Presidi* (Tuscany) and for the
Kingdom of Naples (Martinelli 2006, 96–97; Capasso
1896, 418–419); and in 1575–76, at least 50 pieces for

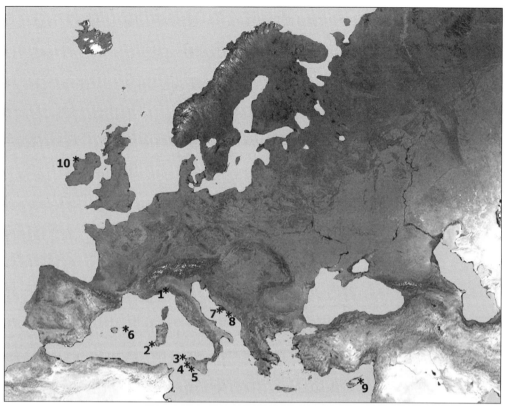

1* Genova /Molo Vecchio: n. 2 Light *Petrieri*; **2*** Carloforte e Calasetta (CA): n. 1 Esmeril (stone), n. 1 Light *Petriere*; **3*** Favignana/Lido Burrone (TP): n. 1 Falconet; **4*** Sciacca/Coda di Volpe (AG): n. 1 Falcon, n. 1 Medium Petriere, 1 Esmeril (stone); **5*** Agrigento/San Leone: n. 1 Demi culverin bastard; **6*** Minorca/Fornells (Balearic Islands - Spain): n. 2 Demi culverins bastard; **7*** Vis [Lissa]/Grebeni (Croatia): n. 2 Medium *Petrieri*; **8*** Dubrovnik/Brsecine (Croatia): n. 1 Medium saker, n. 1 Medium *Petriere* (broken); **9*** Famagusta Bay/Cyprus: n. 1 Heavy saker; **10*** Sligo Bay/ Streedagh Strand (Ireland): n. 1 Heavy saker, n. 2 Medium *Petrieri*.

Figure 6.13. Locating map of sea finds concerning bronze pieces of ordnance from Genoese production.

the city walls and fortress of Palermo (ASG, NA, f. 3150, 30.III.1575, 2.V.1575, 4.V.1575, 26.V.1575, 17.VI.1575; ASPa, TRP, NP, 2382, 1575–76). But this is not sufficient to completely explain the presence in Genoa of seven foundries operating in the early 1570s as attested by a deed of partnership. It was dated 20th March 1572 and includes the seven Genoese gunfounders, Alessandro, Dorino II, Gregorio II and Stefano Gioardi, Giacomo Merello, Gio. Battista Gandolfo and Bartolomeo Sommariva, each one running his own workshop (ASG, NA, f. 2897, 20.III.1572). In my opinion, in this period, the demand that allowed the activity of such a number of manufacturers can be explained only with a sizeable need for naval ordnance.

From notarial records we learn that not only Genoese ship-owners turned to these founders in order to equip their vessels but also foreign ones, like Spanish and Ragusan (from Ragusa/Dubrovnik, Croatia), who frequented the port of Genoa for their trades. See for example, respectively, the medium saker, produced by Dorino II Gioardi in 1582, purchased by Pedro Gonzales from Majorca (ASG, NA, f. 3156, 13.III.1582) and the four pieces cast by Bartolomeo Sommariva in 1571 for the Ragusan ship of Francesco Antonio di Marino Skocibucha (ASG, NA, f. 1800, 21.II.1571). For these reasons, and considering the number of Genoese bronze pieces recovered from 16th century wrecks (see Figure 6.13), it is not rash to think that Genoa

in this period was one of the most productive centres of merchant sea ordnance in the Mediterranean Sea.

But this favourable situation was not destined to last for a long time. The cast iron ordnance, English or western German marketed through Amsterdam – the first exemplars of which began to appear in the Genoese inventories early in the 1580s, replaced the bronze ones more and more quickly aboard the merchant ships. That was only due to reasons of cheapness as an iron gun then cost one fifth of a bronze one of the same weight (Cipolla 1969, 29–32). So at the end of the 16th century, almost all the long range pieces should have been of cast iron and in the first decades of the 17th, no bronze ones could be found aboard a Genoese merchantman (Gatti 1999, 343–344), save for some swivel guns.

For reasons of productive economy, more than for technical ones, it did not however become profitable to set up iron blast furnaces in the territory of the Republic of Genoa, where they continued to use the less expensive, in terms of charcoal, Ligurian *basso fuoco* (low fire) system (Calegari 1979; Baraldi 2005). But the high temperatures needed to melt and cast the iron could not be reached by means of this method. So Genoa continued to produce only bronze ordnance, but the number of gunfounders and workshops were reduced to one in 1616, when the new public foundry had been built.

Appendix

Genoese weight units

Cantaro (100 rotoli)	= 47.649 kg
Rotolo (1½ *libre*)	= 476.49 g
Libra (12 once)	= 317.66 g
Oncia	= 26.47 g

Sicilian weight units

Cantaro (100 rotoli)	= 79.432 kg
Rotolo (2½ *libre*)	= 794.32 g
Libra (12 once)	= 317.73 g
Oncia	= 26.48 g

References

Primary sources

ADGG, AP — Archivio Durazzo Giustiniani di Genova, Archivio Pallavicini.

ASG, AS — Archivio di Stato di Genova, *Archivio Segreto*.

ASG, CGF — Archivio di Stato di Genova, *Camera di Governo e Finanza*.

ASG, FF, MA — Archivio di Stato di Genova, *Fondo Foglietta, Magistrato d'Artiglieria*.

ASG, Mar — Archivio di Stato di Genova, *Maritimarum*.

ASG, MG — Archivio di Stato di Genova, *Magistrato delle Galee*

ASG, NA — Archivio di Stato di Genova, *Notai Antichi*.

ASPa, TRP, NP — Archivio di Stato di Palermo, *Tribunale del Real Patrimonio*, Numerazione Provvisoria

Secondary sources

Baraldi, E. (2005), La ferriera "alla genovese" tra XIV e XVII secolo: In M. G. Meloni (ed.) *Pratiche e Linguaggi. Contributi a una storia della cultura tecnica e scientifica*, ISEM (Istituto di Storia dell'Europa Mediterranea) Cnr, 159–183. Cagliari-Genova-Torino.

Borghesi, V. (1970) Informazioni sulle galee di Andrea Doria nelle Carte Strozziane. In C. Costantini (ed.) *Guerra e commercio nell'evoluzione della marina genovese tra XV e XVII secolo*, 119–205. Genova.

Borghesi, V. (1996), Momenti dell'educazione di un patrizio genovese: Giovanni Andrea Doria (1540–1606). In *Studi e Documenti di Storia Ligure in onore di Don Luigi Alfonso per il suo 85° genetliaco*, 192–213. Genova.

Calegari, M. (1970), Patroni di nave e magistrature politiche: i Conservatores Navium. In C. Costantini (ed.) *Guerra e commercio nell'evoluzione della marina genovese tra XV e XVII secolo*, 57–91. Genova.

Calegari, M. (1979), Il basso fuoco alla genovese: insediamento, tecnica, fortuna (sec. XIII–XVIII), *Quaderni del Centro di Studio sulla Storia della Tecnica del CNR di Genova*, 1, 1–38.

Capasso, B. (1896), Notizie intorno alle artiglierie appartenenti alla città di Napoli dal secolo XV fino al 1648, *Archivio Storico per le Province Napoletane*, 21: 406–424.

Capponi, N. (2006) *Victory of the West – the Story of the battle of Lepanto*. London.

Cipolla, C. M. (1969) *Velieri e cannoni d'Europa sui mari del mondo*. Turin.

D'Albertis, E. A. (1893) *Le costruzioni navali e l'arte della navigazione al tempo di Cristoforo Colombo*. Roma.

Gasperoni, D. (1779) *Artiglieria Veneta*. Roma.

Gatti, L. (1978) Armi da fuoco sulle imbarcazioni genovesi nella prima età moderna, *Studi & Notizie* (Periodico del Centro di Studio sulla Storia della Tecnica – Genova – C.N.R.), 2: 15–23.

Gatti, L. (1999) *Navi e cantieri della Repubblica di Genova (secoli XVI – XVIII)*. Genova.

Giacomone Piana, P. (1997) His Majesty's Galleys. Navi e marinai italiani nella Royal Navy del tardo Seicento, *Notiziario Modellistico*, 1: 3–7.

Grendi, E. (1987) *La repubblica aristocratica dei* genovesi. Bologna.

Guérout M., Rieth E., Gassend J. M. (1989) Le navire génois de Villefranche, *Archaeonautica*, 9. Paris.

Guérout, M., Liou, B. (2001) *La Grande Maîtresse – nef de François Ier*. Paris.

Lo Basso, L. (2003) *Uomini da remo. Galee e galeotti del Mediterraneo in età moderna*. Milano.

Mannoni, T. (1991) Le opere pubbliche nell'ultimo periodo della Repubblica di Genova e nel periodo sabaudo. In Comando 19ª Zona Militare (ed.). *"Forti di Idee" – Aspetti storici, architettonici e militari dei forti di Genova*, 35–42. Genova.

Martinelli, S. (2006) L'arsenale bellico dei presìdi spagnoli di Toscana nella seconda metà del Cinquecento, *Rivista di Storia Finanziaria*, 17: 89–108.

McElvogue, D. M. (2002) A description and appraisal of ordnance from three Spanish Armada transports c 1588, *Journal of the Ordnance Society*, 14: 31–50.

Merli, A., Belgrano, L. T. (1874) Il palazzo del Principe D'Oria a Fassolo in Genova, *Atti della Società Ligure di Storia Patria*, 10/1: 1–118.

Oliva F. (2001) L'assedio del castello dei Fieschi di Montoggio (11 marzo – 11 giugno 1547). Considerazioni tecniche sull'evento. In G. Pistarino (ed.) *Il tramonto dei Fieschi e la caduta del castello di Montoggio, Atti del Convegno, Montoggio 30 agosto 1997*, 37–51 Genova.

Palazzolo, A. (2007) *Le torri di deputazione nel Regno di Sicilia (1579–1813)*. Palermo.

Pandiani, E. (1905) Un anno di storia genovese, *Atti della Società Ligure di Storia Patria*, 37: 1–716.

Pandiani, E. (1935) Il primo comando in mare di Andrea Doria, con uno studio sulle galee genovesi, *Atti della Società Ligure di Storia Patria*, 64: 341–389.

Promis, C. (1841) *Trattato di architettura civile e militare di Francesco di Giorgio Martini architetto senese del secolo XV*. Torino.

Ridella, R. G. (2004a) Un cannone cinquecentesco di fabbrica genovese a Famagosta (Cipro), *Microstorie*, 1: 13–28.

Ridella, R. G. (2004b) Dorino II Gioardi: A 16th century Genoese gunfounder, *Journal of the Ordnance Society*, 16: 27–41.

Ridella, R. G. (2005) Produzione di artiglierie nel XVI secolo. I fonditori genovesi Battista Merello e Dorino II Gioardi. In M. G. Meloni (ed.) *Pratiche e Linguaggi. Contributi a una storia della cultura tecnica e scientifica*, ISEM (Istituto di Storia dell'Europa Mediterranea) Cnr, 77–134. Cagliari-Genova-Torino.

Ridella, R. G. (2006) Il Grifone ritrovato – Un cannone cinquecentesco della Repubblica di Genova nel Royal Artillery Museum a Woolwich (GB), *Ligures*, 4: 158–188.

Ridella, R. G. (2008) «General descritione del'artiglieria che si ritrova nel Regno di Corsica e Isola di Capraia». Bocche da fuoco nelle fortificazioni costiere genovesi di Corsica tra Cinque e Seicento. In M. G. Mele, G. Serreli (eds.) *"Contra Moros y Turcos". Politiche e sistemi di difesa degli Stati mediterranei della Corona di Spagna in Età Moderna, Atti del convegno Villasimius-Baunei, 20–24 settembre 2005*, 289–314. Cagliari.

Ridella, R. G. (2009) Fonditori italiani di artiglierie, in trasferta nell'Europa del XVI secolo. In N. Labanca, P. P. Poggio (eds.) *Storie di Armi, Atti del convegno Brescia 8–10 novembre 2007*, 15–42 Milano.

Bombards in Savona in the 15th and 16th centuries

Furio Ciciliot

Notary documents in the *State Archives of Savona* contain interesting information about the war steel-making industry in Savona (Genoa, Italy) starting from the end of the Middle Ages. Iron ore (called *vena* in the medieval Ligurian Latin lexicon) usually came from the island of Elba and, more occasionally from other mines in Northern Italy. It was worked by numerous *ferriere* and *martinetti* in the inland valleys of Liguria using energy generated by stream water and from vegetable coal.

A medieval corporation of blacksmiths was active in the city of Savona and some of its members specialised in making large iron artefacts, such as anchors and bombards. In almost one hundred unpublished documents there are references to numerous blacksmiths, also known as *bombarderii* – sometimes called *ferrari sive bombarderii* in medieval documents – and to their work between the last decades of the 15th century and the early 16th century.

These newly discovered documents, for which we are making a brief presentation, describe their professional activities and small daily episodes, such as selling or buying homes or work tools or administrative responsibilities in the corporation to which they belonged.

The most interesting documents refer to artillery supplies for Savonese and Genoese merchants. They are also some of the oldest recorded contracts to build bombards.

Some families of bombard makers were identified in the decades between the 15th and 16th centuries. The Cabuto family, one of the most important, consisted of the following members:

- Abramo (22/2/1492–26/2/1501[1]);
- Giacomo (30/8/1479–22/2/1492), probably Abramo's son and the bombard maker for which the greatest amount of information is available;
- Sebastiano Parrino (later called Cabuto, 11/9/1494–12/5/1523), born in the Langhe (currently Piedmont), who changed his name to Cabuto for reasons that are

still unknown; we can consider him to be associated to that dynasty of bombard makers in which, from a certain point on, he is identified as Sebastiano Cabuto. Some historians have emphasised the similarity of the surname Cabuto and that of the navigators Giovanni and Sebastiano Caboto: it would be interesting to determine just how common that name was in the Ligurian area. Even if Sebastiano Caboto and Sebastiano (Parrino) Cabuto are almost the same age, they are obviously two different persons.

- Batta, Sebastiano's son (2/3/1531–26/6/1533);
- Bernardino, Sebastiano's son (10/7/1531–18/7/1553);
- Simone, Sebastiano's son (10/7/1531is the only date for which information is available).

A second dynasty of Savonese bombard makers was based on the Fiorito family, which included:

- Benedetto Cavalerio, known as Fiorito, who came from Stella, about ten km from Savona (4/1/1481–20/12/1518);
- Batta, Benedetto's son, known as Bardella (25/8/1512–15/2/1535);
- Enrico, Benedetto's son (8/4/1531–7/5/1537).

The Cabutos and Fioritos were probably not originally from Savona. It is curious to note how often the two families used nicknames, a rather unusual practice in notary documentation during that period.

Other *bombardieri* were present in Savona during this period but, as this term meant either the makers or the users of those weapons, we do not know if they were embarked on ships, and therefore worked with ordnances, or if they operated in their own local workshops, and therefore were gunsmiths. The following is a list of some of the *bombardieri* even though, at least for now, we still do not have much information about their professional activities:

- Antonio Sucino, from Feglino, west of Savona (mentioned 21/2/1493);
- Gioffredo Zerbino, from Savona (30/8/1497);
- Guglielmo de la Guardia, from Savona (13/2/1516);

---

[1] Dates are written in the format dd/mm/yyyy and refer to the first and last date for which specific information is available for that person while he was still alive.

– Pietro de Massa (6/5/1517);
– Gabriele de Sirio, from Albisola, a town bordering with Savona (19/1/1532);
– Battista Botto, from Verona (1/6/1549).

Considering the large number of referenced bombard makers within a period of just a few decades, we believe that Savona was an important bombard production centre. The referenced bombards were built using the medieval system of staves held together by iron rings.

It is interesting to report a part of one of the more precise construction contracts. On 24/12/1483, Giacomo Cabuto promised Francesco de Bosco to build before next Christmas:

"... *duas bombardas bonas de pedibus octo de tromba pro qualibet ipsarum cum tribus canonibus pro qualibet ipsarum et quas proieci trahere debeant per miliarias duo in circha sive circumcircha lapidem unam penes me notarium infrascriptum ... et postquam confecte erunt ire ad locum Albe ad faciendum eas trahere ...*

... two good bombards with a barrel 8 feet (about 2.5 metres) long, with three removable chambers each, that have to shoot a stone, deposited with me the notary...., over a range of more or less two thousand (paces? in total about 3 km?) and, when they will be built, must be transported to Alba (in Piedmont)..."

We are not sure about the actual range expressed in the decimal metric system because the original document refers to a metrology that was not used very often in Liguria. For the sake of argument, a foot can be considered to have a length of about 30 cm, while a *migliaia* is equivalent to one thousand paces, each (in Liguria) equal to six palms with a length of about 25 cm each (one pace = 1.50 m). The calculation is only hypothetical and a range of about 3 km must be used with much caution since it is considered excessive by ballistic experts, at least based on our current historical knowledge.

Another form of document repeated several times concerns the sale of ordnances. For example, in the following document dated 13/8/1488, Gerolamo Massa received from Giovanni Beltrame:

"... *bombardas decem novem et canonos quadraginta unus a bombardis ex nave Johannis Scarele ...*

... 19 bombards and 41 removable chambers *from the ship of Giovanni Scarella.*"

The dimension of the bombards and the weight of the projectile are specified in just a few cases, as in the following document dated 7/10/1514, in which Battista Fiorito promised Francesco and Giuliano Achini to build within two months:

"... *bombardas duas de cantariis 9,5 singula, de parmis decem singula ... petram ... in pondere librarum 25 singulo iectu in circa ...*

... two bombards weighing about 450 kg (9.5 cantari*) each, with a length of about 2.5 metres (10 palms)* that can shoot a stone ball weighing about 8 kg (25 librae) ..."

As already mentioned, the referenced bombards were made out of wrought iron but, in more recent documents, we also find rare artillery built according to a more modern technology based on the use of bronze, called *metallo* in notary documents. For example, a notary document dated 2/7/1510 refers to a Savonese merchant, Andrea Scarella, who sells ... *duas colubrinas metali* ..., but we do not know if they were built in Savona or if they were made in workshops in other locations.

From the documents in our possession, we believe that Savona was rather important in the field of iron artillery making in the 15th and 16th centuries, but we do not have older references with other areas in Liguria and northern Italy: that's why this documentation, which is reviewed, sampled and examined here only superficially, is so important.

With the development of bronze artillery, our initial impression is that Savonese craftsmen were unable to adapt to the new technology. This historical period coincides with the 16th century during which the Savonese production economy went through a period of stagnation. But all this is now just a working hypothesis.

We hope to study this subject in greater detail in the near future, focusing on three main lines of research:

– to transcribe and publish at least some of the most important notary documents discovered (construction contracts), comparing the bombards with those unearthed;
– to carry out a more analytical analysis of the Ligurian iron industry, taking a more in-depth look at our knowledge relative to how technology was transferred, and to the places and structures in which they worked;
– to become more familiar with the life and professional activities of Ligurian bombard makers, analysing, for example, the public positions held, the customers, the value of private assets and their family and social strategies.

Translation into English by Terrence Agneessens.

***

Appendix

This report is based only on unpublished documents (notary documents) on file in the *State Archives of Savona*. The following also indicate the location of those mentioned in the text and filed in the records of *Notai Antichi del Comune di Savona*. In general, these are small registers, known as *bastardelli* grouped according to the name of the notary public and their date.

The names of the notaries are: Nicolò Bertolotto (*nb*), Simone Capello (*sc*), Vincenzo Capello (*vc*), Federico Castrodelfino (*fca*), Francesco Corsaro (*fc*), Nicolò Corsaro (*nc*), Giovanni Gallo (*gg*), Francesco Guglielmi (*fg*),

Ludovico Moreno (*lm*), Nicolò Priano (*np*), Antonio Ricci (*ar*) e Giacomo Varzi (*gv*).

For Cabutos family: *np* 22/2/1492, *fg* 26/2/1501, *gg* 30/8/1479, *np* 11/9/1494, *fc* 12/5/1523, *vc* 2/3/1531, *vc* 26/6/1533, *vc* 10/7/1531, *vc* 18/7/1553, *vc* 10/7/1531.

For Fioritos family: *lm* 4/1/1481, *gv* 20/12/1518, *sc* 25/8/1512, *vc* 15/2/1535, *vc* 8/4/1531, *vc* 7/5/1537.

For others bombard makers: *np* 21/2/1493, *fca* 30/8/1497, *nb* 12/11/1505, *sc* 13/2/1516, *gv* 6/5/1517, *ar* 19/1/1532, *ar* 1/6/1549.

Other documents of the article: *lm* 13/8/1488, *lm* 24/10/1483, *nc* 7/10/1514, *sc* 2/7/1510.

8

Guns and Profit.
Tuscan Naval Artillery in the 16th to 17th Centuries

Niccolò Capponi

The creation of the navy of the Duchy of Florence and, later, of the Grand Duchy of Tuscany is well known. Starting with the epic-style works by Gino Guarnieri in the late 1920s, passing through the plodding writings of Marco Geminiani and the many contributors of the *Quaderni Stefaniani*, and ending with Franco Angiolini's socio-political studies of the 1990s, every aspect of the Medician naval structure has been examined and dissected, guns included (Guarnieri 1960, 1965; Various authors 1989; Angiolini 1996, 1999; Gemignani 1996). But is this really the case? Is there not, maybe, something that has fallen through the cracks of historical research, not just mere factual details but instead matters that could change our perspective on Tuscany's maritime policy, indeed on the use of ordnance in Early-modern naval warfare? In order to answer these questions, one must take a different angle of investigation, going beyond the strictures imposed by certain "cutting edge" historiographical trends. Technology historians, busy examining scientific developments *in vitro*, or students of logistics, seen exclusively as economic aspects of warfare, tend to forget the main function of a weapon or a weapon-system: namely the destruction, or at least the overpowering of physically hostile people and objects. Yet, in order to obtain this goal any sort of military hardware necessarily needs the human element to work it at the maximum potential, within a specific tactical and strategic frame. The Tuscans' use of naval artillery in the 16th and early 17th centuries is a case in point, as this study shall attempt to demonstrate and at the same time challenge some consolidated knowledge on the matter.

The need for Florence to provide itself with a navy became apparent once the Medici became its ruling princes in 1532, and especially after the Ottoman tactical success at Preveza, in 1539, that settled into the Sultan's hands for the next thirty years the naval initiative in the Mediterranean. The need for a fleet was motivated by the need to protect Florentine subjects living on the coast – and not just from Muslim corsairs, Florence's neigh-

bours being sometimes as troublesome[1] – plus a need for the Medici to become active players on the international check board. However, only in the mid-1540s could Duke Cosimo I turn his attention to the sea, having previously been preoccupied with ridding his domain from a rather stifling Spanish presence (Spini 1980). But fleets could not be built overnight, considering also that Florence lacked a shipbuilding tradition of any significance.

Until the end of the 15th century, the Florentine Republic maintained a galley squadron in Pisa, but financial reasons and the temporary loss of the port of Pisa from 1494 to 1509 had caused Florence to abandon any sort of naval policy, always half-hearted in any case (Manfroni 1985; Mallet 1967); in 1527 the Venetian ambassador in Florence, Marco Foscari, described the Florentine fleet as practically non-existent (Segarizzi 1912–1916, 86).

By the time the Medici had managed to become ruling princes, warfare in the Mediterranean had been completely revolutionized, and, as a consequence, around the 1530s the galley had developed from a mere gun and fighting platform to a complex and versatile weapon-system. Lacking the necessary know-how, the Medici had to look elsewhere to build their fleet.

In early 16th-century Italy, only two places possessed the appropriate facilities for large-scale shipbuilding: Venice and Genoa. However, the former's distance from Florence made it an unpractical source; besides, the Venetians' strategic outlook meant their vessels were ill suited to Florentine needs. Genoa was the only feasible answer, for a number of reasons. It is quite possible that initially Cosimo I had intended his fleet essentially as a costal-protection force, to be employed, if need be, also in amphibious operations in the style of the Iberian monarchs. The Spanish, under whose intimidating wing Cosimo found himself, had a long tradition of such enterprises against Muslim bases in North Africa (Capponi 2006, 72–73). The 1528 agreement between Genoa and Spain had resulted in the Habsburg Mediterranean fleet being made up mostly of Genoese privateers, creating thus a synergy between Spain's strategic outlook and Genoa's political-mercantile needs (Kirk 2005; Lo Basso 2004). For different reasons both the Spanish and the Genoese needed swift vessels, ideal for patrolling and the transport of men or merchandise. The Habsburgs continually needed to bring soldiers from the Iberian Peninsula to Finale Ligure, the beginning of the road to Flanders (Parker 1990), and occasionally carry troops to North Africa. The Genoese, on the other hand, engaged in a lively traffic of precious goods, bullion and the transport of documents, such as diplomatic correspondence, from Italy to Spain. In practice this meant that both Genoese and Spanish galleys, including those of Spain's Italian territories, mounted enough ordnance for defensive purposes, but always preferred speed to hitting power.

At least until the end of the 16th century, Spanish and Genoese galleys appear to have carried a main artillery battery of three pieces. That number appears in a 1575 contract for the sale of four galleys belonging to the Lomellini family of Genoa, and the weight of the ordnance's shot points clearly to them being light pieces: the heaviest gun being a 32-pounder, and the two sakers accompanying the main one on each galley were 4-pounders. The equipment was completed by two or four bronze swivel guns for each galley – (ASG, *NA*, 3150, Notary Domenico Tinello, deed of the 23 April 1575, noticed me by R. G. Ridella). In 1582 the vessels of Doria's squadron had on average a centreline cannon weighing 2000 kg and two 400–600 kg *moiane* (short sakers) on the main batter, plus four 120–180 kg light *petrieri* and swivel guns (ADP, 70/25, int. 9bis "*Inventari delle galere*", 1582; about the Genoese galley ordnance see R. G. Ridella's paper in these volume).

In the following years the iberian galleys seem to carry a slightly lighter ordnance than Doria's ones. An inventory of two Spanish galleys dated 1588 lists for one a 1700 kg centreline piece, a pair of 450 kg *moiane*, four 100 kg *mortarete* swivel-guns, and five large harquebuses; the second sported a 1600 kg main gun, a pair of 250 kg *moiane*, and four 100 kg *mortaretes* (ADP, 76/21, int. 2 "*Inventarii delle due galere di S. Altezza Santa Caterina e Santa Margherita, fatto alla fine di febraro 1588*"). The tactical implications of this type of ordnance setup become evident if one considers that Spanish galleys usually operated in large squadrons, made up of contingents from Spain proper, Naples, Sicily and Genoese privateers, all with a similar armament – the heavy swivel guns adding some extra punch at close quarters without affecting the vessels' sailing performance.[2]

Cosimo I started planning the new Medici navy around the mid-1540s – in May 1546 Cosimo asked for models of the nails used in galley construction (ASF, *MP*, 613, inserto 2, f. 83rv, Pier Francesco del Riccio to Cosimo I, 17 May 1546) – and the first galley was launched from the arsenal of Pisa in October 1547 (ASF, *MP*, 383, f. 352r, Luca Martini to Cosimo I de' Medici, 13 October 1547). In order to accomplish this Cosimo had imported a substantial number of Genoese shipbuilders, but the need to speed matters up caused him to ask the Viceroy of Naples, Don Pedro de Toledo, to furnish him with a ready-made "*light*

and swift" vessel (ASF, *MP*, 5, f. 674r, Cosimo I to Don Pedro de Toledo, 15 March 1547; ASF, *MP*, 1174, ins. 3, f. 32v, Cristiano Pagni to Pier Francesco del Riccio, 4 August 1548). Although Genoa would have been a better place for purchasing galleys, at the time the Genoese were concerned about Cosimo's decision to fortify Portoferraio, on the Isle of Elba, since they suspected the Duke wanted to impose with his navy a stranglehold on the upper Tyrrhenian sea, especially given Cosimo's attempt to take over the state of Piombino (ASF, *MP*, 11, f. 71r, Cosimo I de' Medici to Girolamo degli Albizzi, 28 April 1548; Cappelletti 1897, 159–161). There were concrete fears that the Genoese intended to attack Portoferraio before the fortifications had been completed (ASF, *MP*, 11, f. 122r, Cosimo I de' Medici to Bernardo de' Medici, 5 May 1548; ASF, *MP*, 1169, ins 6, f. 207r (Cristiano Pagni to Pier Francesco del Riccio, 27 February 1550). Until the tensions with Genoa had abated, Cosimo could not tap into that particular source for his ships, while economic and military constrictions meant that only in February 1550 could a new galley be completed in Pisa (ASF, *MP*, 1169, ins 6, f. 207r (Cristiano Pagni to Pier Francesco del Riccio, 27 February 1550).

Cosimo needed Genoa for more than just shipbuilding, since he completely lacked any sort of experienced maritime personnel. Once again the Ligurian area provided the nearest source of expertise and for the greater part of the sixteenthcentury, sailors, coxswains and sailing officers on board Florentine, and later Tuscan, galleys came from Genoa or the surrounding coast. During the early years of its life even the administration of the fleet was in the hands of Genoese naval entrepreneurs, in particular Marco Centurione and later, thanks to an *asiento* stipulated with Philip II of Spain, Giovanni Andrea Doria (Manfroni 242–243, 252–255; Angiolini 1996, 8–9, note 33; Lo Basso 2004, 257). This meant, of course, that Florentine galleys followed closely Genoese patterns for what concerned their tactical employment.

Both Cosimo's request to Don Pedro for a "*swift*" galley and the 1555 inventory of the Florentine fleet are telling in this respect if one looks at the artillery on board. On average, the main gun batteries consisted of a centreline gun, plus a variable number of *sacri*, *petrieri*, and smaller *smerigli* swivel-guns. Indeed, it would be wrong to believe in any sort of standardization, given the hodgepodge structure of the Medicean fleet at that time. For instance, the *San Giovanni Battista* carried a centreline piece weighing 4887 French *livres* (2390 kg) and a *petriere* of 650 *libbre fiorentine* (230 kg) in its main battery, the flagship *San Giovanni* (the Evangelist, in this case) mounted a 4225 French *livres* (2100 kg) cannon, two sakers of roughly 1,400 *libbre fiorentine* (480 kg) each and a 600 *libbre fiorentine* (200 kg) *petriere*. Yet this galley also sported a rather large rowing crew of 181 men, while the *San Giovanni Battista* counted only 125 (ASF, *MP*, 627, registry dated 22 April 1555: for the detailed inventory of these galleys). Logistic needs and potentials were often more telling than a theoretical idea of what sort of artillery a vessel should carry. It should be added that the San Giovanni's three main pieces were French ones salvaged from a shipwreck on the isle of Pianosa two years earlier, a stroke of luck for the Florentines yielding "*four large reinforced cannons and eight* sacres *for galley service, plus twenty-eight smaller artillery pieces, all these guns made of bronze*" – not to mention three-hundred French prisoners of war, ideal rowing material for the muscle-starved Medici fleet (ASF, *MP*, 29, f. 357r, Cosimo I de' Medici to Averardo Serristori, 12 March 1553); a number of the captured French eventually ended up on the rowing bench (ASF, *MP*, 627, passim).

Providing artillery for the navy had become a priority for Cosimo I; however, obtaining the necessary ordnance was not an easy matter. Although Florence had been fabricating artillery since the fourteenth century (Camporeale 2003, 222, n. 95), at the advent of the Medici principate it could not be described as possessing state-of-the-art gun-casting technology; even if the contrary had been true, it lacked the appropriate facilities for such a task. The building of the new fortress of San Giovanni, on the northern section of Florence's walls, provided the Medici with a much needed foundry, but in any case the know-how had to be imported from abroad. In the mid 1540s one of the important fabricants was a certain "*Maestro Janni Franzese*" (Master Jean from France), who in 1549 is recorded to have cast a number of pieces of various sizes "*for the galleys*" (ASF, *MP*, 613, ins. 5, f. 17r, Pier Francesco del Riccio to Cosimo I de' Medici, 20 May 1549). In 1551 a certain "*Maestro Cremonese*", probably Antonio da Cremona, made five pieces "*all of which have turned out perfectly*" (ASF, *MP*, 613, ins. 7, f. 46rv, Pier Francesco del Riccio to Cosimo I de' Medici, 4 December 1551). Antonio da Cremona and his broche Bartolomeo were considered "eccellenti maestri" (ASF, *MP*, 3101a, f. 1179r, Francesco Vinta to Cosimo I de' Medici, 12 August 1549). Overtime the Florentines managed to acquire the needed gun-casting abilities; but the draught of skilled artisans forced the Medici sovereigns to search continually abroad for the necessary personnel, especially Venice, engaging in a hard-nosed competition with other Italian states, Genoa *in primis* (ASF, *Magona*, 2255, n. 5, nnf, Carlo Capponi to Ferdinando II de' Medici 14 November 1563). Not surprisingly, these craftsmen were pampered by the Florentines, in the mid-17th century, an artillery maker receiving an annual stipend of 200 *scudi* (four times the gross amount of a regular infantry soldier), a house, a workshop, plus 20 *scudi* every 1000 *libbre* (340 kg) of ordnance made (ASF, *SFF*, 1928, ins. 38, n. 348, nnf, Andrea Arrighetti to Ferdinando Bardi, 7 February 1658). Apparently the Medici never managed to produce iron pieces of satisfactory quality, being forced to buy them from other countries – England and the Low Countries in particular (ASF, *MP*, 4184, f. 23r, Belisario Vinta to Ottaviano Lotti, 3 September 1605). Also most of the saltpetre used had to be imported, despite the existence of recipes to make it locally, and the same was true of gunpowder. Saltpetre producers enjoyed a number of fiscal privileges, revelatory of their importance in the Florentine defence system (ASF, *MM*, 370, ins. 33,

nnf., Memo by Raffaello de' Medici and Jacopo Corsi, 7 December 1616).

The cost of the navy would be a constant worry for Cosimo I and his successors; yet they understood perfectly well that, to use the words of the Commissioner of the Galleys Piero Machiavelli (son of the celebrated Niccolò) that on the international military check board "*the affairs of the sea are two thirds of the game*" (BNCF, *Magliabechi*, E.B. 15.10, c. 176r (*c.* 1556). Indeed, after that the 1557 peace Cateau-Cambrésis had confirmed for good the Hapsburg's hegemony over the Italian peninsula, Cosimo needed a fleet if he wanted to be taken seriously, and not just considered one of Spain's minions by the other European powers. Unfortunately, in order to obtain from Philip II of Spain the state of Siena in fief, the duke had been forced to agree to send his galleys whenever the king should request them, and also for this reason Cosimo created the military/chivalric order of Saint Stephen: an independent institution under canon law, tied to the Medici ruler through a hereditary Grand Mastership but in no way dependent from the latter's international obligations as duke of Florence and Siena. The origins of the Knights of St Stephen have already been discussed elsewhere, so it would be useless to go over this matter again (Angiolini 1996, 14–24). What has not yet been examined in any depth is the operational side of the question, and how it affected the tactical employment of the Medici fleet.

Cosimo planned the order to be self sufficient financially, and thus not a burden for the ducal coffers. This was to be accomplished thanks to the profits deriving from an extensive patrimony, yet in a pre-industrial economic setting it was unthinkable that military hardware should not yield some sort of profit. Florentine galleys could, indeed, be used for transporting precious merchandise, but Florence lacked the extensive maritime connections of Genoa or Venice. The solution was two fold: rent one's galleys to a foreign power, something Cosimo did with little success and considerable monetary loss up to the late 1560s by loaning his galleys to Philip II (Aglietti 1998; Capponi 2006, 110). Alternatively, vessels could be used for pursuing enemy shipping at sea, thus profiting from the booty obtained, something which also went hand in hand with the Order of St. Stephen's declared goal of defending Christendom. The only people practicing such activities belonged to another religious/chivalric order and independent polity: the Knights of St John of Jerusalem, by then known as the Knights of Malta.

The Maltese built their galleys with different criteria than most other southern European states. While those belonging to Spain or Genoa were intended primarily for patrolling and commerce, those of Malta were essentially hunter/killer weapon systems, preying on Muslim shipping across the Mediterranean (Atauz 2004). Being friars, the Knights upheld the three vows of chastity, poverty and obedience, to which they added a fourth of never retreating from the enemy even when outnumbered three to one (De Caro 1853, 43). This meant having enough fighting men on board and, most of all, the capacity of delivering a sufficient amount of metal to keep an adversary at bay. There is enough evidence that the knights of Malta mounted a five-gun main battery on their galleys already by the mid-1560s (Muscat 1993, 256–325; 1996, 77–113), and it is therefore logical that their colleagues of the order of Saint Stephen should have done the same. Already in 1564 Cosimo I was ordering guns for his galleys at a ratio of twenty-four "major and minor sakers" for every centreline piece produces (ASF, *MP*, 220, f. 33rv, Cosimo de' Medici to Francesco di Ser Jacopo, 19 April 1564). Also thanks to this amount of ordnance at the battle of Lepanto (1571) some outnumbered Florentine galleys would manage to repel repeated Muslim attacks (Capponi 2006, 283–284).

The new ordnance array of the Florentine galleys would pay large dividends in the years to come, allowing the Medici (now Grand Dukes of Tuscany) to pursue their own naval policy and act independently from Spain (Guarnieri 1960; Manfroni 1985: for the military history of the Tuscan navy). In the end, however, the order of St Stephen did not live up to Cosimo I's expectations, his successors having to foot their navy's bill (ASF, *MM*, 264, ins. 29, "*Ristretto delle Entrate Ordinarie e Straordinarie di S.A. Ser.ma, si come di tutte le Uscite Calculate dall'anno 1625 a tutto l'anno 1650*", n.n. ff). Yet the close connections between maritime activities and profit would always be present in the mind of the Medici sovereigns. When in the seventeenth century Grand Duke Ferdinando II tried to create a squadron of sailing ships, he sought to buy heavily armed vessels good for trade as for war (Capponi 2009). The Florentine use of naval artillery should remind us how in the Early modern world, the application of technological developments was motivated not so much by a lofty desire for scientific advance, but more crudely by complex political situations and, just as important, the prospect of concrete financial gain.

Notes

1 The Genoese, in particular, had the habit of raiding the Florentine coast for shipbuilding timber (ASF, *MP*, 181, f. 35r, Duke Alessandro de' Medici to Andrea Doria, 29 May 1534); once Florence managed to reassert its own position, ransacking was substituted by negotiation (ASF, *MP*, 380, f. 99r, Andrea Doria to Cosimo I de' Medici, 24 June 1546). prospect of concrete financial gain.

2 *Colección de documentos y manuscriptos compilados por Fernandez de Navarrete*, 33 vols. Madrid, 1946: VIII, 14, ff. 114r–118r., 1580. For Spanish naval organization in the sixteenth century, see especially: Olesa Munido 1968.

Abbreviations

ADP   Archivio Doria-Pamphili, Rome.
ASF   Archivio di Stato di Firenze.
ASG   Archivio di Stato di Genova.
BNCF   Biblioteca Nazionale Centrale di Firenze.
MM   Miscellanea Medicea.
MP   Mediceo del Principato.
SSF Scrittoio delle Fortezze e Fabbriche.

References

Aglietti, M. (1998) *La partecipazione delle galere toscane alla battaglia di Lepanto*. In D. Marrara (ed.) *Toscana e Spagna nell'età moderna e contemporanea*, 64–66. Pisa.

Angiolini, F. (1996) *I cavalieri e il principe: l'ordine di Santo Stefano e la società toscana in età moderna*. Florence.

Angiolini, F. (1999) *Il Granducato di Toscana, l'Ordine di S. Stefano e il Mediterraneo (secc. XVI-XVIII)*. In *Ordens Militares: guerra, religião, poder e cultura – Actas do III Encontro sobre Ordens Militares*, vol. I, 39–61. Lisbon.

Atauz, A. D. (2004) *Trade, piracy, and naval warfare in the central Mediterranean: the maritime history and archaeology of Malta*. Unpublished PhD Thesis, Texas A&M University.

Camporeale, E. (2003) Telling Time in Florence Cathedral: the Frescoed Clock by Paolo Uccello and Coeval Tuscan Public Clocks, *Interfaces. Image Texte Langage*, 19–20 (2).

Cappelletti, L. (1897) *Storia della città e stato di Piombino dalle origini fino all'anno 1814*. Livorno.

Capponi, N. (2006) *Victory of the West. The Story of the Battle of Lepanto*. London.

Capponi, N. (2009) Non solo remi: la flotta Toscana nel secolo XVII. *Medicea*, 2, 64–70.

De Caro, L. (1853) *Storia dei Gran Maestri e Cavalieri di Malta*. Malta.

Gemignani, M. (1996) *Il Cavaliere Iacopo Inghirami al Servizio dei Granduchi di Toscana*. Pisa.

Guarnieri, G. (1960) *I Cavalieri di Santo Stefano*. Pisa.

Guarnieri, G. (1965) *L'Ordine di Santo Stefano nei suoi aspetti organizzativi tecnici-navali sotto il gran magistero mediceo*, vols I–II. Pisa.

Various authors (1989) *Le imprese e i simboli: contributi alla storia del sacro militare Ordine di S. Stefano P.M., sec. 16.-19: mostra per il cinquantesimo anniversario di fondazione dell'istituzione dei Cavalieri di S. Stefano: 5 maggio-28 maggio 1989*. Pisa. Comune di Pisa, Istituzione Cavalieri di Santo Stefano,

Kirk, T. A. (2005) *Genoa and the Sea. Policy and Power in an Early Modern Maritime Republic, 1559–1684*. Baltimore – London.

Lo Basso, L. (2004) *Uomini da remo. Galee e galeotti del Mediterraneo in età moderna*. Milan.

Mallett, M. E. (1967) *The Florentine galleys in the Fifteenth Century: With the diary of Luca di Maso degli Albizzi, Captain of the galleys, 1429–1430*. Oxford.

Manfroni, C. (1985) La marina da Guerra di Cosimo I e dei suoi primi successori, *Rivista Marittima* XXVIII. IV, 233.

Muscat, J. (1993) The Arsenal: 1530–1798. In L. Bugeja, M. Buhagiar, S. Fiorini (eds) *Birgu: A Maltese Maritime City*, 256–325. Malta.

Muscat, J. (1996) The Warships of the Order of Saint John 1530–1798, In S. Fiorini (ed.) *The Malta Historical Society Proceedings of History Week 1994*, 77–113. Malta.

Olesa Munido, F. F. (1968) *La organización naval de los estados mediterráneos y en especial de España durante los siglos XVI y XVII*. Madrid.

Parker, G. (1990) *The Army of Flanders and the Spanish Road, 1567–1659*. Cambridge.

Segarizzi. A. (ed.) (1912–1916) *Relazioni degli ambasciatori veneti al Senato*. III, part. I. Bari.

Spini, G. (1980) *Cosimo I e l'indipendenza del Principato Mediceo*. Florence.

9

Armed Ships of the Post-Medieval Period in Croatia

Irena Radić Rossi

Introduction

It was an interest in shipwrecks of the pre-modern age that inspired the initiation of organized research and protection of underwater cultural heritage in Croatia. The first underwater archaeological project, using surface-supplied divers coordinated from the surface, took place in the bay of Veliki Molunat south of Dubrovnik (Ragusa) in 1949 (Luetić 1959; 1993; Vrsalović 1974, 26). This was the excavation of a late 18th-century ship that would prove to be of great interest to the maritime history of the Eastern Adriatic coast.

Three other shipwrecks dating to the 16th and 17th centuries were explored in the late 1960s and 1970s, but after the first period of enthusiasm, when many valuable finds had been raised, interest in the study of post-medieval wrecks waned and the projects were never completed. That situation deprived the fields of Croatian and international naval history and nautical archaeology of the most valuable information on post-mediaeval Adriatic shipbuilding, seafaring and trade. At the same time, open access to the sites and the aggressive action of shipworms (*Teredo navalis*) seriously endangered the remains left on the seabed. Even the clamorous discoveries of the famous wreck of Gnalić failed to stimulate future research and conservation of the raised artefacts. And so the situation has continued until the present day, with "old" sites abandoned to their fate and newly discovered sites treated in much the same way as they were over three decades ago.

The UNESCO Participation program 2008–2009 has taken steps to mitigate these trends and to educate a group of young experts in the history and archaeology of these wrecks from the post-mediaeval period. The UNESCO project, *Educational programme in nautical archaeology and history of navigation: The 16th and 17th centuries*, involves various experts, graduate and postgraduate students whose work is coordinated by the University of Zadar, Croatia and the University Ca' Foscari of Venice, Italy. The project aims to reinvigorate the attention of scholars and the organizations responsible for the research and protection of underwater cultural heritage and to refocus efforts on those sites that have been abandoned. These sites, though rapidly disappearing, have great potential to yield stores of knowledge and can serve as innovative pilot projects for the future research and protection of that group of extremely complex and delicate underwater sites.

The sites

Due to the constraints of space, the present overview consists of basic information about the sites and the relevant bibliographies referring to their respective discoveries and surveys, as well as to the raising or recording of artefacts. None of these sites has been systematically excavated or published in detail. It should be emphasized here that only the material from the sites of Gnalić and Suđurađ was studied in a more consistent way, and both shipwrecks have been associated with ships detailed in historical documents.

Islet of Gnalić near Biograd (Figure 9.1/1)

Although officially registered in 1967, the site was discovered in the early 1960s and in the interim much of the material found its way into private collections in Belgium. The first three excavation campaigns were organized in 1967 and 1968, while the next two followed in 1972 and 1973 (Radulić 1970; Vrsalović 1974, 24, 43–44; Petricioli 1981, 37–38). A short rescue campaign took place in 1996 in order to renew the excavation and initiate protective measures of the wreck site (Brusić 2006, 78–80). Due to administrative complications the attempt remained without success.

The ship proved to be a round merchantman approximately 40 m in length (Beltrame 2006), armed with guns and laden with a volume and variety of finished and semi-finished products and raw material of mostly Italian and German origin (Petricioli and Uranija 1970; Petricioli 1973; 1981; Beltrame 2003; 2006; Morin 2006; Davanzo Poli 2006; Lazar and Willmott 2006; Mileusnić 2006; Schick 2006; Stadler 2006; Terzer 2006). Two large iron anchors and eight bronze guns were raised from the seabed. The

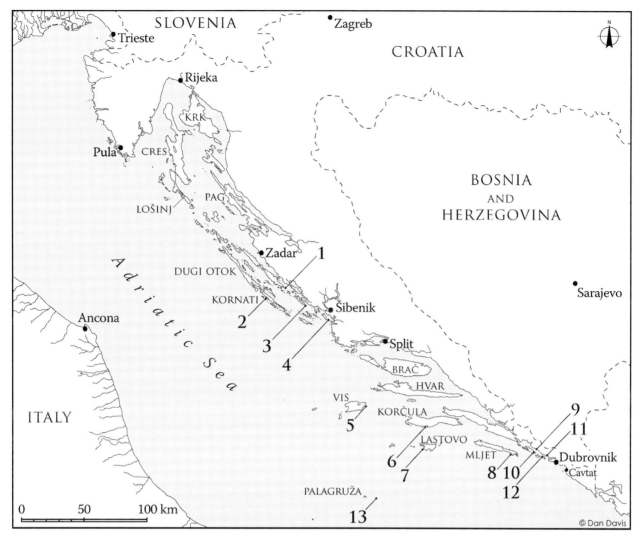

Figure 9.1. Map of sites (D. Davis).

most significant of these is a pair of sakers (length 3,5 m; calibre 91 mm) produced in Venice by Giovanni II (Zuan) Alberghetti in 1582. Three of the remaining guns were identified as *petriere da braga* (stone thrower swivel guns), one as a *moschetto da braga* (small calibre breech-loading swivel gun) and two as *passavolanti* (Morin 2006). The last mentioned guns are not of Venetian origin, but of probable German or French manufacture.

The wooden remains of the ship's hull, identified in several trenches, remain to be excavated and studied in detail (Brusić 2006, 78, fig. 1/2; Beltrame 2006). A large part of the raised material is on display in the Municipal Museum of Biograd. The latest archaeological survey was undertaken in 2005 and confirmed the presence of a large quantity of small archaeological finds in the surface layer and exposed wooden parts of the hull.

Island of Bisaga in the archipelago of Kornati (Figure 9.1/2)

A 17th-century shipwreck near the small island of Bisaga belongs to the group of sites that have been heavily looted for decades and never been researched. The presence of

guns and anchors has been reported (Brusić 1987; 2001, 38; 2006, 82–83), while the material from private collections suggests a cargo composed of porcelain cups of probable Chinese origin and a large quantity of clay pipes. All attempts to initiate archaeological excavation have been without success.

Shallows of Mijoka near the island of Murter (Figure 9.1/3)

The site lies several hundreds metres from the shallows of Mijoka, close to another unnamed shallow. For decades it was known only from a series of interesting finds from private collections (Brusić 2001, 38–40; 2006, 79–83). It was officially registered in 2002, and shortly thereafter the heavily looted remains were covered with protective mesh (Zubčić and Bekić 2003, 76). Rescue excavation began in 2006 and is still ongoing (Zmaić 2007). The reports mention the presence of a "*relatively small anchor*," while local divers remember one "*small bronze stone gun*" with the number 85 indicated by a series of round impressions in the centre of the object.

Among its many spectacular finds (including a goldsmith's

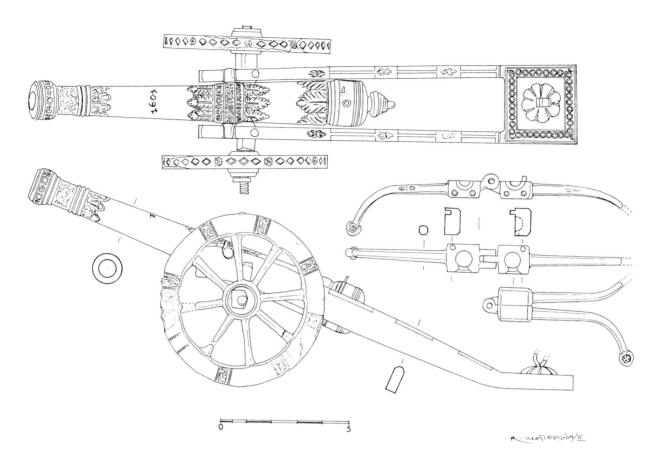

Figure 9.2. Model of brass cannon on a carriage (drawing: K. Rončević).

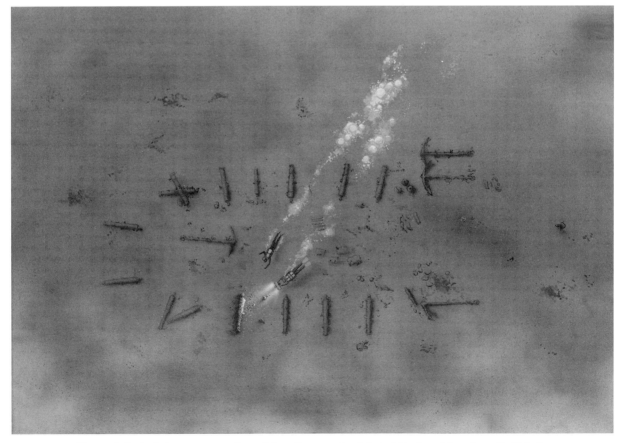

Figure 9.3. Artistic representation of the site near the islet of Greben (drawing: D. Frka).

Figure 9.4. Bronze guns from the site near the islet of Greben (photo: R. Mosković).

Figure 9.5. Bronze gun from the site near the islet of Greben, detail (photo: R. Mosković).

Islet of Greben near the island of Vis (Figure 9.1/5)

The well preserved site with 16 guns was discovered in the 1970s (Frka and Mesić 2003, 142–149). The two bronze *petrieri* (muzzleloading stone throwers) were located at the prow, while 14 cast-iron guns delineated the port and starboard sides of the ship (Figure 9.3). The guns appear to have fallen to their current position after the decomposition of the upper part of the ship's hull. During the archaeological campaign in the 1980s the two bronze guns, pieces of glazed pottery and a copper cauldron were raised and deposited in the archaeological collection at Issa on Vis (Figures 9.4, 9.5). The cascables and breeches with the initials present on the bronze guns suggest a production in Genoa at the end of the 16th century (see Ridella, this volume). The iron guns remain *in situ*.

Islet of Otočac near the island of Korčula (Figure 9.1/6)

The remains of a post-mediaeval shipwreck near the islet of Otočac in front of the village of Brna have been well known among local divers and were officially recorded in 1990 (Radić 1991, 30; Jurišić 2001, 190; Radić Rossi 2005, 43–45; Gluščević 2006, 75). A large quantity of window glass, semi-finished products and raw material can be seen on a plain sandy seabed. One of the striking features of the site is its great number of yellow clumps identified as auripigment (orpiment) or arsenic trisulphide (As_2S_3), which was used as early as the Classical period as a bright yellow pigment. The presence of one iron gun partially buried beneath the sand was also attested. The quality of the seabed and the general aspect of the site suggest the possibility of a well preserved hull.

Cuf Promontory on the island of Lastovo (Figure 9.1/7)

The shipwreck off Cuf promontory was pointed out by the local divers in the early 1990s. The presence of one corroded iron gun, probably a bombard, was attested (Jurišić 2000, 76). During the survey in 2007 other ceramic and metal objects were recorded. They help date the site to the 15th or 16th century.

balances and weights, small sun dials, reckoning counters of Hans Schultes factory from Nuremberg, and more) there is a model of brass cannon on a carriage (Figure 9.2), with the year 1601 incised on the gun itself, and a stamp for casting the associated lead cannon balls (Brusić 2006, 79–83). The site continues to yield many small ordinary and high-value objects intended for trade.

Judging from the dimensions of the site, the small anchor and the lack of guns or cannon of significant size, the ship appears not to have exceeded 10 m in length. The precious and high-value nature of the cargo have prompted the suggestion that this may have been a pirate vessel which sank after having attacked a merchant ship carrying a precious cargo. Until a careful and thorough examination of the cargo is undertaken, this must remain only a tentative hypothesis.

Island of Drvenik near the island of Zlarin (Figure 9.1/4)

On the western side of the island of Drvenik the remains of the battleship from the 16th century were recorded, armed with 6–8 wrought iron stone guns (Brusić 2001, 37–38). To date, no archaeological operation has been organized on the site.

Shallows of Sv. Pavao on the island of Mljet (Figure 9.1/8)

The completely preserved site was discovered in 2006. During the rescue operation seven bronze guns and more than 30 different ceramic, glass and stone objects were raised from the seabed (Miholjek, in press). The wreck is dated to the 16th century. The rescue excavation is still in progress and the material remains unpublished.

Brsečine Bay near Dubrovnik (Figure 9.1/9)

The site, officially registered in 2003, was interpreted as the shipwreck of a vessel that in Napoleonic times transported broken guns for recasting (Jurišić 2005). In the same year one complete bronze saker and four pieces were recovered to prevent their looting. In 2005 another damaged bronze gun was raised. The report mentions an iron stone gun, an anchor and a group of ballast stones on the seabed. Pieces of the ship's hull visible in the surface layer are also reported (Jurišić 2005, 426). A recent examination of the recovered finds has confirmed a date at the end of the 16th or the beginning of the 17th century. Almost all the bronze pieces are certainly of Genoese origin (see Ridella, this volume). It is possible that the sinking of the ship was caused by an explosion or a fire that damaged most of the guns. At the present state of research it is not possible to give a final determination of date and origin.

Bay of Suđurađ on the island of Šipan (Figure 9.1/10)

In 1972–1974 the Naval Museum of Dubrovnik led the rescue excavation of a shipwreck situated near Mali reef at the entrance to the bay of Suđurađ (Kisić 1982). The short term rescue excavation was undertaken in 2000, although no site protection was formulated or put in place (Kisić 2006, 142). The remains of the ship's hull suggest that the vessel's length is about 25 m. Various objects belonging to the ship's equipment and a limited amount of cargo in the form of raw materials were recorded on the seabed. Among the raised objects were two Spanish coins of Philip II (1556–1598) and one of Ferdinand V (1478–1516). Near the bow a small iron gun was found (length about 1.5 m; not conserved), while two larger wrought iron bombards, (length of the first 1.7 m, incomplete, calibre 110 mm; length of the second 2.15 m; calibre 180 mm) were found in the area of the stern. In the 1960s two bronze guns were raised from the site and ended up in private collections. The Naval Museum managed to produce a copy of one of them (length 0.8 m; calibre 50 mm), which was decorated with the emblem of the Ragusan family of Primoević (Primi). During the campaigns of the 1970s, two large anchors were recorded (Kisić 1982, 74; 2006, 131) while the 2000 report mentions the remains of five different anchor pieces.

The identification of the ship as the nava *S. Hieronimo*, which sank in 1576, is confirmed by archival documents as belonging to Jere Primoević, a famous merchant from Dubrovnik (Vekarić 1987, Kisić 2006, 132–133, fig. 5). The documents describe the salvage by divers in 1607 and 1608 of eleven different guns and part of the cargo.

Conserved finds from the site can be seen in the Naval Museum of Dubrovnik.

Drevine in the Channel of Koločep (Figure 9.1/11)

Three brief campaigns at the site of Drevine took place in 1972–1974 (Kisić 1979). Finds raised from the seabed include wooden barrels filled with iron nails, 47 wooden cases full of small objects such as knives, sleigh bells etc., as well as four guns made of cast iron (1. length 1.71 m, calibre 60 mm; 2–3. length 1,86 m, calibre 70–80 mm; 4. length 1.97 m, calibre 80 mm) and other objects of the ship's equipment. Unfortunately, the material has never been studied in detail and just a small portion of it has been conserved (Gluščević 2006, 74–75). During the excavations, pages from 16th-century books reused as elaborate knife binders were discovered. Reckoning counters (jetons) produced by Cornelius Lauffer in Nuremberg from 1686 to 1711 dated the ship to the end of the 17th or the beginning of the 18th century.

The length of the ship itself was estimated at 25–30 m. The survey conducted under the UNESCO Participation program 2008–2009 confirmed the existence of the ship's hull, with clearly visible frames and planks in the surface layer, covered with stone ballast (Radić Rossi and Parica 2009, 79–80). The wood has been seriously damaged by *Teredo navalis*.

Ratac Promontory on the island of Koločep (Figure 9.1/12)

In 1997 local divers pointed out the position of a well-preserved post-mediaeval shipwreck with six iron guns clearly visible on the seabed (Jurišić 1998, 87). A short-term rescue excavation campaign the following year revealed the presence of a cargo composed of glass ware, metal tools, other metal products such as wire or sheet, semi-finished products and raw material (Mesić 1999, 74, 76). Although the site is well preserved and easily reachable by divers, and therefore exposed to looting, it was left without any particular attention until recently (Jurišić 2005, 426).

The official registration of a private collection and new information given by the local divers reveals that the ship contained a great variety of interesting forms of ceramic, glass and metal objects (Radić Rossi 2006), while the survey organized under the UNESCO Participation program 2008–2009 has revealed some well preserved remains of wooden elements of the ship (Radić Rossi and Parica 2009: 80). The work of documenting of the site in detail is in progress.

Galijula Reef in the archipelago of Palagruža (Figure 9.1/13)

A local diver from Komiža on the island of Vis discovered an interesting site near Galijula Reef in the archipelago of Palagruža, which is situated in the middle of the Adriatic Sea. A Roman imperial vessel lies directly underneath a post-medieval vessel, both of which are covered by a modern iron ship. The superposition of the modern ship atop the post-medieval vessel caused some confusion in the

Figure 9.6 (top). Richly decorated smaller gun from Galijula Reef (photo: R. Mosković).

Figures 9.7–9.9. Richly decorated gun from Galijula Reef, details (photo: R. Mosković).

Figure 9.10. Richly decorated smaller gun from Galijula Reef, detail (photo: R. Mosković).

Figure 9.12. Smaller gun from Galijula Reef, details (photo: R. Mosković).

first official reports. Although the site was initially reported as a modern ship transporting much older guns, it appears that they are in fact two different shipwrecks.

In 1987, the diver from Komiža raised a richly decorated gun that has been dated to the first half of the 16th century (Figures 9.6, 9.7–9.9); the second gun came to the surface during the 1988 archaeological survey (Orlić 1988, 42–43; Radić 1990, 216–218; Gluščević 2006, 75), (Figures 9.10–9.12). Both finds are in display in front of the Venetian Tower in Komiža.

Figure 9.11. Smaller gun from Galijula Reef, details (photo: R. Mosković).

Potential sites

The intense utilization of the Eastern Adriatic as a navigation corridor, competition between the Adriatic's maritime trading centres, the abundance of finds in private collections, information on shipwrecks garnered from local divers and fishermen, and a raft of archival evidence – all of these factors point to the probability that many more shipwrecks from the post-mediaeval period remain to be discovered, explored, documented and protected in Croatian waters (Tenenti 1959; Luetić 1972). On the other hand, historical documents testifying to the practice of sailors and divers salvaging ships, tackle and cargo throughout mediaeval and post-mediaeval periods (Vekarić 1987; Brusić 2001, 36–37) may account for their lack of visibility on the seabed.

In the database of the Hvar Heritage Museum the site labelled HVO536 represents one example of a potential shipwreck site that was never archaeologically surveyed (Petrić 2008, 60). The finds from a private collection and the information given by a diver who recalls several guns, two or three large anchors, wooden elements and a number of ceramic wares suggest the existence of a shipwreck preliminary dated to the end of the 15th or the beginning of the 16th century.

Conclusion

The present overview demonstrates the urgent need for a systematic approach to the research, study and protection of post-medieval underwater cultural heritage in Croatia. Several important and interesting sites, such as Gnalić, Suđurađ and Drevine, have already provided valuable information on post-mediaeval trade, but still deserve the serious attention of experts from many different fields and the right solution for an *in situ* protection of the remaining finds. The same statement could be applied to all the other post-medieval shipwrecks, the potential of which is yet to be defined in order to propose an adequate approach to their protection and eventual systematic research. The interest of the international community in integrating existing knowledge, as in the case of the Gnalić wreck (Guštin and Gelichi 2006), has proven to be of great scientific value for stimulating future work.

Completely omitted from all of these programs of research and excavation are reports of hulls and hull construction, as well as detailed studies of ships' equipment. These lacunae have caused a lamentable scarcity of archaeological data that could be incorporated in research on the seafaring and shipbuilding of the post-medieval Adriatic and Mediterranean.

References

Beltrame, C. (2003) Una testimonianza dei traffici veneziani alla fine del Cinquecento. *L'archeologo subacqueo*, IX. 3 (27), 10–14.

Beltrame, C. (2006) Osservazioni preliminari sullo scafo e l'equipaggiamento della nave di Gnalić. In M. Guštin, S. Gelichi, K. Spindler (eds.) 2006, 93–95.

Brusić, Z. (1987) Dio tereta s lađe iz 17. stoljeća potonule kod otoka Bisaga u kornatskom arhipelagu. *Prilozi povijesti umjetnosti u Dalmaciji*, 26, 473–490.

Brusić, Z. (2001) Blago šibenskog podmorja. In Z. Brusić, M. Jurišić & Ž. Krnčević (eds.), *Blago šibenskog podmorja, katalog izložbe*, 17–46. Šibenik, Županijski muzej Šibenik.

Brusić, Z. (2006) Tre naufragi del XVII o XVIII secolo lungo la costa adriatica orientale. In M. Guštin, S. Gelichi, K. Spindler (eds.) 2006, 63–70.

Davanzo Poli, D. (2006) I reperti tessili di Gnalić. In M. Guštin, S. Gelichi, K. Spindler (eds.) 2006, 98–99.

Frka, D., Mesić, J. (2003) *Secrets of the Adriatic sea. Diver's guide on wracks of the Croatian Adriatic sea*. Rijeka, Adamić.

Gluščević, S. (2006) Alcuni ritrovamenti medievali e postmedievali dagli abissi dell'Adriatico orientale Croato. In M. Guštin, S. Gelichi, K. Spindler (eds.) 2006, 59–62.

Guštin, M., Gelichi, S. (2006) The shipwreck at Gnalić. Project The Heritage of Serenissima. In M. Guštin, S. Gelichi, K. Spindler (eds.) 2006, 77–80.

Guštin, M., Gelichi, S., Spindler, K. (eds.) (2006), *The Heritage of Serenissima.* Koper, Založba Annales Mediterranea.

Jurišić, M. (1998) Hidroarheološka djelatnost Uprave za zaštitu kulturne baštine tijekom godine 1996. i 1997. *Obavijesti Hrvatskog arheološkog društva*, XXX/1, 81–90.

Jurišić, M. (2000) Plava grobnica smrtonosnih cijevi. *More Magazin*, 74–77.

Jurišić, M. (2001) Podmorski arheološki lokaliteti otoka Korčula. *Znanstveni skup „Arheološka istraživanja na području otoka Korčule i Lastova", Vela Luka i Korčula, 18.-20. IV. 1991.* Zagreb, Izdanja Hrvatskog arheološkog društva 20, 189–196.

Jurišić, M. (2006) Dubrovački akvatorij. *Hrvatski arheološki godišnjak*, 2/2005, 425–426.

Kisić, A. (1979) Ostaci potonulog dubrovačkog broda iz XVI. stoljeća kod Šipana. *Anali Zavoda za povijesne znanosti IC JAZU u Dubrovniku*, 17, 73–98.

Kisić, A. (1982) Nešto o trgovačkom brodu koji je nastradao u Koločepskom kanalu kod Dubrovnika krajem XVII. ili početkom XVIII. stoljeća. *Anali Zavoda za povijesne znanosti IC JAZU u Dubrovniku*,19–20, 143–163.

Kisić, A. (2006) La nave ragusea del XVI secolo sul fondale marino della baia di Suđurađ sull'isola di Šipan. In I. Radić Rossi (ed.) *Archeologia subacquea in Croazia. Studi e ricerche, 127–145.* Venice, Marsilio Editore.

Lazar, I., H. Willmott, H. (2006) *The Glass from the Gnalić Wreck.* Koper. Annales Mediterranea. Koper, Založba Annales.

Luetić, J. (1959) Stari brodski top izvađen iz mora. *Vijesti muzealaca i konzervatora NR Hrvatske*, 8, 105–106.

Luetić, J. (1972) Havarije bokeljski brodova u spisima pomorskog konzulata – skupštine Dubrovačke Republike od 1629. do 1811. godine. *Godišnjak Pomorskog muzeja u Kotoru*, 20, 133–142.

Luetić, J. (1993) Prvo hrvatsko hidroarheološko djelo. *Večernji list* 3. 10. 1993.

Mesić, J. (1999) Zaštitna istraživanja i rekognosciranja podmorskih arheoloških lokaliteta tijekom 1998. *Obavijesti Hrvatskog arheološkog društva*, XXXI/2, 72–77.

Miholjek, I. (in press) Mljet – uvala V. Dolina i Pličina Preč. *Hrvatski arheološki godišnjak*, 4/2007.

Mileusnić, Z. (ed.) (2004) *The Venetian Shipwreck at Gnalić. Annales Mediterranea.* Biograd na moru – Koper, Zavičajni muzej Biograd na moru.

Mileusnić, Z. (2006) The pottery from Gnalić wreck. In *Guštin, Gelichi & Spindler 2006*: 104–107.

Morin, M. (2006) Le artiglierie del relitto di Gnalić. In M. Guštin, S. Gelichi, K. Spindler (eds.) 2006, 95–97.

Orlić, M. (1988) Rekognosciranje podmorja oko otoka Palagruže. *Obavijesti Hrvatskog arheološkog društva,* XX/3, 42–43.

Petricioli, S. (1981) Deset godina rada na hidroarheološkom nalazu kod Gnalića. *Godišnjak zaštite spomenika kulture Hrvatske,* 6/7, 37–45.

Petricioli, S., Uranija, V. (eds.) (1970) *Brod kod Gnalića – naše najbogatije hidroarheološko nalazište. Vrulje – Glasilo Narodnog muzeja u Zadru 1.*

Petricioli, S. (1973) The Gnalić wreck: The glass. *Journal of Glass Studies,* 15, 85–92.

Petrić, M. (2008) Underwater cultural heritage of the Island of Hvar; A brief statistical overview of sites. In I. Radić Rossi, A. Gaspari, A. Pydyn (eds.), *Proceedings of the 13th Annual Meeting of the European Association of Archaeologists, Zadar, Croatia, 18–23 September 2007,* 41–60. Zagreb, Croatian Archaeological Society.

Radić, I. (1990) Arheološka istraživanja u podmorju istočnog Jadrana u tijeku godine 1988. *Godišnjak zaštite spomenika kulture Hrvatske,* 14–15.

Radić Rossi, I. (2005) Dosadašnji rezultati podmorskih arheoloških istraživanja u zapadnom dijelu otoka Korčule. *Blato do kraja 18. st., Zbornik radova* 3. Blato, 33–48.

Radić Rossi, I. (2006) Il relitto di una nave mercantile presso l'Isola di Koločep. In M. Guštin, S. Gelichi, K. Spindler (eds.) 2006, 71–76.

Radić Rossi, I., Parica, M., (2009) Stručni očevid na podmorskim arheološkim nalazištima dubrovačkog podmorja. *Obavijesti Hrvatskog arheološkog društva,* XL/3, 72–81.

Radulić, K. (1970) Brod kod Gnalića; naše najbogatije hidroarheološko nalazište. In S. Petricioli, V. Uranija (eds.), *Vrulje – Glasilo Narodnog muzeja u Zadru* 1, 4–9.

Schick, M. (2006) The sleigh bell finds from Gnalić wreck. In M. Guštin, S. Gelichi, K. Spindler (eds.) 2006, 110–112.

Stadler, M. (2006) The brass candlesticks, sconces and chandeliers from Gnalić wreck. In M. Guštin, S. Gelichi, K. Spindler (eds.) 2006, 107–109.

Tenenti, A. (1959) *Naufrages, corsaires et assurances maritimes à Venise (1592–1609).* Paris,.

Terzer, C. (2006) The lead seals from Gnalić wreck. In M. Guštin, S. Gelichi, K. Spindler (eds.) 2006, 112–114.

Vekarić, S. (1987) Dva najstarija primjera spašavanja broda u XVII i XVIII stoljeću u Dubrovniku. *Adrias - Zbornik Zavoda za znanstveni i umjetnički rad HAZU u Splitu* 1, 65–71.

Vrsalović, D. (1974) *Istraživanje i zaštita podmorskih arheoloških spomenika u SR Hrvatskoj.* Zagreb, Republički zavod za zaštitu spomenika kulture.

Zmaić, V. (2007) Redni broj: 200; Lokalitet: Pličina Mijoka. *Hrvatski arheološki godišnjak* 3/2006, 376–377.

Zubčić, K., Bekić. L. (2003) Podvodna i kopnena arheološka istraživanja Odjela za zaštitu arheološke baštine u godini 2002. *Obavijesti Hrvatskog arheološkog društva* XXXV/1, 75–83.

10

Did Naval Artillery Really Exist During the Modern Period? A Brief Note on Cannon Design

Javier López Martín

Underwater archaeology and artillery are related to each other. The former strongly contributes to the study of the latter, adding more pieces to our knowledge as they are discovered. On the other hand, cannon contribute to our dating of shipwrecks as they provide a *terminus ante quem* for when the ship was sunk. When cannon are not dated, clues can be provided by distinctive features inscribed in pieces such as mottoes and coats of arms, which can also give a precise framework for their production. However, not all the pieces provide such information. It depends on the material they are made from.

When the piece recovered is made of wrought iron, the possibilities are less reliable; they are usually not dated as the iron is not as easy to embellish with inscriptions or highly ornate motifs as is bronze. Thus, such pieces lack the gunfounder's name and place of manufacture. Furthermore, iron has no protection against corrosion and it is soon corroded. They can, however, bear a type of mark which could be ascribed to specific areas of production. On the other hand, artillery made of bronze is usually inscribed with both the date of manufacture and the gunfounder's name, representing valuable information for the shipwreck in which it is found.

Bronze cannon were among the first artefacts to be recovered from a sunken ship. This was because of the economic value of bronze and also its resistance to sea-corrosion. The prices of the alloy were continuously rising during the Modern period, reaching the highest prices when demand for artillery increased, though it never was a serious obstacle for its production. Bronze can be re-cast and there were huge quantities of scrap metal, sculptures and cannon of old design which could be broken down and smelted again into new pieces. Therefore, the recovery of artillery from the sea was also an important target to achieve.

Diego Ufano inserted in his *Treatise of Artillery* (Brussels 1613) an illustration of a diver recovering a piece of bronze (Figure 10.1). The diver, using a primitive diving suit, is binding the dolphin lugs of the cannon to a hook with ropes. On the surface, a boat equipped with a device similar to a carpenter's brace, is ready to raise the piece.

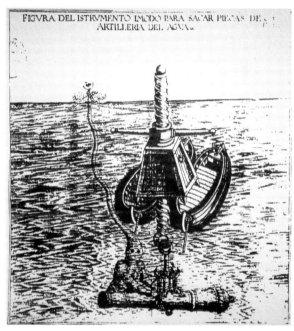

Figure 10.1. Figvra del instrvmento i modo para sacar piecas de / artilleria del agva. Tratado de Artilleria. Diego Ufano (Brussels 1613, 237).

Similar devices must have been in use for a long period before Ufano's time, and they must have been very effective as there are records that confirm the recovery of cannon from shipwrecks during the early Modern period.

This is the case of the warship *Engelen*. It was built in Denmark between 1509 and 1512, and lent to Charles V (then Charles I) for his landing in Spain. She burnt on 2 July 1518 in the port of Pasajes, near San Sebastián. Forty-six pieces of artillery were recovered from the ship within the following days: thirty-one of iron with thirty-six chambers, and fifteen of bronze with fifteen chambers. Some pieces were retrieved "*half melted*". Among the cannon salvaged were three cast iron guns with fourteen powder chambers made with the same material.

A surviving bronze bombard, the so-called *Pluckeroseken*

Figure 10.2. The Pluckeroseken. *Museo de San Telmo, inv. H45. L: 244 cm, cal: 21.2 cm.*

Figure 10.3 (left). A cast iron hailshot piece from the Mary Rose, no. 80A0544; side view. Figure 10.4 (right). Front view of the hailshot piece with four original dice recovered from the site.

(little rose), was recovered during dredging operations in 1936 in the port of Pasajes. It is now at *Museo de San Telmo*, San Sebastián (Figure 10.2). It might have been retrieved from the wreck of the *Engelen*. The piece, made in two parts, has no trunnions and shows that a bombard designed for the battle field was still onboard a ship probably at the beginning of the 16th century. It is important to bear in mind that it still has the same shape as the great bombards in use a hundred years before the *Engelen* sunk.

Artillery was a key point in the construction of vessels because of the changes in the shape of the hulls as well as the adoption of new-style loopholes on lower decks and carriages to accommodate guns. However, a high percentage of pieces recovered from wrecks correspond

to different cannon types, design of which was made exclusively for their use on land. Wrought iron cannon recovered from early European and American shipwrecks do not differ from others used in land sieges or castle defences. These are bombard, port-pieces or *cerbatana* types. This is the same with bronze artillery excavated from underwater sites. In theory, naval artillery can be considered as any cannon ready to use onboard warships. Strictly speaking, however, pieces specifically designed for use on board vessels were made in only a few cases. According to their design, only a small range of pieces were made for use at sea.

One of the earliest examples could be four small pieces recovered from the *Mary Rose*. They are cast iron muzzle-loading pieces designed to fire "hailshot", a form of grapeshot. They have a flat rectangular body divided by mouldings at the muzzle, middle and end of the barrel, which narrows towards the breech. Behind the vent-field moulding it expands cylindrically to form a socket for a wooden stock designed to enable handling of the gun. There is a hook on the underside of the barrel to counteract the recoil (Figure 10.3). The shape of the piece bears a relationship to its position of use within the gundeck and this perhaps suggests an evolution designed predominantly for shipboard use. One gun was loaded with 20 iron cubes shaped like 'dice', and the radiograph of another shows that it contains about 30 iron dice (Figure 10.4). The length of the guns run from 41.5 to 44.4 cm and the rectangular bore has a calibre of 5.8 × 2.6 cm approximately.

According to the fleet artillery inventory of 1546, the so-called *Anthony Roll*, which lists the ordnance within 58 vessels, the *Mary Rose* was equipped with 20 hailshot pieces out of 76 iron guns. Small ships such as pinnaces have just two hailshot pieces. The maximum is for the 1,000-ton *Harry Grace à Dieu* with 40 of them on board. The total number of hailshot pieces listed is 459 out of 1,814 guns of iron. Hailshot pieces are far less common in castles or land fortifications, where just 76 are listed (Hildred 2003).

As the *Mary Rose* sank in Portsmouth on 19 July 1545 it is quite possible that these small cast iron pieces were from the first cast iron production initiated in 1543 by Peter Baude, a French gunfounder established in Houndsditch (London), and Ralph Hogge, an iron founder to the King. Both worked together with the clergyman William Levett, initiating cast iron muzzle-loading cannon production for the Ordnance Office.

A surviving drawing may have been a precedent of these pieces. It was made by Leonardo da Vinci. At the top and bottom of a folio of the Windsor Collection appear two cannon designs that have been designated as naval ordnance, merely because the piece at the bottom is on a boat surrounded by water (Figure 10.5). In each case the discharge is of hailshot, and the cannon bodies have

Figure 10.5. Leonardo da Vinci. Windsor Collection, fol. RL12632r.

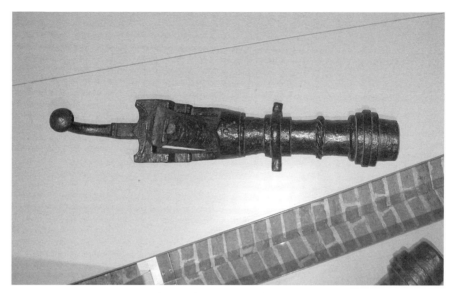

Figure 10.6. Leger Museum, inv. 13335. It shows the triple and sugarstick rings, the mark and the tail curved up.

a peculiar flat rectangular shape. In fact, the similarities between these drawings and the hailshot pieces recovered from the *Mary Rose*, which, as mentioned previously, were loaded with dice for grapeshot, is remarkable. The pieces from the *Mary Rose* could have been designed specifically for shipboard use and Leonardo's designs are compatible with this assumption. This is a unique case in which an original drawing made by Leonardo might be sustained by archaeological evidence. The *Mary Rose* pieces are also a fresh indication that guns similar to Leonardo's designs actually existed, though there would not be a direct link between them.

According to Diego García del Palacio's *Instrucción Naútica para el uso de las Naos* (Mexico 1587), pieces with separate chambers might be used in the upper deck only. Otherwise the smoke produced restricted aiming and the use of cannon. Muzzle-loaders, cast in one piece, may have been placed on lower decks, as the smoke was expelled from the muzzle and therefore outside the hull.

Muzzle-loaders, designed for land use and mainly placed in lower decks, were combined with other pieces which seem to form a specific typology for naval use: the swivel gun, made for close anti-personal fighting and placed on the upper decks. This type usually refers to medium or small breech-loading cannon with a tail or tiller at the rear end designed to enable handling of the gun. On the back, it has a hole or chamber holder to place the chamber. It could be made either wrought in iron or cast in bronze with different designs. They have been studied in different articles (Howard 1987; Smith 1995; 2004); however, none of these papers tried to confront their shape and marks. Six major categories can be distinguished from the point of view both of their design and inscribed marks.

The first category is formed by a group of 26 wrought iron breech-loading swivel guns, spread worldwide, which exhibit similar typology irrespective of the overall length. Some of them even present similar marks. Gun marks have been grouped in Table 10.1. They have three main

characteristics (Figure 10.6):

–   three rings, or a triple ring, form the first hoop (from the muzzle), being higher the ring placed on the middle;
–   in ten of the guns studied the next reinforcement is always a spiral-forged hoop or sugarstick ring; ten others do not have this, and five have been cut down or broken, or the image used has too low a resolution to determine if it exists;
–   all the preserved tails or tillers are curved up at the end to create a control handle.

There are other pieces that seem to form a different category (Figure 10.7). They are larger, lacking both the triple and sugarstick rings, and generally have a straight tail. Surprisingly, they have the same type of marks (grouped in Table 10.2). Four other examples at the Rijksmuseum and the Scheepvaart Museum in Amsterdam have not been included due to the absence of marks. However, their shape is the same. It is important to note two main features within both categories:

–   the strong resemblance between marks. Eleven marks out of 14 have dots at the ends. Only the marks on the pieces from the Molasses Reef Wreck and Berlin differ;
–   the marks were stamped on the same place of the guns and some of them also have dots located at both sides and the rear end of the breech.

These models of swivel guns might have come from related workshops within the same production area, perhaps in the Low Countries. Many of them have been ascribed to the Netherlands or have been related to a Dutch wreck. The mark stamped three times on the *Stuerghewalt*, a basilisk rather than a swivel-gun, belongs to Jan Fyck, a German master who worked in s'Hertogenbosch (Netherlands). The Zeebrugge bombard, a wrought-iron piece, was recovered with other important metal objects (*e.g.* candleholders, coins, cannon and bullets) off the coast of Zeebrugge

Table 10.1. (Drawings not to Scale).

Piece	Triple Ring	Sugarstick Ring	Main Mark(S)	Tail
Molasses-39 ①	No	No		straight
Deutsches Historisches Museum Berlin-431	alternate	yes		broken
Royal Armouries Tower of London Al.53.2	yes	yes		broken
Heeresgeschichtliches Museum Vienna-17	yes	yes		curve
Musée Royal de l'Armée et d'Historire Militaire Brussels-1096 ②	yes	yes		curve
Leger Museum Delft-13335	yes	yes		curve
Museu Militar Lisbon-A4	yes	no		curve
Museu Militar Lisbon-A5	yes	no		curve
Museu Militar Lisbon-A6	cut	cut		curve
H. L. Visser Collection 100	Yes	No		curve

① After Keith (1987, 203). ②I could not distinguish well this mark because of the showcase.

(Belgium) (Vandenberghe 2006, 19). The marks could have belonged equally to the masters, owners, guilds or workshops. If all these pieces are not from the same area of production, it is amazing that various masters in different areas stamped the same type of marks in the same place on the guns. The production of wrought iron pieces in the Low Countries during the second half of the 15th century was large scale, especially in Liège. They were of a type that proliferated throughout the continent. However, none of the wrought iron Spanish or Italian guns supposedly from the same period have this type of mark.

These countries seem to form the area of production for the third category of swivel guns, though the evidence is more tenuous than in the case of the pieces attributed to

Table 10.2. (Drawings not to scale).

PIECE	MAIN MARK(s)	TAIL
Musée Royal de l'Armée et d'Historire Militaire Brussels-23	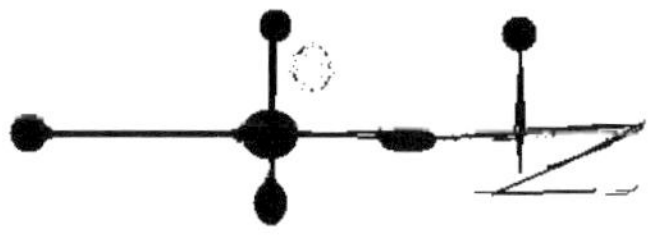	straight & curved at the end
Leger Museum Delft-50245	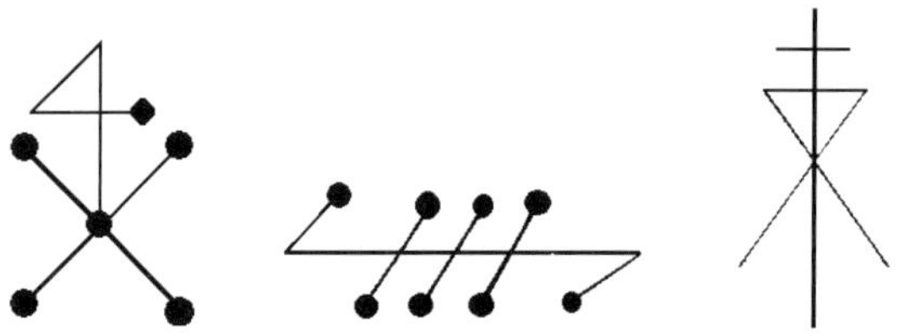	only half of the tail is curved
Nederlands Instituut voor Scheps-en onderwater Archeologie, Lelystad (no number)		straight
Museo Histórico Militar Seville-2728	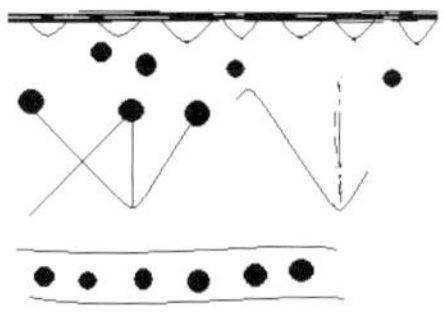	straight
Hertogenbosch The Netherlands (the "*Stuerghewalt*")	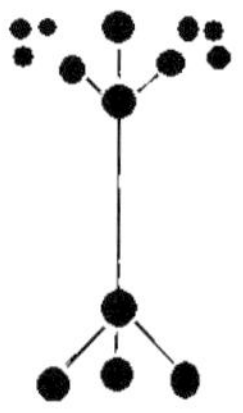	(this mark is stamped three times on the piece)
The Zeebrugge bombard Zeebrugge Port Authority building ③		(the mark is stamped above the touch hole)
Museo Histórico Militar de Canarias Sta. Cruz de Tenerife 78		straight

③   Drawing by Axel Biront, private communication February 2009.

the Netherlands. The swivel gun of this typology is always made in wrought iron, with reinforced rings, straight tail, and the walls of the breech chamber form right angles (Figure 10.8). This type is associated with wrecks of Iberian or Mediterranean tradition. Nine swivel guns of this typology were recovered from the Brescou-2 site, off Cap d'Agde (Languedoc-Roussillon, France). No wreck has been found, suggesting that the objects were jettisoned. They could also have been made in Italy, which is the area of production of the fourth category or type of piece: the composite swivel gun.

Its barrel is made from bronze whereas the breech chamber holder is made from wrought-iron (Figure 10.9). It seems that these pieces were made for Venice, though the workshops could have been located in Venice, Genoa, Naples or even Sicily. Many examples bear the Lion of St Mark (in all varieties) and the letter *X* for the *Consiglio dei Dieci*, which could have ordered the castings. Sometimes the initial(s) of the master gunfounder appears below the Lion of St Mark (*e.g.* the letter *A* for Alberghetti or *N. C.* for Nicolò di Conti). In guns without these marks, the weight helps to ascribe them to a Venetian or Italian workshop. It is always inscribed on the upper side of the barrel near the chamber holder.

Figure 10.7. Museo Militar de Sevilla, inv. 2728. The piece is larger than the piece showed in Figure 10.6, has a straight tail and lacks both the triple and sugarstick rings.

Figure 10.8. Heeresgeschichtliches Museum, inv. 81439, 81436 and 81499. The gun on the left has lost the tail.

Figure 10.9. Ulster Museum, inv. 6.8. A composite gun. It has a bronze barrel whereas the breech chamber holder is made from wrought iron.

Figure 10.10. Museo Storico Navale, inv. 947. It shows the moulding at both sides of the chamber holder.

Table 10.3. (drawings not to scale)

PIECE	MARK / SHIELD	MOULDING
Museo Provincial Cadiz (no number)		No
Tolosa ④		No
Rahmi M. Koç Müzesi Istanbul ⑤		No
Koločep Private collection Dubrovnik		No
Brescou-2255 ⑥		No
The Hellenic Maritime Museum Piraeus ⑤		No
Palace of the Grand Master Rhodes-533 ⑤		No
Palace of the Grand Master Rhodes-534 ⑤		No

Table 10.3 continued

Museo Storico Navale Venice-1004		No
National Historical *Museum* Athens-1 ⑦		No
Musée de l'Armée Paris-17		No
Athlit site ⑧		No
Athlit site ⑧		No
Musée de l'Armée Paris-52		No
Musée de l'Armée Paris-53		No
Askeri Müzesi Istanbul-233		No

Table 10.3 continued

Askeri Müzesi Istanbul-421		No
Museu Militar Lisbon-G5		No
Museo Naval Madrid-1408		No

④ Recovered from the wreck of the Tolosa, sunk in Dominican Republic in 1724. Letters within the shield for San Francisco Xavier?

⑤ After R. B. Smith (1999, unpaginated).

⑥ After Jézégou (2001, 34).

⑦ After R. B. Smith (2000, unpaginated).

⑧ Information and photographs kindly supplied by Sa'ar Nudel, arms researcher, 11 Sept. 2003.

The fifth category of swivel guns is entirely cast in bronze. Pieces within this category have the weight inscribed in the same format and they may have the Lion of St Mark. However, there is a single feature which allows further identification. It is a lineal moulding located at both sides of the chamber holder, a peculiar motif for the swivel-guns made, provisionally, in Italy only (Figure 10.10). This assumption needs further confirmation. Guns with this moulding can also bear the master's name or initial, which mainly corresponds again to different members of the Venetian families of gunfounders such as the Alberghetti and the Di Conti. A swivel gun cast by the Sicilian Federico Musarra in 1559 presents a similar moulding. This might indicate that it was a feature spread throughout Italian workshops. This unique moulding might help to ascribe swivel-guns to Italian and Venetian workshops as more pieces with identical moulding are retrieved from shipwrecks. It is known that Musarra cast four bronze *mezzi cannoni* for the Royal galleys in 1529 (Palazzolo 2003) and he could have also cast swivel guns with this moulding since then. However, this is pure speculation.

The sixth typology of swivel guns is quite similar, though pieces within this group always lack this moulding (Figure 10.11). Instead of this, they bear a shield at the middle of the chase with a master, guild or workshop mark inside it (Figure 10.12). Sometimes the shield is blank as the workshop did not inscribe its mark, or the gun was sold without a selected owner or client. However, these marks are unlike those inscribed on the wrought iron swivel guns mentioned above, though, again, there are remarkable

similarities between them. Eighteen pieces of this category have been located (grouped in Table 10.3). There must be further examples.

If all the marks grouped in the tables are compared, it is clear that two great different types of marks are found in two main different typologies of swivel guns. Marks contained in the first two tables may correspond to wrought iron pieces, mainly presumably from Northern Europe. The other marks are inscribed in pieces supposedly from the Mediterranean area. They have been ascribed to Turkish workshops, though the non-Arabic letters used would reject this theory. They could have been made in workshops based in Italy, the Balkans or within the area of influence of the Republic of Ragusa, a competitor with Venice for maritime power. There is nothing to link them to Spain.

Portugal also made swivel guns in bronze, such as the *berços, falçaos*, and *çaos*. These models were made under designs which may be among the oldest in use, at least since 1525. The gunfounder Luis is recorded working that year at Cochim (South of Goa): "*de falquões pedreiros que quá faz Luys ... xiij peças*" (Lima Felner 1862–1931, 12). They could have also been made in Europe with similar shapes since the beginning of the 16th century or even earlier. Portuguese swivel guns usually bear the symbols of the Monarchy, the *Esfera Armilar* and the Portuguese coat of arms. However, these pieces, round or facet-shaped, lack the moulding present on Italian pieces at both sides of the chamber holder.

It is the same with Dutch pieces made from 1602 for

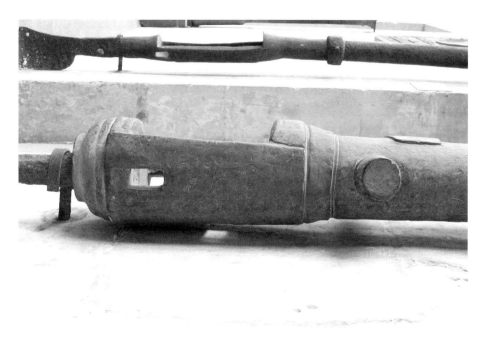

Figure 10.11. Musée de l'Armée, inv. 17. This type of piece lacks the peculiar moulding.

Figure 10.12. Detail of the shield on gun showed in Figure 10.11.

the United East India Company (V.O.C.), which bear the initials of the Company combined with the initials of its five chambers (Amsterdam, Rotterdam, Delft, Hoorn-Enkhuizen and Middelburg), in all varieties. Likewise, pieces of the West India Company (G.W.C.), created in 1621, also bear the initials of the Company and its chambers (Amsterdam, Rotterdam, Hoorn, Middelburg and Groningen). Unlike Portuguese pieces, Dutch guns usually bear both the gunfounder's name and place of manufacture, allowing a complete identification. The shape of Portuguese and Dutch pieces, always made in bronze, follows the same format, different from the designs used throughout the Mediterranean, mainly unsigned and undated.

Conclusions

To sum up, it can be said that artillery used on board warships of the Modern period always followed a shape previously designed for land use. Even guns made *specifically* for naval use, such as those made within Venetian and Genoese workshops, fundamentally followed this design. Both from surviving examples and pieces recovered from shipwrecks it seems that only swivel-guns and the hailshot cast iron guns from the *Mary Rose* were made for naval use. The former were made in various materials with different shapes. Some of them present unidentified marks, which have been ascribed to different areas of production.

Acknowledgments

I would like to thank Axel Biront, independent scholar, for supplying me with information on the Zeebrugge bombard; to Max Guérout, *Groupe de recherche en archéologie navale-GRAN*, for reminding me of the Brescou-2 site, to Odile Bérard-Azzouz, chief curator *Musée de l'Éphèbe*, Cap d'Agde, and to Irena Radic Rossi, *Croatian Conservation Institute*, Zagreb, who supplied me with photographs of the Koločep gun.

References

Collecção de Monumentos Ineditos para a Historia das Conquistas dos Portuguezes em Africa, Asia e America (1862–1931) (6 vols.). Rodrigo José de Lima Felner (ed.). Vol. V–III, *Lembranças das cousas da India em 1525*. Lisbon.

Jézégou, M.-P. (2001) *Hérault, Carte archéologique*. In Bilan Scientifique du Département des Recherches Archéologiques Subaquatiques et Sous-Marines (DRASSM) 1997, Ministère de la Culture et de la Communication, pp. 32–41.

Lima Felner (1862–1931) *Collecção de Monumentos ineditos para a Histoira das Conquistas dos Portuguezes em Africa, Asia e America.*

Hildred, A. (2003) Report on the artillery of the *Mary Rose*, draft 2 (unpublished).

Howard, F. (1986) Early ship guns. Part I: Built-up breech-loaders. *The Mariner's Mirror* 72, 439–53.

Howard, F. (1987) Early ship guns. Part II: Swivels. *The Mariner's Mirror* 73, 49–55.

Keith D. H. (1987) *The Molasses Reef Wreck*. Ann Arbor (unpublished).

Palazzolo, A. (2003) Cannoni e Fonditori in Sicilia nel XV e XVI secolo. *Rassegna Siciliana di Storia e Cultura* 20 (e-magazine, unpaginated).

Smith, R. B. (1998) *Three swivel guns in the Turkish Military Museum*. Lisbon.

Smith, R. B. (1999) *16th century swivel guns in Greece and Turkey. Including a piece in private collection*. Lisbon.

Smith, R. B. (2000): *16th century swivel guns in Spain, Greece, Bulgaria and Cyprus and two bronze pieces in the* Akbar Nama. Lisbon.

Smith, R. D. (1995) Wrought iron swivel guns. In M. Bound (ed.) *The Archaeology of Ships of War. The International Maritime Archaeology Series* (Vol. I), 104–113. Shropshire.

Smith, R. D. (2004) Bronze breech-loading swivel guns: a preliminary survey. In G. Groenendijk, P. de Gryse, D. Staat, H. Bronder (ed.) *A Farewell to Arms: Studies on the History of Arms and Armour – Liber Amicorum in honour of Jan-Piet Puype, former senior curator of the Army Museum Delft*, 167–80. Delft.

Vandenberghe, S. (2006) Major finds from the Zeebrugge site. In M., Pieters, G., Gevaert, J., Mees, J., Seys (ed.) *Colloquium: To sea or not to sea - 2nd international colloquium on maritime and fluvial archaeology in the southern North Sea area, Brugge (Belgium), 21–23 September 2006. Vlaams Instituut voor de Zee (VLIZ): Special Publication* 32, 19–20, Oostende.

Stowed or Mounted
The Spanish Armada of 1588 and the Strategic Logistics of Guns at Sea

Colin Martin

Introduction

The sea can be used as a medium for warlike activity in two ways. The first involves the transport of military personnel and hardware to attack a terrestrial objective. This exploits the capacity of water craft to carry bulk over distance, and the ability to apply concentrated violence at a chosen landing point, often enhanced by the element of surprise. The principle is the same whether the operation involves a small-scale viking raid on an undefended coastal monastery, or a major amphibious task-force such as that deployed on D-Day in 1944.

The second approach is to create a weapons system integral with the ship so that it can engage other vessels in ways which exploit its technical and tactical advantages. An example of such a combination is the early modern Mediterranean galley with its forward-mounted ordnance, applied by pointing itself towards an enemy like a fighter aircraft (Guilmartin 1974, 295–303). A broadly contemporary symbiosis evolved in Atlantic Europe in the broadside-armed sailing ship, which sought to outmanoeuvre its adversaries and position its batteries of guns where they could be used to maximum effect (Cipolla 1965; Parker 1996).

Both approaches were combined in the strategic intentions, proposed tactics, and logistical planning of Spain's unsuccessful attempt to invade England in 1588. The Armada was conceived as an invasion task-force, modelled on the successful amphibious landing on Terceira in 1583 in the final phase of Spain's annexation of Portugal. This operation had been mounted from Lisbon, where the requisite military force was assembled together with all the provisions, weaponry, munitions and supporting services it needed to ensure a successful outcome of the land campaign when the troops came ashore. Shipping requirements were determined by the need to transport the combined force to its objective, defend its integrity while at sea, and provide close support for the landings and subsequent advance along the coast. The task-force was commanded by the marquis of Santa Cruz, an experienced officer who was a master of the complex mix of logistics

and rigid battle-drills which characterised galley warfare (Guilmartin 1974, 221–252). The Terceira operation was an unqualified success and the assault on the beach, with the troops disembarking from their purpose-built landing-craft supported by galley squadrons working close inshore, is graphically represented in the Escorial's Hall of Battles (Guilmartin 2002, 119, 155).

The victory at Terceira was also commemorated in contemporary souvenirs, one of which has been recovered from the Armada wreck *La Trinidad Valencera* (Flanagan 1988, 133). It is an ornate metal bowl, decorated in relief with Spain's warrior patron Santiago mounted on his charger with sword-arm raised. But the foes beneath his horse's hooves are not the usual group of defeated Moors. They are the swirling waves of the Ocean Sea, the new theatre of naval activity which Spain's maritime prowess now dominated under her protective saint. The architect of this strategic shift from Mediterranean to oceanic amphibious warfare was Santa Cruz, and the successful outcome of the Terceira campaign provided him with a model for a more ambitious venture which Philip II ordered him to prepare – an Armada against England.

In his proposals for the invasion of England, Santa Cruz envisaged a much-enlarged version of the Terceira operation, involving almost 100,000 men and over 500 ships totalling 110,000 tons (Duro 1884, 250–319). Shortly afterwards an alternative plan was put forward by the duke of Parma, commander of Spanish forces in Flanders, who proposed that 20,000 of his crack troops should cross the Channel in landing craft under cover of darkness and strike for London (Martin and Parker 1999, 93–94). Both plans were viable, though each carried risks. The sheer magnitude of Santa Cruz's proposal created formidable problems of cost, scale, and attrition during its assembly, while Parma's depended on total secrecy, without which his unprotected barges might be intercepted and annihilated at sea. Philip II sought to resolve the issue (and bring the cost to manageable proportions) by combining both plans to create a much smaller Armada (30,000 men and 130 ships totalling 60,000 tons) which would rendezvous with Parma's troops

Figure 11.1. Armada wreck sites in Scotland and Ireland: 1. Santa Marìa de la Rosa *(Guipuzcoa); 2, 3,4.* Lavia, Juliana, *and* Santa Marìa de Vizon *(all Levant); 5.* Trinidad Valencera *(Levant); 6.* Girona *(Galleasses); 7.* San Juan de Sicilia *(Levant); 8.* El Gran Grifón *(Hulks).*

off Flanders and escort them across the Channel. In spite of the concerns of his senior commanders, both of whom feared that the new plan's complexity and the difficulty of communication between its two disjointed parts would almost certainly lead to misunderstanding, confusion and disaster, the king insisted that his compromise solution should be adopted. He was confident that the plan enjoyed God's approval and any difficulties would be overcome by divine support. Events proved Santa Cruz and Parma right, and blame for the Armada's failure (which he accepted) rests squarely with Philip II (Martin and Parker 1999).

From the historian's perspective the Armada is an extraordinarily well documented operation, and the

copious paperwork generated by the fleet's assembly and associated policy matters survives virtually intact in the royal archives at Simancas. To this may now be added a growing resource of archaeological evidence derived from the investigation of some of the ships wrecked during the Armada's disastrous return voyage around the British Isles (Figure 11.1). These include the Guipuzcoan vice-flagship *Santa Marìa de la Rosa* (Blasket Sound, SW Ireland) (Martin 1973); the galleass *Girona* (Lacada Point, Co. Antrim) (Sténuit 1972); the hulks flagship *El Gran Grifòn* (Fair Isle, Shetland) (Martin 1998, 28–45); the Levant squadron's *San Juan de Sicilia* (Tobermory, Mull, off W. Scotland) (Martin 1998, 11–27); three ships of the Levant squadron (Streedagh Strand, C. Sligo) (Birch and McElvogue 1999); and the Venetian ship *La Trinidad Valencera*, also of the Levant squadron (Kinnagoe Bay, Co. Donegal) (Martin 1979). The wreck of *La Trinidad Valencera* was located in 1971 by the City of Derry Sub-Aqua Club and subsequently investigated in association with the writer between 1971 and 1985. This ship served both as a front-line fighting unit and as an invasion transport carrying soldiers and military equipment, including part of a siege artillery train, and the wreck has provided extensive evidence of these two distinct but interdependent aspects of the Armada's composition. This paper considers the evidence of the ship's armament.

La Trinidad Valencera *(Martin 1979; 1983)*

The Venetian merchant ship *La Trinidad Valencera* (a Spanish corruption of her Italian name *Balanzara*) was requisitioned early in 1587 by Spanish authorities in Sicily to convey troops and war materials to Spain, where they were required for the forthcoming Armada. Together with five other Italian and Ragusan ships she arrived at Cartagena in May 1587, and by 18 June the *Valencera* was at San Lucar, where she was listed with an armament of 28 guns of unspecified types and sizes. After reaching Lisbon she was embargoed to take part in the Armada itself, an act against which her master (and perhaps part-owner) Horatio Donai protested vigorously but in vain.

In the muster held at Lisbon on 7 January 1588 the ship was allocated to Martin de Bertendona's Levant squadron, and by 19 March she was described as ready and equipped for sailing. A document dated 14 May lists various items of siege artillery and associated equipment loaded on board *La Nave Valencera*, including three 40–pounder *cañones*

de batir each provided with two sets of land carriages. A Turkish gun of similar type, described as '*sin peso*' (*i.e.* with no weight mark stamped on it), was also stowed.

There is some confusion about the number of guns finally carried by the ship. In his interrogation after capture by the English, the *Valencera's* senior officer, Don Alsonso de Luzon, refers to '*4 cannons of brass*' as distinct from the ship's original 28 while his second-in-command, Baltasar Lopez del Arbol, confirms that the vessel carried '*32 pieces of brass whereof 4 were cannons of the king, the rest belonging to the ship being of divers kinds...*'. An addition of four battery cannons to the *Valencera's* original armament would make the total of 32 which both de Luzon and del Arbol attest, but the figure is ten short of the 42 guns with which the ship is credited in the final muster at Lisbon on 9 May 1588. The larger figure may be an exaggeration or, more probably, an unrealised intention, as Corbett (1898, 20) believed, citing the deposition of an Armada deserter who reported that '*the ships of Italy, nominally the largest, were badly provided with artillery*'. Nonetheless *La Trinidad Valencera* was, in comparison with the rest of the fleet, heavily armed. Her gunpowder quota of 125 *quintales* (5750 kg), listed in the 9 May muster, was only 15 *quintales* (690 kg) below that of the Armada's flagship *San Juan de Portugal*, which carried the largest ration in the fleet.

Thus armed, with a rating of 1100 tons, and carrying a complement of 79 seamen, 281 soldiers from the Neapolian *tercio* (which de Luzon commanded), together with a large contingent of officers and gentlemen adventurers, *La Trinidad Valencera* was the most powerful member of the Levant squadron, whose ten large converted merchantmen were all of Mediterranean origin. The

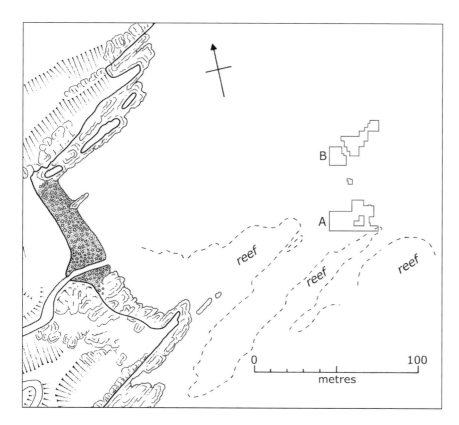

Figure 11.2. The Trinidad Valencera *wreck site in Kinnagoe Bay, Donegal. The areas A and B are the excavated zones shown in Figure 11.3.*

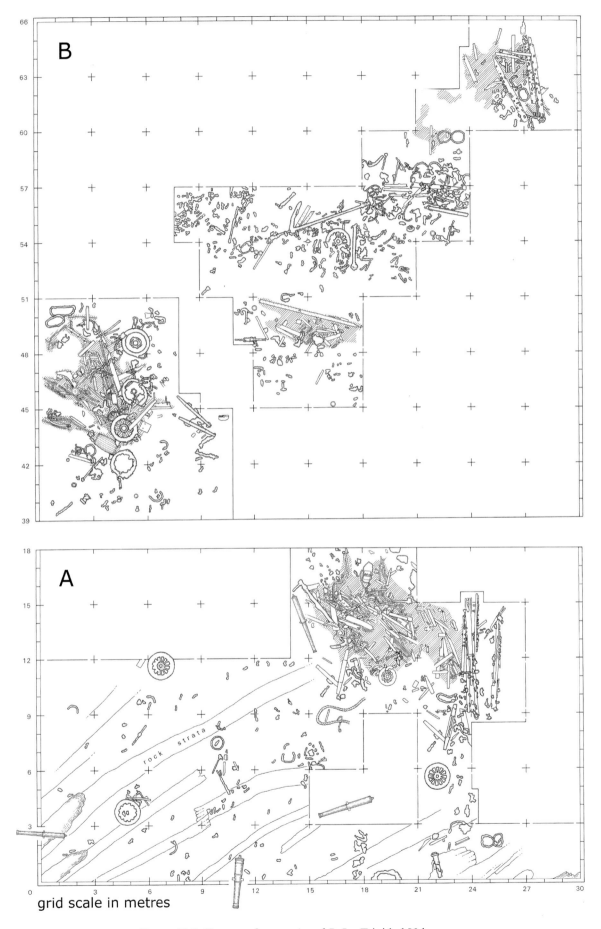

Figure 11.3. Excavated zones A and B, La Trinidad Valencera.

importance attached by the Spaniards to vessels of this type when gathering the Armada together gives a clear insight to their intended battle tactics. In his 1586 proposals Santa Cruz had earmarked a number of great-ships from Ragusa, Venice, Sicily, and Naples for the invasion fleet while the squadron's commander, Martin de Bertendona, writing to Philip II on 27 February 1588, states why he thinks his massive Levanters will be crucial in the forthcoming campaign. Although he admits that their *grandeça* – a word which implies overbearing magnificence as well as sheer size – may carry considerable risks in facing the Atlantic weather, it will give them, thinks Bertendona, an overwhelming tactical advantage when it comes to close-quarter battle. The capital ships of the Armada were to be, in effect, mobile fortifications filled with troops and their equipment, a Mediterranean-rooted concept of naval warfare diametrically opposite to the mobile *"weapons platform"* strategy adopted by the well-gunned and manoeuvrable front-line ships of Queen Elizabeth's navy.

The Armada's formation as it advanced along the English Channel towards the rendezvous with Parma was arranged to provide defence without the fleet becoming dispersed or deflected from progress towards its objective. Following the precepts of galley warfare in the Mediterranean the ships were arrayed like an army on land, with a central core or main battle flanked by extended wings on either side. Most of the vessels had instructions to keep formation on the flagship at all costs, failure to do so being a capital offence for the officer responsible. But an ingenious defensive device protected the formation from attack by heavily gunned sailing ships. Scattered through the fleet were 20 or so powerfully armed and nobly officered ships, *La Trinidad Valencera* among them, which were authorised to act on their own initiatives whenever the formation as a whole was threatened. In this way an immediate response to any attack, led by courageous and high-spirited aristocrats, was guaranteed, and no further orders were needed to set it in train. Meanwhile the main body would plod on towards its objective, its formation intact, with gaps in its ranks to which the aggressive *"troubleshooters"* might return when their business was complete (Martin and Parker 1999 15–17).

At first the English were nonplussed by the Spaniards' tight defensive formation, vigorous response to attack, and inexorable progress – *"we durst not adventure to put in amongst them, their fleet being so strong"*, wrote Lord Admiral Howard in worried frustration. In fact the fleets were tactically stalemated. The English, whose ships were more manoeuvrable and had heavier guns, could keep clear of danger and dictate the range at which they fought, but could not physically overwhelm their adversaries. On the other hand the Spanish troubleshooters were unable to engage in the close combat and boarding actions in which their superior military strength would have been likely to prevail.

Early in the fighting the *Trinidad Valencera* and Don Alonso de Leiva's *Rata Encoronada* (the Genoese merchantman *Santa Maria Incoronata*, built by *Gio. Maria*

Ratti in 1571. Information from R. G. Ridella), also of the Levant squadron, were detached as independent battle-groups with two Neapolitan galleasses attached to each, though for reasons which are not clear these powerfully armed units were not effectively deployed in combat. After the rendezvous with Parma had failed, the *Valencera* was one of the twenty or so ships which fought in Medina Sidonia's close support in the final battle off Gravelines, so saving the now retreating Armada from destruction.

Following Gravelines there was no alternative but the perilous north-about route around Britain and into the Atlantic for the long southward run to Spain. Autumn was approaching, and the equinoctial gales of that year blew early and with unusual violence, driving many of the returning Spanish ships towards the western coasts of Scotland and Ireland. On 14 September *La Trinidad Valencera* grounded on a reef close to the eastern end of Kinnagoe Bay, County Donegal, and two days later she broke up and sank.

The wreck site (Martin 1979)

The main area of wreckage lies 150 m offshore, adjacent to a reef complex which runs from the shore and rises to within 4 m of the surface close to the wreck (Figure 11.2). Here the ship evidently grounded. On discovery the visible remains comprised a spread of wreckage extending northwards from the reef for 65 m over a flat sandy sea bed at a depth of about 10 m. Wreckage spill among the reef continued southwards for another 30 m. The visible wreckage included two anchors, five large spoked wooden guncarriage wheels, three wooden axles, and seven bronze guns, one of which lay in the broad gully which runs through the reef.

Excavation of the sandy deposits north of the reef revealed several discrete deposits of organic material, sealed in scour hollows which had evidently formed around the hull while it was still partially intact, filling again when the upstanding structures disintegrated. The deposits were exceptionally well preserved and contained a broad sampling of the ship's contents, including military equipment and weaponry (Figure 11.3). These finds form the basis of a detailed analysis of the ship's fighting capacity.

The siege train (Martin 1988; 2001b)

In February 1588 the Venetian ambassador to Spain reported *"they have embarked twelve heavy siege guns and forty eight smaller ones, with a double supply of gun carriages and wheels for the field batteries..."*. Most of the twelve heavy pieces were carried by the capacious ships of the Levant squadron. Three full *cañones* were loaded aboard *La Trinidad Valencera*, and are described thus:

> *"...one cast bronze* cañon de batir *from the Flemish foundry, having on the first reinforce a shield with the royal arms picked out in paint and an inscription reading* Felipus Rex. *Behind the vent are three inscriptions, one reading 'Juan Manrique de Lara ordered me to be cast' and another recording the date 1556. The gun*

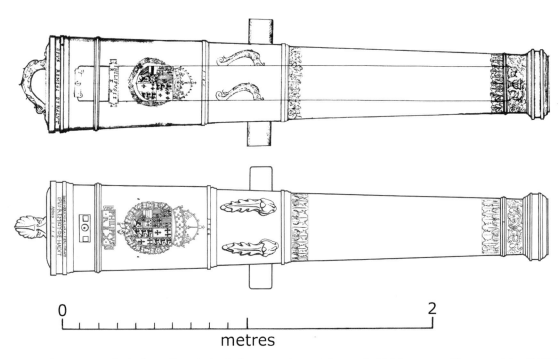

Figure 11.4. The Remigy de Halut cañon de batir *bearing the weight mark 5186: top, as illustrated in 1587 (Archivo General de Simancas, Planas y Diagramas, V-18); bottom, as recorded in 1987 (top illustration courtesy of the Director, Archivo General de Simancas).*

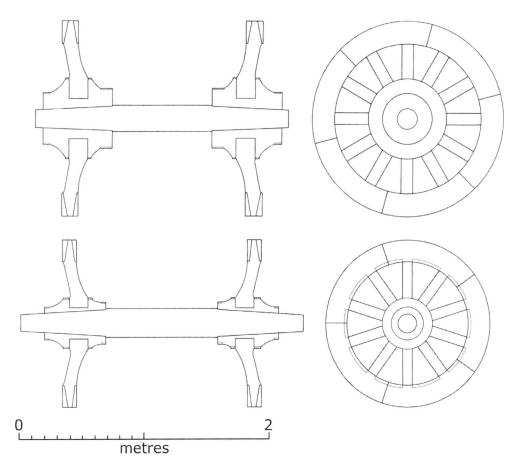

Figure 11.5. Undercarriage assemblies for the cañones de batir, La Trinidad Valencera.

weighs 5186 libras and fires a cast-iron ball weighing 40 libras".

The other two *cañones* were identical except for their individual weights, recorded as 5316 and 5260 *libras*. All three have been recovered from the wreck, and their weight marks match those recorded in the document. As noted in the inventory, the guns carry the arms of Philip II and the date 1556 – the first year of his reign. At the time he was consort to Mary Tudor, queen of England, so her arms are incorporated in the escutcheon. The Flemish gunfounder, un-named in the lading document, is revealed as Remigy de Halut, master of the king's foundry at Malines near Antwerp. Juan Manrique de Lara was Captain-General of Artillery at the time. Specifications common to all the pieces are:

> Bore 0.184 m. Shot diameter (5% windage) 0.175 m. Shot weight (by the Spanish estimate) 40 Castillian *libras* (18.4 kg). Overall length 2.92 m. Muzzle to breech ring 2.68 m. Calibre: length 1:14.5. Average gun weight 2416 kg (5254 Castillian *libras*). Shot gun-weight 1:131.

Gun weights were established after casting and marked on the barrels. This was in part an accountancy procedure to ascertain the amount of metal used in each piece but also, since even guns cast to the same specification were unlikely to have exactly the same weight, a means of identifying individual pieces. The accuracy with which this operation was conducted was confirmed by a controlled weighing of the 5316 piece, which yielded a unit value very close to the expected 460 g Castilian *libra*. By a remarkable coincidence the gun marked 5186 can be identified with the weight recorded in a scale drawing of a Remigy *cañon de batir* dated 1587. The 16th century drawing shown in Figure 11.4 has been scaled for comparison with a modern record of the actual gun. The proportions of the original drawing are remarkably accurate, though there are minor discrepancies in the treatment of the decoration and inscriptions. The three guns' dimensions, as well as their weights, fall within one percent of their median values, a level of uniformity on a par with modern heavy castings. This shows that 16th century manufacturing processes, when conducted within self-contained parameters under state control, were capable of working to repeatable standards of conformity.

Each *cañon* had been provided with two dismantled sets of field carriages for service ashore. It appears that these were manufactured specially for the campaign. On 17 October 1587 Juan de Acuña Vela, the incumbent Captain-General of Artillery, informed Philip II that his men were cutting timber to make wheels and carriages for the fleet's *cañones de batir*, and a week later he reported the necessity of making wheels of unseasoned wood because of the urgency with which they were needed.

Ten large spoked wooden wheels and six axletrees have been located on the wreck (Figure 11.5). The wheels are of two types. One (Type A) has 12 spokes and a diameter of 1.5 m, while the other (Type B) is of 10-spoke construction and spans 1.3 m. It seems likely that 12-spoke wheels, of which five have been identified, are carriage wheels, while the smaller 10-spoked ones belong to limbers.

On both wheel types the spokes are of cleft oak. The naves are turned out of elm heartwood. Those for the carriage wheels are 0.62 m in diameter and 0.55 m wide, reinforced with iron bands at the hub ends and at either side of the spokes. A tapered hole accommodates the axle bearing, and rectangular mortices house the tenoned spoke ends. All the felloes are of ash, and each is mortised for two spokes. Thus a carriage wheel has six felloes, a limber one five. The butt-ends of the felloes are set tangentially to the wheel arc, and joined to their neighbours with dowels. An unused felloe blank – presumably one of the spares noted in the Spanish inventory – was recovered. No mortises or dowel holes have been cut in it and, in comparison with the felloes on the assembled wheels, which are sound and well made, the spare is shoddily derived from a blank of ash which includes the sapwood and presents a waney edge at two corners.

The wheels were clamped around their rims with short iron strakes, each starting at the centre of a felloe and ending on the centre of its neighbour in order to span the joint. The strakes were secured to the felloes with iron clamps. The angle at which the spokes are set gives the wheels a noticeable 'dish', or concave appearance. This concavity faces outwards: that is, the apex of the shallow cone thus formed sits on the inside of the axle arm. Such an arrangement, which had been the general practice in Europe since *c.* 1500, absorbs wheel stresses more evenly and improves rotational stability.

Of the five axletrees recorded on the wreck three were too severely damaged to allow accurate measurement. One, however, was almost completely free of abrasion and concretion, and appeared from its condition to be an unused spare. Another, although somewhat abraded and partly obscured by concretion, retained enough of its original surfaces for its primary dimensions to be obtained. The two axles are of different lengths and proportions, and it is likely that Type A, which is shorter and stubbier, is for carriage assemblies, while the longer and more slender Type B is for limbers. Both are of ash.

The Type A axle is smoothly and accurately made, with a bed 0.8 m long and 0.22 m square, save for a 0.065 m chamfer along its two lower corners. Symmetrically-placed arms extend 0.6 m on either side, tapering from a distance of 0.18 m at the slightly stepped shoulder to 0.13 m at the end. That this type of axle is for the main carriage assemblies is suggested by the bed length, which closely matches the trunnion span of the Remigy *cañones de batir*. A wrought iron bar is set into the underside of the axle along its full length and secured to the axle ends by cup-like fittings over the hubs. Integral upper and lower clout plates extend from the hub caps to reinforce the axle arms and reduce friction and wear on the axle and rotating nave (Figure 11.6).

The bed and arms of the Type B axle are rather longer,

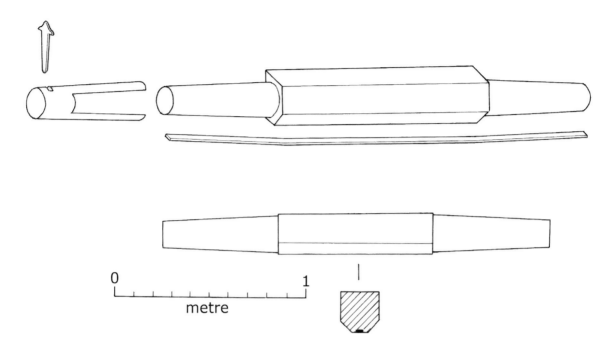

Figure 11.6. Main carriage axle (bottom) and exploded diagram of parts (top).

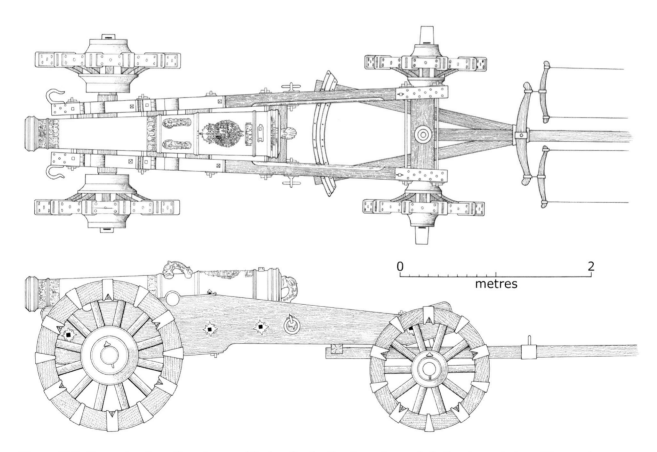

Figure 11.7. Reconstruction of carriage and limber for the Remigy cañones de batir, *shown in travelling mode.*

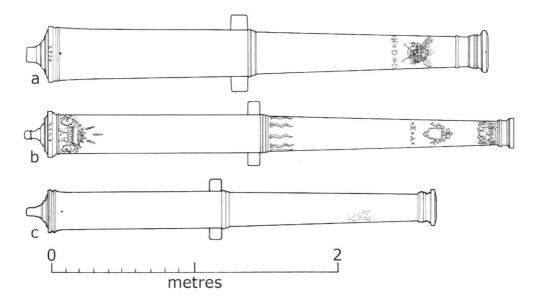

a

b

c

0   2

metres

Figure 11.8. Venetian guns from La Trinidad Valencera.

and seem to be intended for the smaller diameter 10-spoked wheels of the postulated limber assemblies. The greater length of this axle was doubtless conditioned by the splay of the trail, and the need to accommodate the turning radius of an articulated limber. Like the Type A axle, the Type B example appears to have been fitted with a countersunk iron bar on its underside, and to have had similar hub caps and clout plates.

Luis Collado (1592, f.21) describes a guncarriage axle with characteristics very similar to those recorded from *La Trinidad Valencera*. Set into its under surface, he writes, is an *anima*, which he describes as "...*a true iron bar ... set into the wood of the axle, as wide as the same is long*". The function of the *anima* (which he sometimes calls a *contraexe*, or counter-axle) was, he explains, to prevent overheating, wear, and shearing of the axle stubs. The end fittings were called *mangas*: these were iron hub-caps which reinforce the axle ends and provide a solid seating for the linch pins. Iron plates extend from the *mangas* at top and bottom to serve as bearing surfaces for the wheel. These components are clearly the *animas* and *manguetas* of the inventoried *Trinidad Valencera* axles, and visible in the examples from her wreck.

No hollow (downwards inclination) or lead (forward toe-in) – the stabilising offsets which were to become common in later periods – is apparent in the set of the axles. Thus the wheel discs ran parallel to one another. These arrangements would have greatly increased the axles' strength, particularly against shearing stresses at the arm/bed interfaces. It is not clear when counter-axles were introduced, though it seems that the *Trinidad Valencera* examples are the earliest to be reliably identified. They may be seen as a technically elegant response to what had been, from at least the mid-15th century, a major problem in the design of heavy-wheeled vehicles, which were prone to failure at the weak point between the square-sectioned bed and the rounded axle arms. Perhaps this is why new carriages were built for the Armada's *cañones de batir* in

1587, for by this time the Remigy guns' original mountings would have been more than 30 years old and, in addition to being worn out, were probably regarded as obsolete too.

Sufficient evidence thus exists for replicating the carriage and limber undercarriage assemblies, but no trace was found of cheeks (side pieces) or transoms (cross members). However a drawing in the Simancas technical papers dated 1592 shows the side view of a field carriage, while the Venetian artillery writer Pietro Sardi (1621) provides extensive information on the components, fittings and construction of such mountings. The proportions of the *cañon de batir* carriages, moreover, are defined by the guns for which they were made. A resolution of these data permits a full and probably accurate reconstruction to be attempted (Figure 11.7). A limbered-up configuration is shown, with the gun mounted in a travelling position some distance behind its firing position at the front of the carriage. This arrangement was necessary to shift the centre of gravity closer to the middle of the articulated assembly for vehicular stability in transit.

The reconstruction shows the extender piece and swingletrees for the first pair of horses, and the draft pole running between them. Nine further pairs would probably have been required to draw the 5–tonne rig, making it about 30 m long. This underlines just how cumbersome a heavy artillery train was, and how advantageous it was to employ water transport wherever possible.

The ship's guns (Martin, Parker 1999, 269–274)

Of the 28 guns belonging to the ship, five have been identified on the wreck. Three are bronze muzzle-loaders. There is also a composite bronze and wrought-iron *petriera da braga*, or breech-loading swivel gun (a Spaniard would have called it a *falcon pedrero*), and the wrought-iron breech-block of a similar but larger piece. The pieces are described individually below. Shot-weights are estimated on the basis of 5% windage and an arbitrary specific mass of 7.0.

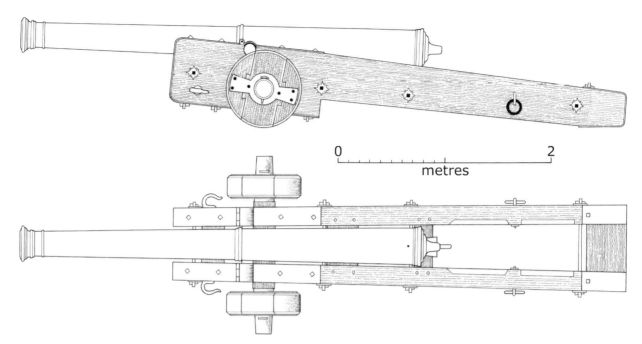

Figure 11.9. Reconstruction of two-wheeled sea carriage recorded on the Trinidad Valencera *wreck site in 1987, with hypothetical gun mounted.*

1. (Figure 11.8 a) Bore 0.124 m. Shot diameter 0.118 m. Shot weight 6.2 kg. Overall length 3.25 m. Muzzle: base ring 3.1 m. Calibre: length 1:25. Weight mark 2950. Estimated weight 1392 kg. Shot: gun-weight 1:224.

    The chase of this piece is decorated in relief with crossed olive and palm branches with the with the motto SENPER (*sic*) set in a scrolled cartouche. The founder's initials N D C spaced with rosettes appears below it. The initials are probably those of the Venetian gunfounder Niccolò di Conti.
2. (Figure 11.8b) Bore 0.095 m. Shot diameter 0.090m. Shot weight 2.67 kg. Overall length 3.45 m. Muzzle: base ring 3.27 m. Calibre: length 1:34.4. Weight mark 2529. Weight by weigh-bridge 1194 kg. Shot gun-weight 1:447. The marked weight unit resolves to 472 g, identifying it as the Venetian pound. A motif which appears to represent swans and crustacea supporting a vase emitting flames is moulded in relief around the touch-hole. Three darts of flame are placed above it. More flames encircle the rear end of the chase, just forward of the trunnions. Towards the muzzle end of the chase there is a floriated shield, with no internal device, below which the letters Z A appear within rosette spacers. There is further foliation around the muzzle. The initials are of Zuanne Alberghetti, a prominent Venetian gunfounder.
3. (Figure 11.8c) Bore 0.076 m. Shot diameter 0.072 m. Shot weight 1.37 kg. Overall length 2.92. Muzzle: base-ring 2.77 m. Calibre: length 1:36. Estimated weight 874 kg. Shot gun-weight 1:638.

    This gun had lain exposed on a rock outcrop and has suffered from severe abrasion and pitting, particularly on its left side. It is of similar proportions to 1 above, and bears the abraded traces of a similar escutcheon on the chase together with the terminal letter C. It is probably another product of the Niccolò di Conti foundry.

Sea carriage (Figure 11.9)

In 1987 the remains of a sea carriage were found adjacent to the main site, and it was recorded *in situ* before being consolidated with sandbags. The assembly lay right way up, and although its upper part had been reduced by erosion the buried lower elements were in good condition. Both cheeks and all four transoms were present and the axle was in place, with one of its arms intact. The other was missing, as were both wheels.

No associated gun was found, but the proportions of the piece can be reconstructed from the width and splay of the cheeks, the trunnion recesses, and the position of the third transom on which the breech ring would have rested. The diameters of the missing wheels are estimated from the height of the axle to be about 0.70 m, and a solid tripartite construction based on contemporary sources has been chosen for the reconstruction (Figure 11.9). Though it is impossible to be precise about the missing gun's bore, 0.12 m is a reasonable estimate, which would give it a shot-weight of around 6 kg. The reconstructed gun is 3.96 m long, and the combined assembly measures 5.8 m from muzzle to trail. It is assumed that the carriage, like the ship's guns, is of Venetian origin.

More than one eye-witness claimed that during the Armada battles, the English rate of fire was double that of the Spaniards (Martin and Parker 1999, 198), and this may have been due in part to the design of the carriages. The

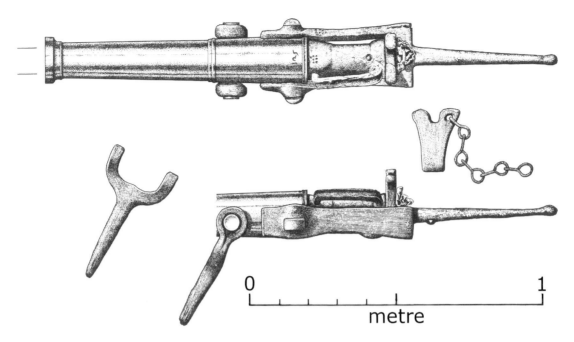

Figure 11.10. Petriera da braga *(swivel gun) from* La Trinidad Valencera.

long trails, in particular, would have made them difficult to manoeuvre within the confines of a gundeck. "*The fashion of those carriages we use at sea*", wrote Sir Henry Mainwaring in the 1620s, "*are much better than those of the land, yet the Venetians and Spaniards and divers others use the others in their shipping*" (Manwaring and Perrin 1922, 119). During comparative trials in 1988 a replica of the *Valencera* carriage took twice as long to load and run out as a compact four-wheeled truck carriage of the kind used by the English (Martin 2001a, 383–399).

Breech loaders

4. *Petriera da braga* (swivel gun) (Figure 11.10). Bore 0.086m. Shot diameter 0.082. Shot weight (stone specific mass 2.6): 0.75 kg. Barrel length (including *mascolo*): 1.2 m. Overall length (including tiller): 1.73 m. Calibre: length (barrel and chamber) 1:14. Weight mark (referring to the bronze barrel only): 125. Total weight (estimated) 160 kg. Shot gun-weight 1:213.

    The barrel is cast in bronze but the gun's other fittings – breech stirrup, removable breech-block, wedge with attachment chain, aiming tiller and mounting swivel – are made of wrought iron. The piece is preserved as its gunner left it, ready for action, in 1588. It has a stone shot in the barrel, a charge (stoppered with a wooden plug) in the breech, and a twist of hemp in the touch-hole to keep the priming dry. A folded pad of leather has been inserted behind the wedge to ensure a tight fit. Nine punch-holes relate the breech-block to the gun, which has a similar pattern of marks on its right-hand side. Guns of this kind could be reloaded much more quickly than muzzle-loading types, and were extensively used as anti-personnel weapons.

5. Wrought-iron chamber with lifting rings for a similar but larger gun of 0.15 m calibre. Stone projectile: *c.* 4.6

kg . Length: 0.61 m. Estimated weight of chamber: 100 kg. If barrel was bronze (no iron guns are mentioned in association with the ship), it may have been one of the 31 bronze *medios cañones pedreros* firing shot of between 10 and 16 Castillian *libras* (4.6–7.4 kg) issued jointly to five of the Levant squadron's ships including the *Valencera* on 26 September 1587 (Martin 1983, 114).

Gunners' rules and shot gauges (Figure 11.11)

A wooden gunner's rule was recovered from the wreck of *La Trinidad Valencera*. This simple device was intended to relate the diameter of a gun's bore to the weight of roundshot appropriate to it. Progressive scales are marked on either side, one evidently calibrated for iron projectiles and the other for lead. By assuming constant specific gravities for each of these materials (cast iron 7.3 and lead 11.4) calculations can be applied which, if the instrument is correctly scaled, should reveal the value of the weight unit involved and its consistency across the range of shot-sizes given. However the fourteen shot sizes given on the iron side of the scale, covering balls weighing nominally from one to 120 pounds, resolve into units ranging in value from 241 to 367 g, a variation far too great to allow any particular weight standard to be identified. The calibrations clearly have no basis in rational mathematics. Calculations for the lead-calibrated scale reveal an even greater error on the part of the instrument-maker, who has evidently worked on the false assumption that the relative mass of lead to iron can be expressed in the same linear proportions. The resulting units resolve into patently spurious values of between 82 and 131 g.

At the level of an individual gunner aboard a particular ship these errors would not of themselves necessarily been misleading. Gunners' rules were complemented by annular

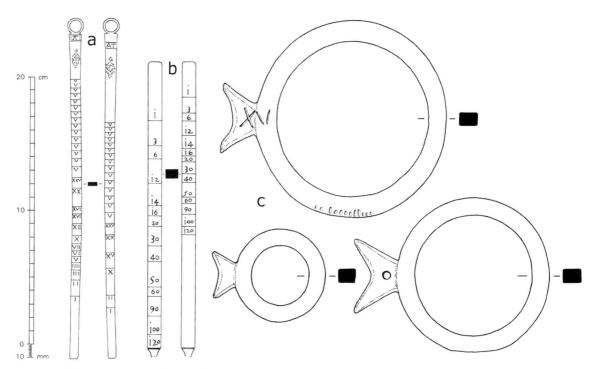

Figure 11.11. *a) brass gunner's rule from the* San Juan de Sicilia; *b) wooden gunner's rule from* La Trinidad Valencera; *c) wooden shot gauges from* La Trinidad Valencera.

wooden gauges matched to the shot-weight graduations, of which three have been recovered from *La Trinidad Valencera*. They accurately match the 1, 12, and 16 divisions on the rule's scale, so if the rule was used to gauge the shot required by measuring across a gun's bore, and the corresponding gauge applied to checking the diameter of an appropriate ball, the errors would cancel one another out. Had all gunners' rules and gauges in the Armada been to this common standard, and had the same erroneous but consistent standard been applied to the processes of manufacturing and distributing roundshot, no difficulty would have been experienced in matching projectiles to bores. But this was not the case. Another Armada gunner's rule from the *San Juan de Sicilia*, a fellow-member of the Levant squadron, has been recovered from her wreck in Tobermory Bay on the west coast of Scotland. Though it carries errors quite as serious as those recognised on the *Trinidad Valencera* rule, they are of different and unrelated kinds. The two instruments articulate, so to speak, in different and untranslatable languages. The problem of relating bore size to shot weight and diameter in early modern gunnery as well as its relevance to wider questions of standardisation, repeatability, popular mathematical understanding and the growth of industrialisation, will be explored in a forthcoming paper.

Conclusion

In many respects *La Trinidad Valencera* can be seen as a microcosm of the Armada as a whole. Her primary function was as a bulk carrier, for which her origins as a grain ship suited her. On board were 300 soldiers together with their weaponry, munitions and provisions, and also elements of a heavy artillery siege train. This military cargo was a self-

contained element of the integrated force whose strategic purpose was to land in England as a back-up to Parma's troops in support of the *blitzkreig* on London.

But her secondary role as a warship was complemented by her function as an invasion transport. The ship's fighting potential while at sea focussed on the need to defend the task force without impeding its progress towards a terrestrial objective, and she had been nominated as one of the free-ranging 'trouble-shooters' charged with protecting the formation as a whole. As a front-line combat unit, the *Valencera* relied mainly on her cargo – the superior numbers, quality, and equipment of her soldiers. Short of sinking the *Valencera* by artillery fire alone – an almost impossible feat – an Englishman was effectively powerless against her in ship-to-ship combat, for if he came too close he would almost certainly be overwhelmed by the superior military force on her decks and fighting tops.

To prevail in such close-quarter actions the Spaniards deployed specialised close-quarter weapons, of which the *Valencera's* breech-loading *Petriera da Braga* is a fine example. Her wreck has also yielded incendiary firepots (*alcancias*) and a wooden fire trunk (*bomba*). These would have supported the troops in the aggressive boarding tactics by which they hoped to overwhelm individual enemies without hindering the Armada's progress towards its objective (Martin 1994).

The role of a ship's guns in such an action was to fire a salvo at very close range, just before ship-to-ship contact was made to launch a boarding assault. This is how galleys normally fought. The guns were prepared at leisure before battle was joined by crews of soldiers. Once the guns were loaded, the troops took up their battle-stations on deck and aloft, leaving the gunners to fire a single crucial salvo just before the assault went in. Guns were just one element in the Armada's aggressively structured defensive posture, and not the main one. They should certainly not be seen as the dominant part of an integrated weapons system in its own right. In 1588 the seeds of that future naval revolution were being sown – tentatively and with more than a hint of desperation – by the other side. The Armada conflict was not so much an historical turning-point as a foretaste of what was to come (Rodger 1996).

References

Note: References to unpublished primary documents will be found in the sources listed below.

Birch, S. and McElvogue, D. (1999) *La Lavia*, *La Juliana* and the *Santa María de Vison*: three Spanish Armada transports lost off Streedagh Strand, Co. Sligo: an interim report. *International Journal of Nautical Archaeology* 28.3, 265–276.

Cipolla, C. M. (1965) *Guns and Sails in the Early Phase of European Expansion, 1400–1700*. London, Collins.

Collado, L. (1592) *Platica Manual de Artilleria*. Milan.

Corbett, J. S. (ed.) (1898) *Papers rating to the navy during the Spanish War 1585–1587*. London, Navy Records Society.

Duro, C. F. (1884) *La Armada Invencible* (vol. i). Madrid.

Flanagan, L. (1988) *Ireland's Armada Legacy*. Dublin, Gill and Macmillan.

Guilmartin, J. F. (1974) *Gunpowder and Galleys: Changing Technology and Mediterranean Warfare at Sea in the Sixteenth Century*. Cambridge, Cambridge University Press.

Guilmartin, J. F. (2002) *Galleons and Galleys*. London, Cassell.

Manwaring, G. E. and Perrin, W. G. (eds.) (1922) *The Life and Works of Sir Henry Mainwaring*, vol. II, London, Navy Records Society.

Martin, C. J. M. (1973) The Spanish Armada Expedition. In D. J. Blackman (ed.), *Marine Archaeology* (Colston Papers No. 23), 439–461. London, Butterworths.

Martin, C. (1979) *La Trinidad Valencera*: an Armada Invasion Transport Lost off Donegal. *International Journal of Nautical Archaeology*, 8.1, 13–38.

Martin, C. J. M. (1983) *The Equipment and Fighting Potential of the Spanish Armada*. Unpublished thesis, University of St Andrews.

Martin, C. J. M. (1988) A Sixteenth Century Siege Train: the Battery Ordnance of the 1588 Spanish Armada. *International Journal of Nautical Archaeology*, 17.1, 57–73.

Martin, C. J. M. (1994) Incendiary Weapons from the Spanish Armada Wreck *La Trinidad Valencera*, 1588. *International Journal of Nautical Archaeology*, 23.3, 207–217.

Martin, C. (1998) *Scotland's Historic Shipwrecks*. London, Batsford.

Martin, C. (2001a) De-particularizing the particular: approaches to the investigation of well-documented post-medieval shipwrecks. *World Archaeology*, 32.3, 383–399.

Martin, C. (2001b) Before the Battle: Undeployed Battlefield Weaponry from the Spanish Armada, 1588. In P. W. M. Freeman, A. Pollard (eds.), *Fields of Conflict: Progress and Prospect in Battlefield Archaeology*, BAR International Series 958, 73–85. Oxford,

Martin, C. and Parker, G. (1999) *The Spanish Armada* (second edition). Manchester, Manchester University Press.

Parker, G. (1996) The *Dreadnought* Revolution of Tudor England. *Mariner's Mirror*, 82, 269–300.

Rodger, N. A. M. (1996) The Development of Broadside Gunnery, 1450–1650. *Mariner's Mirror*, 82, 301–324.

Sardi, P. (1621) *L'Artiglieria*. Venice.

Sténuit, R. (1972) *Treasures of the Armada*. Newton Abbot, David and Charles.

12

"A Jewel of Great Value": English Iron Gunfounding and its rivals, 1550–1650

Ruth R. Brown

I hope in the course of this paper to give an overview as to how so many guns on ships from the mid 16th until mid- 19th century – in the Mediterranean as well as the world's oceans – came from two of the most northerly kingdoms in Europe which dominated the trade in cast iron ordnance.

In 1619 John Keymer wrote confidently that England's iron ordnance was "*a jewel of great value far more than is accounted, by reason that no other country could ever attain unto it, although they have essayed it with great charge*" (Thirsk and Cooper 1972, 469). This situation was in the very process of change as he wrote, helped by the British government's successful attempts to control the manufacture of iron ordnance and its sale to the wider world. In the late 16th century there had been at least half a dozen founders producing cast guns in ironworks in southern England and Wales, but by the 1630s there were only two furnaces left, both controlled by the Brown family (Brown 2005; 2006). Already Dutch money and Flemish experience had created a rival industry in Sweden and by 1649 Henry Robinson lamented that, "*though our want of foresight (neighbouring nations) bereft us of our peculiar prerogative of furnishing all foreign parts with iron ordnance...*" (Thirsk, Cooper 1972, 54).

There had been some limited success in northern France and in southern England in producing cast-iron guns in the earlier part of the 16th century; by the mid-1540s, however, in the last years of the reign of Henry VIII, English founders had begun to produce long muzzle-loading iron guns similar to cannons cast in bronze on a regular basis. Those involved included Peter Baude, a French or Walloon founder of bronze cannons, who had been in Henry's service for a number of years and the local Parson, William Levitt. In the early years the cast iron ordnance were intended for the new fortifications round England's southern coasts. The industry was concentrated mainly in the Weald, the southern part of England lying across the Kent-Sussex border. The furnaces were often close to major waterways, so that the guns could be shipped either up towards the Thames to London, or across the English Channel to Europe. This was to create a permanent temptation, as we will see (Figure 12.1).

Bronze was expensive; its materials of copper and tin often had to be imported from abroad, then transported to the foundries which were often situated in urban locations, thus easily overseen by authorities. By contrast, iron casting was a rural industry. Its main advantage was cheapness; it was carried out in the same area where the iron ore occurred naturally and could be mined and water used to power the furnace bellows. Cast iron guns were not better guns, but they were cheaper guns. And there was the potential to cast many more iron guns than had been possible with bronze guns.

Between 1546 and 1573 the English iron gunfounding industry grew from a single furnace to an industry involving several works and founders. The Tudor government's use of the new iron cannons was mainly limited to fortifications because the Navy preferred bronze for its ships; the

Figure 12.1. Cast-iron demi-culverin from Pevensey Castle, Sussex, now in the Museum of Artillery, Woolwich, c. 1550.

Figure 12.2. Cast-iron demi-cannon perrier at Groenlo, the Netherlands, c. 1570.

Figure 12.3. Cast-iron saker or minion, Enkhuizen, c. 1595.

inventory taking after Henry's deaths show only a few cast iron guns in service. However other uses quickly developed for the new weapons, and they soon formed the main armaments for merchant ships, while others were destined for export. Already by 1557 the ambassador of the Duke of Mantua reported that "*There is a great quantity of artillery in the Tower… I counted them roughly, and estimated about 250 brass pieces, and 600 of iron, some of which are cast like those of brass*" (*CSP – Ven*: Vol. 6, 1668).

In 1573 the government's gunfounder, Ralph Hogg, wrote to the Privy Council of England, claiming that when cast iron cannons had first been introduced, they had only been intended for royal service, but now founders in Kent and Sussex were producing guns to sell abroad and that three quarters of their products were being exported without a licence. He demanded the crown protect his monopoly, not only for himself, but to prevent them falling into the hands of England's enemies. This problem was already agitating Elizabeth's government. By 1570 disquieting

rumours reached Lord Burghley of English iron cannons being openly available in Spain (*CSPD-EI*: vol. 1, 638). Ten years later, when the relations between the two countries were deteriorating the English representative in San Lucar wrote that "*all nations were furnished with ordnance from England. We shall find the smart of it if we brave any of them to enemies*". (*CSP-For Eliz*: Vol. 14, 284–302).

The result of Hogge's complaints was a major attempt to control export and production. Over 40 named individuals had to deposit bonds of £2000 each to prevent them exporting cannons without a licence (*CSPD-EI*: vol. 1, 474–76).

It was also suggested that in future, guns should only be cast for English service (*CSPD-EI:* vol. 1, 476). However this could never be a serious policy; in the 1570s and 1580s Elizabeth's government used access to guns as a reward or a bribe, granted to allies, such as the French Protestants or Dom Antonio, the Portuguese pretender (*CSP-For Eliz*: Vol. 16, 314–324; *CSP Sp (Sim)*: vol. 3,

280–299). In February 1599 the Queen allowed the town of Emden to buy 24 cast-iron guns, since they had "i*n times of dearth done good service by sending us corn*" (*CSPD-EI*: vol. 5, 161). While Frederick II of Denmark was granted a licence to purchase and export 100 iron culverins, the Spanish representatives were unsuccessful in buying guns for Hapsburg forces (*CSP-For Eliz*: Vol. 10, 427–436; *CSP-Sp (Sim)*: vol. 2, 491–492).

However the largest single destination abroad for English guns was the Netherlands. Barely a year after the attempts to stop the exports, in March 1575 the prince of Orange requested leave to buy 300 iron guns for Dutch ships (*CSP-For Eliz*, Vol. 11, 19–40). The Spanish ambassador could only complain bitterly: "*The Ghent people have taken from here 4,000 crowns worth of cast iron artillery, and when I complain they tell me that the Queen considers the States her friends.*" (*CSP-Sp (Sim)*: Vol. 3, 139–152). Dutch purchases often involved hundreds of guns at a time (eg 200 light guns in July 1576 (*CSP-For Eliz*: Vol. 11, 346–356); 60 tons of ordnance in 1577 (*CSP-For Eliz*: Vol. 12, 403–440.); 40 pieces of various calibres for Ghent in 1581 (*CSP-For Eliz:* Vol. 15, 26–38). Many can still be found in the fortifications surrounding Dutch towns today.

Throughout the 1580s the international situation worsened, Spain was affronted by Elizabeth's open help to the Dutch rebels (including the ease with which they could buy artillery) and the execution of Mary Queen of Scots. And the supply of cast-iron ordnance became increasingly political, with the potential invasion of England by the Spanish armada. A report for the English secret service in May 1588 stated that 2,431 pieces of ordnance had been gathered for the Armada, included 934 cast-iron guns – of which it must be assumed many had originated from the Weald (*CSP-Sp (Sim)*: vol. 4, 275–286). Some years later, an Englishman informed Sir Francis Walsingham that two Spaniards had attempted to bribe him to deliver "a great quantity of iron ordnance, either in Hamburg, Rotterdam or Calais'. When he had refused, they simply contacted some Dutchmen instead. His concern was that "the Ordnance was for furnishing the Armada' (*SPD-EI*: vol. 3, 339–40). The Dutch also warned the English government that guns were finding their way into Spanish ports and eventually onto Spanish ships (*CSP-For Eliz:* Vol. 18, 549–561). As we shall see, there were various ways in which the guns cast in the furnaces of Kent and Sussex could end up on in the Mediterranean.

The activities of 1588 lead to another close examination of iron gunfounding and sales. Again the gunfounders had to promise not to cast ordnance without a licence, or sell to foreigners or export guns overseas and to inform the Master of the Ordnance each month of how pieces had been cast. In August 1589 the local authorities at Sussex and Kent were instructed to check the cast-iron guns at the furnaces (*APC*: vol. 18, 7).

One method to restrict exports was to control the sizes; although the government allowed 6 sakers, relatively light calibres, to be exported to the Netherlands, 6 larger guns

were refused because they were of "*too great a size*" while the Magistrates of Veer were only allowed their 25 guns when they assured the English authorities that they were strictly for their own defence (*APC*: vol. 19, 463; *CSP-For Eliz*: Vol. 3, 116; *CSP-For Eliz*: Vol. 1, 205). In September 1590, the orders were clarified, with founders being forbidden to cast iron pieces larger than a minion without permission. Increasingly the government were refusing to let larger calibre guns be sold abroad. However in the debate on restricting the export of ordnance held in the House of Commons in 1601, it was explained that founders got round the size restrictions by casting guns to a heavier weight, but only reaming them out to a lesser size; once abroad they would be bored out to their true nature.

Guns for whom exports were approved included the King of Denmark (*CSP-For Eliz*: Vol. 1, 422; SP 46/22/fo 17); Count Edzard of east Friesland (*CSP-For Eliz*: Vol. 2. 412); the Margrave of Brandenburg, in exchange for masts (*CSP-For Eliz*: Vol. 3, 466) the Duke of Luneburg (*CSPD-EI: Vol. 5*, 12); the governor of Brest (*CSPD-EI:* Vol. 5, 56); the Duke of Holstein (WYL100/PO/6/XII/1) and the Grand Duke of Tuscany (*CSP-Ven*: Vol. 10, 298–307).

However as the controls tightened, ways round them, both legal and illegal were found. There were many ways that guns could move. Some ironfounders, not bound by bonds, merely converted their ironworks to cast cannons (*APC:* Vol. 20, 5). Others bypassed the regulations by appealing to those further up the network, the Master of the Ordnance or the monarch.

Of course gun-running existed then, with cannons being moved directly from the furnaces near the south coast straight to a ship and wafted across the sea. There are rumours from before the Armada to the time of the Napoleonic wars of guns finding their way from British furnaces into enemy hands. However it is difficult to know exactly how this was done because of its illegal nature and even where records have survived, interpreting them is difficult because someone has something to hide. Late in the summer of 1591 the Privy Council ordered the arrest of "*Norry of Shordishe*" for transporting ordnance "*to her Majesty's enemy's as to other places*" with the request the local magistrates discover "*who and when he has sold ordnance to in the last 12 months*" (*APC*: Vol. 21, 430–1).

Exporters could obtain a legitimate licence, but then lie about the ultimate destination: an English agent abroad reported that

> "*A Netherlander at Calais boasted that, although export of iron ordnance from England was prohibited, he would soon get English guns to sell in Holland. A friend of his in London had obtained licence to take out 80 pieces under colour of fitting out some new Dutch pinnaces. He hoped to have most of these*" (*CSP-For Eliz*: Vol. 1, 188).

In October 1590 an Irish merchant William Herbert was accused of selling guns to Spain which had been intended for La Rochelle (*APC*: Vol. 20, 61).

It was easy to load guns onto a ship and claim they were

the ship's armament, then sell them abroad. This seems to have been the ruse used in 1577 when Mr Golston of Plymouth, sold a quantity of cast-iron pieces with their accoutrements to Spanish and French customers (*CSP-For Eliz*: Vol. 12, 1–15). To counteract this, a system of registering and deposit was introduced in March 1586 to ensure the guns which went out as ships" armaments were brought back again (*APC*: Vol. 14, 45). Even then, one captain managed to sell his ship with its ordnance to the Genoese in 1629 (*APC*: Vol. 45, 212–3). The Privy Council also banned the practise of the owners of Dutch-built ships claiming they belonged to Englishmen or denizens and could therefore buy English guns (*CSPD- JI*: Vol. 3, 619).

Another way to access cast-iron guns was beyond the control of Queen Elizabeth and her government- this was to seize the ship at sea or in foreign ports and just take the ordnance. This was a regular occurrence, both by foreign governments and by pirates (*CSPD-EI*: Vol. 3, 284). In 1624 it was noted that 50 pieces of ordnance shipped to the Netherlands had been captured by pirates, while earlier in 1602 the King of Denmark sold to Spain 700 cannons taken from English and Dutch ships in Danish waters (*CSPD-JI*: Vol. 4, 186; *CSPD-EI*: Vol. 6, 183).

In the 1590s, the government began a new policy of using their control of the export of iron ordnance to raise money by selling the right to issue licences. In November 1592, two Flemish merchants and the English iron master, Henry Neville, were given a monopoly to export Iron guns for twenty years. Limits to weight of the cannons were set (LR 15/301). However the partners soon fell out (*CSPD-EI*: Vol. 3, 156). In addition, this new policy was regarded with some suspicion in some areas: suggesting the foreigners involved might be "*instruments of Spaniards or other enemies*" (*CSPD-EI:* Vol. 3, 339–40). However others believed that allowing some exports cut down on the blatant smuggling, claiming it had halved the amount of guns illegally exported (with the relevant gain of revenue to the crown) (*CSPD- JI*: Vol. 5, 416).

This was followed in January 1600 by giving Thomas Browne, the Queen's gunfounder, and a colleague permission "*to export custom free*" old and unserviceable "*cast-iron ordnance*" in exchange for replacing them with "*a like quantity of new, good and serviceable iron ordnance of such weight, bore and strength as required for service*" (*CSPD-EI*: Vol. 5, 388).

These perceived abuses led in 1601–2 to a more serious attempt by Parliament to control the transportation of iron ordnance. These include stricter controls, restraining the number of gunfounders and limiting how many guns they could produce, and to keep a yearly account to whom the ordnance was sold. Gunfounders were to mark on every piece they cast. A gun market was set up at Tower Hill which was to be the only place guns could be sold, while stricter records would be taken of merchant ships' armaments (*CSPD*-EI: Vol. 6,172).

Overseas customers still wanted English cannons; their reputation was much appreciated. A spy in Denmark wrote to Walsingham in 1582 about 200 culverins and sakers and shot purchased for the King of Denmark, noting they were all "*very well proved with double charge three times shot off at least*". In 24 July 1595, the Dutch representative asked if five guns for which he had paid custom could be replaced as they had burst on first proof (*CSP-For Eliz*: Vol. 6, 105). In June 1613 the Privy Council approved a license for 200 iron guns for Elias Tripp since the Dutch merchant stated that Thomas Browne was the only founder able to supply him with sufficient guns (*APC*: Vol. 1, 92). Shortly after this, John Browne, his son, claimed to employ 200 men, and that more than half of the ordnance manufactured by him has been bought and exported by the Dutch under license. (*CSPD- JI:* Vol. 3, 12).

At this point there were still four other gunfoundries working in Sussex, and another in Wales.

A constant irritation to the government in London was the presence of the iron gun foundry in south Wales, so far from the capitol's jurisdiction. In July 1591 the authorities were already aware that merchants from Hamburg were taking Welsh guns out through Bristol – "*the enemy have had too much of our ordnance within these last 15 years'* (*SPD-EI*: Vol. 3, 73). In October 1592 it was rumoured that two Irish ships had loaded guns from there without license (*SPD-EI*: Vol. 3, 284). By 1602 the government was forced to severe action: they stated that

"*Edmond Mathews to be put down for casting ordnance at his furnace near Cardiff, whence it may easily be carried into Spain; for five or six years last, most that he has made has been stolen beyond the seas, and as the officers of that port are poor, and dare not displease him, that place is very unfit for casting ordnance*" (*CSPD-EI:* Vol. 6, 172).

However 20 years later in May 1614, the furnace, now operated by the Dutch Peter Semayne was accused of transporting iron ordinance into the Low Countries out of Cardiff (*APC*: Vol. 1, 427). It seems it was finally destroyed during the great backlash a few years later.

However the situation changed after King James of Scotland inherited the throne of England; he wished to restore good relations with Spain, while relations with the Dutch cooled, particularly as both countries had ambitions for trade outside Europe. From 1614 until the end of the decade there were constant appropriations of what were claimed to be illegally exported cannon. The British government had begun to grow uneasy about the vast numbers of iron guns heading to the Amsterdam market. A request in the summer of 1618 from the Admiralties of North Holland and West Friesland and from Venice for permission to ship ordnance was greeted with the tart response that they could when England had enough to supply its own needs (*APC*: Vol. 35, 69). On the other hand the Spanish ambassador was allowed to export 100 iron guns, which outraged public opinion. This led to one of the last and most successful restrictions of trade which Order in Council, made by the King's express command, for preventing the unlawful export of iron ordnance in 1619–20 (*CSPD- JI*: Vol. 3, 55).

Figure 12.4. Cast-iron demi-culverin, probably cast by John Browne, c. 1620. Derry, Northern Ireland

In July 1620 things had come to a head. The Venetians were just trying to buy cast-iron guns and the Ambassador wrote:

> *"I have discovered that these last months, his Majesty, perceiving the great quantity of artillery being exported from these realms, and that it is also being used to the detriment of the ships and interests of his subjects, chiefly in the East Indies, where they have suffered so greatly".*

It was decided to grant no more licences for the immediate future and reduce the number of furnaces casting guns from seven to two. This policy was indeed put into action and gun exports from England plummeted (*CSP-Ven*: Vol. 16, 318).

A combination of the legislation and the ambition of John Browne, the King's gunfounder, lead to more success. By the time Civil war broke out in Britain in the 1630s, Browne and the English policy had successfully whittled away at the other furnaces and gunfounders, so that Browne was left in triumphant control. However as we shall now see, Browne was to lament his Pyrrhic victory. Thus by the 1620s, Europe's supply of cast-iron guns had been heavily curtailed, but the genie could not be returned to the bottle. And with this we now turn to how the Dutch and Swedes succeeded in thwarting the English attempts at control.

It had been suggested by some Englishmen that restricting the export of cast guns would encourage other, possibly hostile, powers to establish their own industry: *"Metal for guns can be had elsewhere, in Westphalia, and if no guns could be had from England, they would be manufactured there"* (*CSPD-JI*: Vol. 5, 416). This was born out by events.

Within a short space of time, other states, having looked at the cast iron guns with envy, began to consider how to secure a more reliable supply. The quickest way was to establish their own industry by persuading experienced English workers to move abroad. As early as 1574, Lord Burghley heard from Spain that Phillip II's officials had inquired from some Englishmen there

> *"whether they had skill in casting such iron pieces as come in the English ships, and whether their iron would run to make the like ordnance. To which he answered that he thought that this iron would not well run for*

that purpose, but that in England they 'melted' it with some other privy metal. Hears that about Bilbao they have already cast falcons and falconets" (*CSP-For Eliz*: Vol. 10, 471–481).

Fifty years later in 1625 the gunfounder, Nicholas Stone, asked the Master of the Ordnance to stop a French spy from leaving the country with one of his workers. (*CSPD-JI*: Vol. 4, 489). In 1627 John Browne complained that a Frenchman had attempted to entice away his workmen. This time he was apprehended and questioned by the authorities (*ACP*: Vol. 42, 368). The following year attempts were made to entice Brown's workmen to Scotland (APC: Vol. 44, 71–2; *CSPD-CI:* Vol. 23, 429). In 1628 the authorities became concerned when a catholic spy was found snooping round the Tower of London and the ordnance for sale at Tower Hill (*CSPD-CI:* vol. 3, 255; 328; 343)

Although these attempts were thwarted, others proved more successful and knowledge of iron-casting technology began to spread. In 1620 a report stated that the author had seen much good iron ordnance cast at Liege and Courland, and thinks English ordnance would hereafter be in little request (*CSPD-JI*: Vol. 3, 115). In 1623 another report gave details of *"ordnance manufacture in Germany, Holland and Sweden. At first the pieces used to break in the proving, but are now much amended."* The author suggested unless English ordnance was allowed to be exported, the foreign ironworks would take their place (*CSPD-JI:* Vol. 4, 123).

However it was already too late. In the far north, in Sweden, the wishes of the new Vasa dynasty coincided with the needs of the new Dutch state. The Netherlands had an increasing demand for artillery – its continued existence depended on guns to arm its walled cities, its shipping and its army, as well as supplying its markets. Increasingly the Dutch trading fleets, of which the VOC (the Dutch East India Company) was the most famous, needed guns for their ships and settlements and to impress, bribe or threaten foreign potentates. Already by 1609 the VOC's 9 ships were armed with 601 cast-iron guns out of a total of 1029 (Sint Nicolaas 2004, 151).

In Sweden the Dutch entrepreneurs found a sympathetic government – the recently established Vasas were keen to play a part on the European stage. They, too, had need of armaments, experience and finance. Sweden had natural resources in abundance – vast untapped quantities of iron

Figure 12.5. Cast-iron 18 Pounder Swedish finbanker, Tynemouth Castle, England, 17th century.

Figure 12.6. Cast-iron Swedish 12 Pounder Finbanker, Jodhpur, India.

and copper, as well as water power. Thus while the British government was trying to close its gunfoundries, the Vasa were actively promoting them on Swedish soil.

The earliest examples of the Dutch, or to be more accurate, Flemish, involvement in the exploitation of Sweden's rich mineral resources was in the 1580s when Willem de Wijk established a gun foundry at Finspång. However this was a false start and it was not until 1618 when Willem de Besche built two new furnaces there that we come to the true start of the Swedish iron gunfounding industry. This time there was financial backing from Louis de Geer, whose family had come from Liege, and his brothers-in-law, Elias and Jacob Tripp, the most important arms dealers in Europe – cast iron guns were but a small part in their business. We have already met Elias as one of the Browne family's most important clients. Protestant ironworkers from Liege, which remained under Spanish catholic control, had moved to the independent United Provinces and so were available to put their experiences into establishing iron industries in new territories – Germany, Russia and Sweden.

With sound financial backing, experienced workers and guaranteed markets, Swedish cannon quickly began to make inroads into the markets which previously the English had effortlessly dominated. At first De Geer and Trip could rely on their contacts in the Netherlands to

ensure that the price was lower than the English guns.

The De Geers and Trips' involvement in Sweden was at first limited to financial backing, but in 1627 with the blessing of Gustavus Adolphus, De Geer visited the country for the first time. He went on to establish four new gun foundries and received a monopoly for cannon production throughout Sweden, not unlike the position of John Browne in England (Malmberg 1963, 5–9). By 1630 de Geer was exporting a thousand guns a year, mainly through Amsterdam. After 1631 the relations between the Trips and de Geers soured and they split up their business partnership. De Geer established some of his family in Sweden, at Finspång and Leufsta. This period of expansion exactly coincided with the contraction of the English gunfounding industry.

By the 1630s the annual production of Sweden's furnaces had increased from 64 guns weighing 45 tons to 219 guns weighing a total of 162 tons (Cipolla 1965, 154). By 1650, the foundries in Sweden were producing 1,500–2,000 tonnes of cannon each year. Quality was also an issue. An English agent had noted gleefully in 1623 that large numbers of the Swedish guns had failed at proof (Cipolla 1965, 61). However soon the Swedish foundries were using what we might think of as modern sales techniques, with attention to detail, making sure they supplied their own proofmasters and also exploited branding; they marked their iron products, both bars and cannons with letters indicating where they were produced. Colbert noted that the cannons with the highest reputations were marked with the F (Finspong) H (Huseby) and G (possibly Julita) and these cannon were accordingly more expensive (Cipolla 1965, 156).

Thus by the 1620s and 1630s we have on one side a contracting English industry, reduced to few markets, restricted exports and only one founder in two furnaces, working under a hostile government, while on the other an expanding Swedish industry, with both practical support as well as government encouragement.

For several years it seemed that the manufacture of iron ordnance in England lay in the balance. By 1631 John Browne was aware of how much a threat the new northern works were to his business, complaining of how Tripp and his Swedish guns had made the price of ordnance fall from 15 guilders to 8 (*APC*: Vol. 46, 297–8). Browne wrote repeatedly to the government, stating how

"the making of iron ordnance was first found out in this kingdom, and foreign kingdoms used to be supplied at the will of this state, but within a few years Sweden has endeavoured by underselling to engross the markets beyond the seas."

He complained how the "King of Sweden, to draw the manufacture of iron ordnance and shot into their country, gave certain Dutch men woods and mines, and the benefit of their slaves, by which means such multitudes of ordnance and shot have been made there, and of such goodness, that all the world is by them supplied which heretofore was furnished from this kingdom." He added that the privileges granted to his Swedish rivals meant they were easily able to undersell him. These complaints by Browne became a running thread in his dealings with the government. In July 1635 Browne wrote that he now made few guns for export and that the home market was not enough to keep his men in employment and feared that the industry must die out in England (*CSPD-CI*: Vol. 8, 288).

Thus Brown began searching for new markets. In 1631 he asked permission to export 4 demi-culverins and their shot to Italy (*CPSD-CI*: Vol. 5, 195). In 1633 he persuaded the Admiralty to lend him a naval gunner to send to Marseilles and Genoa, to proof some pieces of ordnance that he had sent there. He was worried that otherwise they would be proofed abroad

"with a far greater proof than is used here, and by that means would break most of the pieces sent to the writer's exceeding loss, and to the great disgrace of the English pieces, by which the manufacture would be greatly condemned. The Swedish merchant sends a gunner along with his pieces to prevent this danger" (*CPSD-CI*: Vol. 5, 531; 554).

This was agreed to and his absence was noted as lasting about 10 months.

Browne developed a new product – a lighter, shorter type of gun, called a drake, which he claimed combined the advantages of bronze with the advantages of cast-iron, but not its cheapness. These guns were popular for a number of years; at the end of the 1620s the Venetian state made

Figure 12.7. 'Roaring Meg', cast-iron demi-culverin, given to the City of Londonderry in 1642 by the Fishmongers Company of London.

inquiries about buying them when the export restrictions seemed to be lifting, but were told that their sale was restricted first to the English government, then to English customers only (*CSP-Ven*: Vol. 21, 571).

It was the policies of the English Parliament that allowed the English iron industry to again rival the Swedish industry. During the Civil War, it was decided to greatly increase the number of ships in the Navy, building new additions every year, all needing new guns. To meet this target, the government ended the Browne family monopoly and encouraged the establishment of new gun foundries. This, with the relaxing of export laws, meant that by the late 17th century there were again two competing national iron industries, supplying the world with iron guns (Brown 2000, 55).

Exporting of iron guns was again seen as something to be encouraged, particularly as it hit Britain's new enemy – the Dutch. England once more used its artillery supply as a diplomatic tool; in 1660 the Portuguese ordered 100 iron guns, while the Admiralty of Amsterdam ordered guns in Sweden a few years later in 1664 (SP 89/4; *CTB*: Vol. 1, 121; *CSP-Ven*: Vol. 34, 67). In the 1680s the Dutch ambassador sourly noted that the Envoy from Bantam was shown round Prince Rupert's gun-foundry at a time when Anglo-Dutch relations were at a low ebb while Venice itself purchased iron guns from England, and was allowed to export some of Prince Rupert's guns.

This success had profound effects on European and world history. The existence of a rival second great iron industry allowed for the beginning of an arms race, unleashing the power latent in the West's navies. As the use of cast-iron guns spread, navies grew, both in ship numbers and sizes. Mastery for the continent was no longer just fought on the fields of Europe but also on the world's oceans. Other attempts to establish cast iron founding industries met with varying successes – the ironworks set up in Germany largely failed to survive, probably because of the Thirty Years war while Denmark's works in Norway had some limited success. Later in the 17th century, France began producing its own iron guns. However none of these were able to make much headway into the monopolies enjoyed by Britain and Sweden in this sphere. In fact one of the reasons why the world was able to support two rising iron industries was the great worldwide demand for cast-iron guns, from the Far East to the New World.

I hope this short introduction has gone some way to explaining how it is that the Mediterranean, like other parts of the world, is today still littered with guns from the furnaces of the north of Europe. Wherever there is trouble, you will find arms dealers. This was as true in the Mediterranean in the past as it is today.

References

Primary sources

APC	*Acts of the Privy Council of England* Vol. 12–46 1896–1964. London
CSP-For Eliz	*Calendar of State Papers Foreign, Elizabeth.* Vol. 1–23, 1863–1950. London.
CSP-Sp (Sim)	*Calendar of State Papers, Spain (Simancas)* Vol. 1–4, 1892–1899. London.
CSP-Ven	*Calendar of State Papers Relating to English Affairs in the Archives of Venice*, Vol. 6–38, 1877–1947. London.
CSPD-CI	*Calendar of State Papers Domestic – Charles 1.* Vol. 1–24, 1858–1897. London.
CSPD-EI	*Calendar of State Papers Domestic-Series of the reign of Edward, Mary and Elizabeth.* Vol. 1–7, 1856–1871. London.
CSPD- JI	*Calendar of State Papers Domestic – James I.* Vol. 1–5 1857–1872. London.
CTB	*Calendar of Treasury Books* Vol. 1, 1904. London.

Secondary sources

Brown, R. R. (2000) Notes from the Office of the Ordnance: the 1650s. *Wealden Iron Research Group Bulletin* 20 (second series), 39–55.

Brown, R. R. (2005) John Brown, gunfounder to the King Part 1. *Wealden Iron Research Group Bulletin* 25 (second series), 38–61.

Brown, R. R. (2006) John Brown, gunfounder to the King Part 2. *Wealden Iron Research Group Bulletin* 26 (second Series).

Cipolla, C. (1965) *Guns, Sails and Empires. Technological Innovation and the Early Phases of European Expansion 1400–1700.* London.

Malmberg, A. (1963) *Finspong through the centuries.* Finspång.

Sint Nicolaas, E. (2004) Three colonial guns and their story. *A farewell to arms, studies on the history of arms and armour*, Legermuseum, Delft.

Thirsk, J., Cooper, J. P. (eds.) (1972) *17th Century Economic Documents.* Oxford.

Ships and Guns of the Tudor Navy 1495–1603

Robert Douglas Smith

Introduction

The 16th century witnessed the greatest change in the armament of the ships of the English Navy of any period before the end of the 19th century. At the end of the 15th century, royal ships were armed with many small guns, mainly anti-personnel weapons. A hundred years later they carried a complement of heavy cannon capable of firing a significant weight of shot. This short article is an attempt to chart the changes through the period and pinpoint just when they occurred. That this is possible is because, from the end of the fifteenth century to the beginning of the seventeenth, a number of inventories survive which detail the guns aboard the ships of the English Royal Navy. And, while the earlier inventories present us with some problems of interpretation, the group as a whole provide an unrivalled opportunity to review the changing armament of English ships through the century. Of equal importance is that they can provide the background to understanding the changes in tactics and warfare at sea, not just in England but in other European states.

Most of the inventories are lists of ships and how many guns of different types were aboard each of them.[1] Although the very first list from 1495 contains details of only two ships, from 1514 onwards the inventories deal with many more, for example 58 ships are listed in the 1546 inventory, ensuring that we are dealing with the broader picture of English naval armament. The inventories I will discuss date from 1495, 1514, 1540, 1546, 1558, 1576 and 1603.[2] The information from these lists can be supplemented by a number of other documents recording what cannon were owned by the state, what was required to arm a ship or ships, or what was in store. In addition, cannon from dated or known wrecks can help shed further light on the subject.

1495[3]

The first of the inventories, dated 1495, is contained within documents listing the stores and equipment of just two ships – the *Sovereign* and the *Regent*. What is significant is that only two types of guns are listed – serpentines, made of both iron and bronze, and stone guns (see Table 13.1).

Table 13.1 The guns on the Sovereign *and the* Regent.

	Sovereign	*Regent*
Serpentine – iron	109	151
Serpentine – bronze	1	30
Stone gun – iron	31	–

The problem we are presented with is just what these names are referring to. From the large numbers of serpentines listed it seems likely that they were small and it is tempting to think that the stone guns were larger; unfortunately, however, at present we cannot really be sure of this. Contemporary illustrations show a type of gun which may be a serpentine – a small calibre (approximately 50–75 mm) iron barrel with a separate powder chamber mounted on a wooden bed, the whole supported on an iron swivel. An example was found on an unidentified wreck discovered on the Goodwin Sands in the 1980s.

Though we only have a small amount of information, it seems likely that the tactics used at sea, at the turn of the 15th century, were based very much on ships coming alongside to enable the soldiers to fight one another. There does not appear to have been guns of sufficient size to inflict severe damage on the actual ships themselves.

1514[4]

Within twenty years there appears to have been a decisive change in the way that ships engaged and this is well illustrated by an inventory of 1514. From just the two ships at the end of the 15th century there are now thirteen and they are armed with a far more varied range of artillery which numbers some 783 iron and 68 bronze pieces (Table 13.2).

At first sight there are a bewildering number of different types of guns – some 23 varieties ranging from bombards to handguns (hackbuts). However on closer examination many of these 23 can be reduced to 4 basic variants – stone gun, serpentine, sling and murderer – plus a small group of miscellaneous pieces. What is also apparent is that the armament of the ships was now far more mixed with both

Table 13.2. The inventory of 1514.

		Henry Grace à Dieu	Trinity Sovereign	Gabryell Royle	Kateryn Forteleza	Grete Barbara	Grete Nicholas	John Baptist	Mary Roose	Petyr Pome Granett	Grete Elizabeth	Crist of Grenewich	Kateryn Galie	Roose Galie	TOTALS	
Bronze	Bombard	1													1	
	Curtow	1	3	1	1				5						11	
	Demi-curtow		3	1											3	
	Culverin	2	3										1		7	
	Falcon	6	2	6	2	8		1	2	2					29	
	Falconette								3						3	
	Serpentine	1													4	
	Vice piece	4													4	
	Murderer								2		2				4	
	Sling half										2				2	
	Unspecified	1							1	1					3	
Iron	Great gun of iron	18	7					10		5	16				59	
	Great stone gun	2		2											4	
	Stone gun	22		7	13	2	1		26	6	11	15	6	1	108	112
	Serpentine double					2		18		26				3	55	
	Serpentine single			15		1		4		4	56	3			83	
	Serpentine unspecified	122	62		26	13	11	12	28	6		23			321	
	Serpentine small									25	28				53	512
	Sling double	1								2					2	
	Sling ordinary		4	2	4		2	2		1		3	2	3	26	
	Sling half				2				2		2				6	
	Sling ringed														1	35
	Great murderer								1	6	6				13	
	Murderer			3	14	10			3						30	
	Murderer small						5								5	
	Murderer unspecified											8		4	12	60
	Top gun								3	1		1			9	
	Capstan gun									2					2	
	Pot gun									4					4	
	Hackbush														0	
	Falcon			2											2	
	Falcon half											1			1	
	Organs			12											12	
	Cast-iron piece						2	1	2						5	
	Sling cast														2	
	TOTALS	181	84	51	62	36	21	50	78	91	123	54	9	11		

smaller and larger guns, some of which are now capable of inflicting damage on a ship's structure.

Unfortunately it is not always clear exactly what some of the guns listed were, how big they were or how large a shot they were capable of firing. Within the lists of bronze guns some are clearly of large calibre – the bombard, curtows, and culverins were all of large size for example. However the largest number of bronze pieces were the falcons, which are small guns more useful against men then wooden hulls.

Of the iron guns the large number listed can be reduced to four types – stone gun, serpentine, sling and murderer. The serpentines are probably the same guns as those in 1495 – small anti-personnel guns supported on a swivel – but what were stone guns? The name probably refers to the fact that they were loaded with stone shot but we have little more information about them or their size. Some were probably large, the great stone guns, but it is unclear if they were always so. In recent years a gun was recovered from a wreck found in off the coast near Poole in Dorset. The wreck has been tentatively dated to around 1520 and it is possible, though not conclusive, that this might be a stone gun. It has a bore of 17 cm (7 inches) and is mounted on a wooden bed with a separate breech chamber. Still inside the barrel is a stone shot. The other major types in the 1524 list, the sling and the murderer, are difficult to identify at this period with any certainty.

What is clear though from this inventory, is that the armament of the royal ships had undergone significant change over the years since 1495. The larger ships were being armed with larger guns – guns capable of inflicting damage to an enemy ship. However there were significant numbers of smaller guns showing that coming alongside and boarding were still the primary tactics for ship-to-ship conflict though now it may have been possible to inflict structural damage on the enemy before the serious business of hand-to-hand fighting got underway. We can deduce that ships were armed with a variety of armament which allowed them to make significant damage to other ships, but also able to use earlier boarding forms of sea warfare.

1540

The next inventory, dated 1540, lists 10 ships armed with a total of 546 iron and 86 bronze pieces (Table 13.3).

What is immediately obvious is that the number of different types of guns has gone down dramatically. Now instead of the plethora of gun names seen in the 1514 list we have just seven types of iron guns and eight types of bronze. And within those groups there is also more uniformity. Of the seven type of iron gun there are just 4 basic divisions – port piece, sling, fowler and base. The slings are described as being a double sling, a single sling (sometimes called a whole sling), and a quarter sling. It is unclear exactly what these refer to, though it is likely that they refer to the weight of the shot fired – the double sling firing shot twice the weight of the sling and the quarter sling, a quarter. Similarly there are double and single bases – the former probably firing a shot twice the weigh

Table 13.3. The inventory of 1540.

| | Bronze | | | | | | | | | Iron | | | | | | | |
Ship	Cannon	Demi cannon	Culverin	Demi culverin	Saker	Fawcon	Fawconette	Fowler	TOTAL	Port piece	Double sling	Single sling	Quarter sling	Fowler	Double base	Single base	TOTAL
Lion					1	2			3	7		2		2	2	20	33
Swepestake					5	2	1		8	9		4		2	8	16	39
Genet					1	1			2	6	2	3		4	6	21	42
Primrose				2	3	1	1		7	10	6			2	17	10	45
Small Galye	2			6	2				10	10	4	3			30	10	57
Great Galye	5			2	4	2			13	12		2			50	10	74
Trentye Herre		1		1	2	1			5	11		7		1	30		49
Mynyon		2		1	4	2			9	9		6		2	33		50
Peter	2	2	1		5			4	14	10		4	5	5	52		76
Mary Rose		4	2	2	5	2			15	9		6		6	60		81
TOTALS	9	9	3	14	32	13	2	4	86	93	12	37	5	24	288	87	546

of the latter. The 8 bronze guns fall into 5 main categories – cannon, culverin, saker, fawcon and fowler.

Although at first sight there appears to be significant change between 1514 and 1540, a closer examination reveals that the situation is so greatly different. Ships were armed primarily with smaller calibre weapons, more useful for anti-personnel use, than with larger guns. However there is definitely increase in the numbers of larger guns and, more importantly, a move towards a more uniform and less diverse complement of pieces. Tactics of fighting at sea would appear not to have changed too much – the larger ships able to inflict some damage on an enemy vessel though there is still a greater emphasis on anti-personnel weapons and boarding.

1546[5]

In 1546 an inventory of the King's navy was made by the then Clerk of the Ordnance in the Tower of London, Anthony Anthony. This inventory lists the armament of each vessel below a coloured image of the ship. It lists the *"Ordenaunce, artillery, munitions, habillimentes for warre, for the arming and in the defence of the sayd shippe to the see"*, as well as the tonnage, and numbers of men separated into soldiers, mariners and gunners. No less than 58 ships

of all sizes are listed with a total of 1815 iron and 256 bronze pieces. See Tables 13.4a and 13.4b.

At first sight this inventory appears very complex and confusing, listing, as it does, so many different types and names for guns, both iron and bronze. It does seem to indicate a dramatic rise, since the 1540 inventory, of the different categories of guns. A possible explanation is that the enormous explosion in the size of the navy has meant that every weapon in store has been brought out to arm them all – there were 10 ships in 1540 and nearly 60 in this list.

Of the iron guns, 11 variants are listed of 9 different types – the sling having two further categories, the demi and quarter sling. The most common iron gun was the base, making up almost half of all the iron guns listed. This seems to occupy the space/use of the serpentine of the earlier inventories; the base was essentially again a short range anti-personnel weapon. The second most common gun, making up just over a quarter of the assemblage, is the hailshot piece. And here modern excavation, from the wreck of the *Mary Rose*, has helped to identify what a hailshot piece is – a short, small calibre weapon which fired a charge of small anti-personnel pellets – similar in appearance and use to the later blunderbuss. This means

Table 13.4a. The iron guns from the inventory of 1546, the Anthony Roll.

Ship	Demi culverin	Fawconette	Saker	Port piece	Fowler	Sling	Demi sling	Quarter sling	Base	Top piece	Hail shot piece	Total
Henry Grace à dieu				14	8	4	2		60	2	40	130
Mary Rose	3			12	6	2		1	30	2	20	76
The Peter				16	4		2	2	66	2	20	112
The Mathew				16		2		2	48	2	2	72
The Great Bark				10	6	2	2		30	1	20	71
Jesus of Lubeck				4	4	10			12	2	20	52
The Pauncey				12	9		4		24	1	20	70
Murrian				4		4			12	1	6	27
Strufe				6	2	4			12	1	12	37
Mary Hambrough				6	2		2		12	1	12	35
Christopher			1	2			2		12		12	29
Trinity Harry	1			10	4		5		12	1	12	45
Samuel Barke				12			5		46	1	12	76
Sweepstake					4		4		29	1	12	50
Mynnion				12	3	4			33	1	12	65
Lartyque		1					3	4	8	1	4	21
Mary Thomas		1		2			5		10	1	4	23
Hoye Barke				2	2			2	6		6	18
George				2			1		8		4	15
Mary Jamye		1		2			5		10		4	22
Grande Masterys				2	2		2		12	1	12	31
Anne Gallante						1			12	1	12	26
The Harte	3		2	4		2			12	1	12	36
The Antelop	3		2	4		2			12	1	8	32
The Tegar	4			4				2	12		4	26
The Bulle	4			4				2	12		4	26
The Salamander				8	3		2		17	1	12	43

Table 13.4a continued.

Ship	Demi culverin	Fawconette	Saker	Port piece	Fowler	Sling	Demi sling	Quarter sling	Base	Top piece	Hail shot piece	Total
The Unicorne			1	2	2		3		12	1	8	29
The Swallowe	1			6			3		20	1	12	43
The Galie Subtille				2					14		12	28
The Newe Barke				9	6		1		20	1	6	43
The Greyhounde							3		12	1	6	22
The Jennet	1		2						10	1	6	20
The Lyon				3	3			3	18		4	36
The Dragon			2		2		4		20		6	34
The Phawcon								2	20		4	26
The Sacar					2				12		2	16
The Hynde								3	14		4	21
The Roo									12		6	18
The Phenyx				2				2	10		4	18
The Marlion									8		4	12
The Less Penace		1	1		2				6		3	13
The Bryggenden									10		2	12
The Hare									12		4	16
The Trege									12		4	16
The Double Rose									6		4	10
The Flowre de Luce									7		4	11
The Portquilice									6		4	10
The Harpe									6		3	9
The Clowde in the Sonne								1	6		3	10
The Rose in the Sonne									6		4	10
The Hawthorne									6		3	9
The Ostrydge Fethers									6		3	9
The Fawcon in the Fetherlock									8		4	12
The Maydenhede									6		3	9
The Rose Slype									6		3	9
The Sylver Flowre									5		3	8
The Sonne									7		3	10
Total	20	1	14	197	78	37	60	26	892	31	459	1815

Table 13.4b. The bronze guns from the inventory of 1546, the Anthony Roll.

Ship	Cannon	Demi cannon	Culverin	Culverin perier	Long culverin	Short culverin	Demi culverin	Saker	Cannon perier	Minion	Fawcon	Fawconette	Curtall	Double base	Chamber piece	TOTAL
Henry Grace à dieu	4	3	4				2	4	2		2					21
Mary Rose	2	2	2				6	2			1					15
The Peter		2	2				4	4			2					14
The Mathew		2					5	3								10
The Great Bark		5	2				3	2								12
Jesus of Lubeck	2		2				2									6
The Pauncey		4	2				3	4								13
Murrian			2				2									4
Strufe			2				2									4
Mary Hambrough							2	2			1					5
Christopher			2					1			1					4

Table 13.4b continued.

Ship	Cannon	Demi cannon	Culverin	Culverin perier	Long culverin	Short culverin	Demi culverin	Saker	Cannon perier	Minion	Fawcon	Fawconette	Curtall	Double base	Chamber piece	TOTAL
Trinity Harry		1						4								5
Samuel Barke		2	1				1	5	2							11
Sweepstake		2	1				3	2								8
Mynnion							1	1			2					4
Lartyque										1						1
Mary Thomas										1						1
Hoye Barke											1					1
George							1	1								2
Mary Jamye										1						1
Grande Masterys		2	4					1								7
Anne Gallante					2	2	2						1			7
The Harte		1	3													4
The Antelop		1	3													4
The Tegar			1				2									3
The Bulle			2				2	1								5
The Salamander			2				2	4								8
The Unicorne			1				1	2	1							5
The Swallowe		1					1	4								6
The Galie Subtille	1							2								3
The Newe Barke							1	3	1							5
The Greyhounde			1					2	2		2	1				8
The Jennet			1					2								3
The Lyon								2			1					3
The Dragon								1						1		2
The Phawcon								4								4
The Sacar								2								2
The Hynde								1								1
The Roo				1			2							2		5
The Phenyx								2								2
The Marlion										3	1					4
The Less Penace											1					1
The Bryggenden											1	2				3
The Hare								1								1
The Trege																0
The Double Rose							1									1
The Flowre de Luce							1	1								2
The Portquilice								1								1
The Harpe								1								1
The Clowde in the Sonne							1	1								2
The Rose in the Sonne							1									1
The Hawthorne								1								1
The Ostrydge Fethers								1								1
The Fawcon in the Fetherlock							1				2					3
The Maydenhede								1								1
The Rose Slype								1								1
The Sylver Flowre								1								1
The Sonne								1			1					2
Total	9	28	40	1	2	2	49	85	8	6	19	3	1	1	2	256

that some three quarters of the iron guns, a total of 1351 pieces, were short-range anti personnel weapons.

Just over one tenth of the iron guns are a type called a port piece, a category which, until relatively recently, could not be positively identified. However, as with the hail shot piece, excavations of the wreck of the *Mary Rose*, has shown them to be large calibre, around 20 cm (8 inches), wrought-iron guns which fired stone shot. Excavation has also shown that they were seen, at the time, to be as important as the large calibre bronze guns as both were mounted on the main gundeck side by side.

The 15 different types of bronze guns cans be split into 9 separate categories. Of these, the commonest types were the demi-cannon, shooting a cast-iron shot of 32 lb, the culverin firing a shot of 18 lb and the saker, firing the much smaller shot of just under 6 lb. What is remarkable about the 1546 inventory is the huge number of ships and the huge range of guns listed. However it does not show a significant change in the way that ships were armed. Most of the guns were still of small calibre and many were purely for anti-personnel use. In warfare at sea, boarding was, still very much as previously, viewed as the predominant tactic though the possibility of doing some damage to the enemy's hull had increased.

1558[6]

This inventory differs from the others in that instead of listing the armaments of individual ships, it is a summary of the guns for the whole fleet and those held in store (Table 13.5).

It is interesting on a number of counts. First there is now a separate listing for cast iron cannon though the numbers are quite small. The wrought iron guns are again dominated by the smaller types – some two-thirds are bases of various types – but the hailshot pieces of the 1546 inventory have almost completely disappeared.

The bronze guns are very similar to those in the earlier list with the emphasis on smaller calibre guns – over half are sakers or smaller calibre pieces.

This listing then shows the continuity of the preceding years. Ships are armed with large numbers of smaller guns augmented by a complement of larger calibre pieces both iron and bronze.

1576[7]

The next inventory is dated 1576 and shows a real change from the one taken less than 20 years previously (Table 13.6).

Twenty-one ships are listed as armed with 152 iron and 639 bronze guns. And here we can see the first change – from a predominance of iron (that is, of course, wrought iron), to that of bronze pieces. But there are other equally significant changes. There are now just 3 types of iron gun – fowler, base and top piece, although in fact only 2 top pieces are actually included. All three types are small calibre anti-personnel weapons. However it is the bronze gun categories that show real change. Though there are 13 different names, there are just 8

Table 13.5. The inventory of 1576.

	On ship	In store	TOTALS
Brass			
Cannon	0	0	0
Cannon perier	16	6	22
Demi cannon	14	2	16
Culverin	30	7	37
Demi culverin	54	8	62
Saker	80	6	86
Minion	20	2	22
Fawcon	41	16	57
Fawconnet	9	1	10
Total	264	48	312
Cast iron			
Demi culverin	13	3	16
Saker	25	5	30
Fawcon	8	0	8
Fawconnet	2	0	2
Total	48	8	56
Forged iron			
Port pieces	62	32	94
Fowlers	71	23	94
Whole slings	0	3	3
Demi slings	9	20	29
Quarter slings	11	24	35
Top pieces	3	1	4
Double ring bases	6	3	9
Double bases	128	33	161
Single bases	355	94	449
Single ring bases	0	11	11
Wagon bases	46	0	46
Double of iron	0	6	6
Flawmouthes	0	8	8
Total	691	258	949

types of bronze guns. But something more significant is also going on. Now almost half of the bronze guns can be classed as the large calibre guns – culverins or cannon. It appears that the armament of the ships was getting heavier with more guns of a larger calibre. And interestingly the port pieces, formerly made from wrought iron, are now also made from bronze.

So it would appear that in the twenty years prior to 1576 the major change to the armament of ships occurred. Now, instead of a preponderance of smaller guns, mostly anti-personnel weapons, ships are now armed with large calibre guns capable of inflicting damage on the hulls of their enemy's hulls. The tactics of sea warfare are now more based on firing a significant weight of cast iron shot at your enemy from a longer range. This is not to say that boarding was not important but it is clear that more of the fighting, the destruction and softening up of the enemy, could be done first. It must always be remembered that although beating the enemy was of paramount importance, capturing an enemy ship was also a much desired outcome

Table 13.6. The inventory of 1603.

	Demi cannon	Demi cannon perier	Cannon perier	Culverin	Culverin perier	Demi culverin	Saker	Minion	Fawcon	Lizard	Fawconette	Fowler	Port piece	Forged fowler	Base	Double base	Top piece	TOTAL
Elizabeth Jonas	8		4	6		8	7	2	2			4	4	8	22			75
Tryumpe	8		5	14		7	10	2	2			4	2	4	2			60
Beare	6		6	13		12	12	2	2					6				59
Victorie	6		4	14		4	4	2						8	2			44
Hoape	1		2	7		10	4	4	1		1	2	4	6	6			48
Marie Rose	4		2	8		6	8						2	4	4			38
Slip and Marie	4		2	4		6	13	2	2			2		9		2		46
Lion	4	2	2	6	1	7	6	2	2			8	2					42
Elizabeth Bonaventure	2		2	5		10	8	2	2			1	3	4	5			44
Dreadnought			2	4		8	6	4	4			8						36
Swiftsure			4	4		9	6	2	2			6						33
Anteloppe				2		7	9	2	2				4	2	8			36
Swalloe						4	13	3	6		1			4	6	2	2	41
Foresight						10	9	4				1		2	2			28
Gennet						4	9	4	5					6	2			30
Aid						2	13		6		1	6						28
Bull						7	8	2	2					4	2			25
Teigre						6	10	3						4	2			25
Achates							2	2	8			2			2			16
Handemaide							2	2	7		2	4						17
Barke Boolen							1		6	1	2			2	8			20
TOTALS	43	2	35	87	1	127	160	46	61	1	7	48	21	73	73	4	2	791

Table 13.7.

	Bronze pieces													Iron guns					
	Cannon perier	Demi cannon	Culverin	Culverin perier	Demi culverin	Saker	Minion	Fawcon	Fawconette	Curtall	Port piece	Fowler	**Total**	Culverin	Demi culverin	Saker	Minion	Fawcon	Total
Elizabeth Jonas	3	2	18		13	19	1					2	**58**						0
Tryumph	4	3	19		16	13						4	**59**						0
Beare	2	6	21		16	12							**57**						0
Merehonor		4	15		16	4						2	**41**						0
Arke Royal	4	4	12		12	6					4	2	**44**						0
Guardland			16		12	2					2	2	**34**		2	2			4
Due Repulse	2	3	13		14	6					2	2	**42**						0
Waspyte	2	2	14		10	4					2	4	**38**						0
Defiance			14		14	6					2	2	**38**						0
Mary Rose		4	10		7	4					4		**29**	1	3				4
Elizabeth Bonaventure	2	2	11		14	4	2				2	2	**39**						0
Nonperalia	2	3	7		8	12					4	4	**40**						0
Lyon		4	8		12	9		1				8	**42**		2				2
Victorie												7	**7**	8	9	2			19
Raynebowe		6	10		7	1						4	**28**						0
Dreadnought	2		4		11	10		2				4	**33**						0
Swiftsure	2		5		8	6		2				4	**27**		4	3			7
Hope	2	4	9		12	4					4	2	**37**						0
Vauntguarde		4	14		16	4	2	2					**42**						0
St Mathias	4	4	16		10	2	3	2					**41**		6	2	1		9
St Andrewe			4	2	7	3	1			2		4	**23**	2	14	4	1		21
Antiloppe			4		5	4		1			2	2	**18**		8	4			12
Adventure			4		11	7						2	**24**						0
Advantage					6	8	2						**16**				4		4
Crane					2	2	6					2	**12**		4	5			9
Tremountara						12	7						**21**						0
Quittance					4	4	2	2				2	**12**	2	2	3	4		11
Answeare					2	2	2	2				2	**10**		3	4			7
TOTALS	31	55	248	2	265	170	26	16	0	2	28	69	**912**	13	57	29	10	**0**	**109**

– a prize was worth a lot of money from which all the crew, from master to cabin boy, benefitted financially.

1603[8]

The final inventory, dated 1603, lists the armament of 28 ships, and shows that the changes continued through the last quarter of the century (Table 13.7).

The first change is that the cannon on ships were either made from bronze or from cast iron and that wrought-iron guns were no longer used in the Royal Navy. Even those guns which were traditionally made from wrought iron, for example port pieces and fowlers, were now made of bronze. However, of the 1021 guns listed, just 36 are made from cast iron – 9 culverins, 20 demi-culverins and 7 sakers. What is interesting is that, though the English had been successfully producing cast iron artillery since the 1540s, the navy still preferred to use bronze pieces. And in fact, it was not till the 1640s that they were to move away from bronze and arm the fleet with cast iron cannon.[9] Interestingly there are still quite a number of different types of guns though the number of unusual pieces was now very small.

However the major change is that the ships were armed predominantly with 'big guns – almost two thirds of the total armament are large calibre guns: cannon, culverins and demi-culverins. At the beginning of the seventeenth century, ships had become floating fortresses, capable of firing a very significant weight of cast-iron shot. And it is here where the seeds of the later pre-eminence of the English navy can be traced. Though large guns and firepower were never the only way to success at sea, the experience gained over the last decades of the sixteenth century were probably very significant.

Conclusions

This very brief survey of the inventories from the late fifteenth to the early sixteenth centuries has allowed us to chart the changes in ships' armament over the sixteenth century. For the first fifty years they were armed predominantly with large numbers of smaller guns, the majority of which were made from wrought

iron, augmented by a small – but increasing – number of larger guns.

Between the 1550s and 1576 there was a significant change. Now there are far fewer iron pieces and ships were armed primarily with bronze guns. Increasingly too these pieces were larger and heavier in size than before and it is clear that ships were changing and becoming more like floating artillery platforms. And this continues through the last quarter of the century, till by the beginning of the seventeenth century, the ships of the Royal Navy were armed predominantly with great numbers of large calibre bronze guns. What is equally important is that the royal ships were armed with bronze and not cast iron cannon – a move which does not occur until the 1640s.

Notes

1 It has been necessary to simplify some of the inventories in the tables which accompany this article as the originals are often very complex and in a short article it is not always possible to provide every small detail. This in no way affects the overall argument put forward in the discussion.
2 There are a few other inventories but this group provides the basis to understand the changes in armament through the century. An inventory of 1547 for example is extensive but adds nothing new to that of 1546.
3 The lists of ships stores from which these figures are taken can be found in Oppenheim, M., *Naval Accounts and Inventories of Henry VII 1485–8 and 1495–7.* Naval Records Society, volume 8, 1896, page 194, 205.
4 National Archives, Kew, PRO E 36/13
5 The inventory is now in two parts, one held at the British Library, London, Additional MS 22047, and the other, and larger part, is preserved in the library of Magdalene College, Cambridge, Pepys library 2991.
6 National Archives, Kew, SP12/3 ff.136–139
7 National Maritime Museum, Greenwich, CAD/C/1
8 British Library, London, Royal MS 17a XXXI
9 See Brown, R. R., 'The thundering cannon: guns for the English Navy in the 17th century'. In *A farewell to arms, Studies on the history of arms and armour.* Legermuseum, Delft, 2004

The British Sea Service Mortars

Some Notes on their Evolution with Particular Reference to the Drawings of Albert Borgard, *c.* 1700

Martino Ferrari Bravo

Introduction

This paper examines some aspects of the circulation of technology that backed the development of the sea service mortar and its inseparable sailing platform, the bomb vessel, in late 17th-century to early 18th-century Britain. Although some fine works on the bomb vessel are available (Wray 1977; Goodwin 1989; Ware 1994), a late 17th-century document attributed to Lieutenant-general Albert Borgard (1659–1751), one of the foremost officers in the history of the Royal Artillery, can supply some interesting information on the evolution of sea service mortars. The notebook, containing twenty-five plates of different pieces of artillery – mostly mortars of late 17th century – was accurately executed and still represents a rare visual document on these specific ordnances. The notebook (MD/3026) is currently displayed in the Firepower Museum at Woolwich and is titled *"Drawings of Venetian Artillery in the manuscript of Lieut-General Albert Borgard"*, but does not contain any reference to Venetian ordnances. The drawings, (part in colour and with measurements) were bound and first studied in 1867 by Colonel F. Miller, an R.A. officer. The notebook was among the few documents that survived a German air raid in 1941 – although with some visible damages – that partly destroyed the Royal Artillery Library (now James Clavell Library), when many other precious documents were lost forever. In 1992 the manuscript was examined and partly reproduced by Adrian Caruana. The importance of this document, which is attributed to Borgard (but not signed by him) is found in the variety of mortars of different design that were drawn by the author during the first decades of his exceptional 44–year military career. Other sources that have been used for this paper are the letters of the British military engineer, Jacob Richards (bapt. 1664, d. 1701), currently conserved at the British Library (Stowe ms 444 to 452). Richards played an important role in developing a revolving mortar bed that improved the efficiency of the system mortar-vessel.

A new form of warfare: mortars and vessels, 1680s–1730s

In 1686, both Richards and Borgard, even if under different flags, were at Buda during the siege that saw new technologies in mortar and shell design being experimented, while the mixed provenance of the officers who were fighting the Ottomans permitted a European circulation of these developments. In late 17th-century Britain, Richards and Borgard were possibly the most knowledgeable officers in terms of land and sea mortars and both of them were granted the command of squadrons of bomb vessels during operations against the French ports (1693–95) and in the siege of Vigo (1702). The bomb vessel, invented by the French in 1681 and promptly adopted by the Republic of Venice as well as England, was the result of a phase of artillery – and particularly mortar – development in Europe. Defined as a *"floating siege engine"*, this small vessel required the skills, the crews and the technology of both the artillery and the navy. The idea of mounting a couple of land mortars on a vessel allowed a maritime power to be projected from the sea against coastal fortifications or towns, but also to exercise a heavy psychological pressure on civilian populations who were hit by explosive (shells) or incendiary (carcasses) projectiles. A new form of warfare was performed by a vessel that *"brought together the concepts of revolving gun mounting and explosive shells"* (Ireland 2000, 118), a military innovation that can be compared with the shock produced by the air raids of the past century. Although the great enthusiasm for this weapon system gradually faded after the first decade of employment (Candiani 2008), it did represent an important progress in naval warfare and a significant example of the integration between craft and gun, the former specifically built for the latter, a scheme that would last until the first half of 19th century. Mounting a mortar on a naval craft had basically three advantages: to stay outside the range of coastal batteries, to fire at 45 degrees, thus over obstacles, and finally to shoot explosive or incendiary shells (Wray 1977, 246). The maximum range for a 13-inch mortar was about

Figure 14.1. Bronze 12-inch mortar and iron bed, Spanish, dated 1724. Cast by Voie-Y-Abet of Seville, gourd shaped chamber (Tower of London, XIX.142, © Board of trustees of the Royal Armouries).

3,750 yards and a 10-inch could fire at about 3,500 yards. If a 32pdr had a theoretical range of 3,250 yards (while the actual range was much less) this meant that the bomb vessels could stay clear of coastal defences (JCL, notes of Caruana, MD1501). These advantages had to be matched with some technical difficulties, the solution of which made the Royal Navy perhaps the most efficient user of a weapon system adopted both by Atlantic and Mediterranean navies. The main technical problem that had to be dealt with was the tremendous vertical recoil of the ordnance. The vessel on which the mortar was mounted needed to be able to absorb it, while the rigging had to be adapted in order to leave enough space for firing the mortars, thus compromising the balance while on sail. At the same time this specialised, strong craft had to maintain sufficient manoeuvrability and speed to accompany a squadron. The French's initial choice of a Dutch *galliot* as a model for their *galiote à bombes* was probably influenced by the characteristic short length and broad beam of that craft that made her a stable platform for mortars (Goodwin 1989, 7). In Britain, better flexibility from such a specialised craft was obtained through a ship rigging that allowed these vessels to sail with the rest of the fleet, once they had landed their mortars (Rodger 2004, 223). The bomb vessel was usually an extraordinarily strong craft; the *Carcass* and *Racehorse* (a converted bomb vessel) for instance, were used in 1773 in a polar expedition on which Nelson served (Knight 2005, 25–42). After the 1750s, no more *bombs* – as they were called in the Royal Navy – were rigged as ketches, unlike among the French who stuck to this rigging for many decades. Using mortars at sea was an extraordinary combination of naval and artillery knowledge: the complexity of firing at a high angle on an unstable platform required the presence of Royal Artillery personnel on board (2 officers and 4 non-commissioned officers to

each vessel). These men were called Bombardiers, the rank being instituted specifically for this purpose in 1686. In Britain the bomb vessel continued to be manned both by the Navy and the Royal Artillery until 1804 and other navies had similar arrangements. But in the Royal Navy this coexistence sometimes generated hierarchy problems: the RA colonel in charge of the operations for instance, was expected to answer only to the Admiral, according to his orders, and this often generated confusion in the command of a naval squadron.

The mortar bombardment had increased in importance during the reign of Louis XIV, as a technique 'more connected with mathematical science' (Hall 1952, 56); in the late 17th century, however, the knowledge about ballistics was still relying substantially on experience. In a 1693 Spanish military handbook, a trigonometric formula was provided to assist bombardiers in adjusting the mortar, although a first trial still had to be made in order to estimate the range of the projectile at a given elevation (Escuela de Palas 1693, I, 204). Even in 1716 the technical skills and experience of the bombardiers counted more than the support of science, the theory being 'vitiated by the multitude of uncontrollable technical factors' (Hall 1952, 56). The increase in the range of land mortars, which made their use at sea more convenient, was enabled by the development of a non-cylindrical chamber in 1679. The invention, attributed to a Spanish officer called Antonio Gonzalez (d. 1687), was immediately adopted by the French (*Escuela de Palas* 1693, 204). The short barrel of mortars allowed greater flexibility in the choice of shape of their chambers. Practical problems like cleaning a non-cylindrical cannon chamber for instance, could easily be sorted out by hand in a mortar (*Memorias* 1802, 61). Gonzalez first designed an elliptical chamber followed by a spherical one, to be used both for cannons and mortars. While the increased velocity of the gas expansion permitted by the spherical chamber in cannons implied some complications, it represented a great advantage for mortars. The dangerous effect of stronger recoil on the bed had been partially minimised by changing the position of the trunnions, which were moved on the breech (on the pattern of the Trabucco-mortar). The Spanish Artillery apparently stuck to this solution for some decades; a 1724 12.6-inch Spanish mortar, now displayed in the Armouries of the Tower of London, possesses a gourd-shaped chamber (Figure 14.1). A more advanced version was proposed by Iacomo (or Jacomo) Roca (the Genoese *Giacomo Rocca* the elder, 1648–1730. Information from R. G. Ridella) which had the trunnions in the centre (like a howitzer) and the chamber was a combination of a sphere and a cylinder, as explained in the above-mentioned Spanish military handbook, where the simultaneous presence of different patterns of mortars is also evidenced; mortars were extremely expensive to cast and they tend to last long before being replaced or re-cast (*Escuela de Palas* 1693, I, 204). The French were prompt in adopting and possibly developing the spherical chamber technology that was first used to bombard Algiers in 1682. The shape of the chamber of the mortar rapidly evolved, as can be seen in Borgard's drawing in the notebook of the

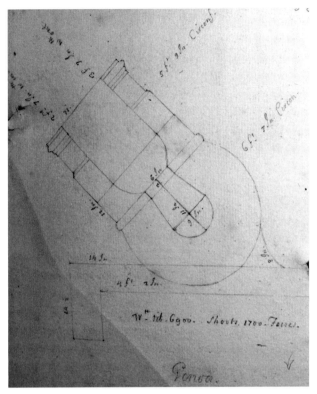

Figure 14.2. 12.5-inch mortar marked Genoa (JCL, MD/3026, Albert Borgard's notebook, plate 16).

mortar employed against Genoa, in May 1684 (Figure 14.2). Borgard, a Dane, joined the Army of Louis XIV in 1692, when he could study the design of their artillery (Baigent 2004, 658, Hime 1885, 129–158). The spherical or non-cylindrical chamber allowed the mortars a superior range of fire, well off the range of defence batteries. According to J. Peter "*les chambres sphériques ou en poire devaient s'avérer plus résistantes que les chambres cylindriques, d'ailleurs rarement bien coulées*". In 1683 the English shipwright Edmund Dummer was among the first to recognize the power of this technology, during his two-year voyage in the Mediterranean. He described and drew some *galiotes a bombes* after assisting at their testing off Toulon. Dummer explained the increased firepower of their guns:

> "*The Chambers of their Mortars are Concave, not Strait Bored, or Cyllindricall, & as they are Cast standing Angular to the greatest Random on a Table of the same Metall*".

He said elsewhere:

> "*The chambers of these mortars are not straight or cylindrical but concave and oval, and charged with loose powder and is the only reason why they have so much overshot the cannon of Algier and Genoa*" (BL, King's ms 40).

Less than ten years later, in 1692, Dummer, still young and unknown, was to become the new Surveyor of the Navy, the "*Navy's principal warship designer*" (Rodger 2004, 218–9). But Dummer was not the only Englishman

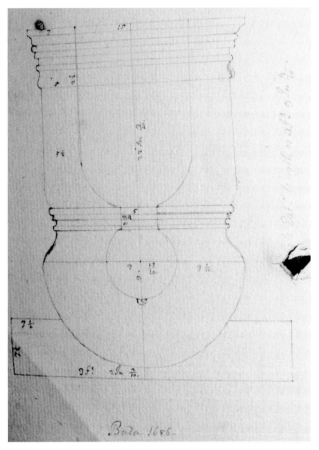

Figure 14.3. 15-inch mortar marked Buda 1686 (JCL, MD/3026, Albert Borgard's notebook, plate 24).

to witness the power of the new "*Spanish pattern mortar*". The military engineer Jacob Richards also recognised their performance during the siege of Buda in 1686, where he gained a good knowledge of their design and also of the Spanish innovative shells. At that time about twenty English officers were present at Buda, for Charles II was then making strong efforts to gather information on continental military practice and fortification. Richards was instructed to improve himself in "*Forreigne Parts beyond Seas, to be employed at his returne as one of His Majesty's Engineers in England*" (BL, Stowe ms 474, 1 r). He was also required to make "*as many draughts of places and fortifications*" and to present his journals to the Master-General of the Ordnance, who at that time was Lord Dartmouth. Once in the allied army in Vienna, Richards could visit their ordnance stores (BL, Stowe ms 474, 9v). Examining the Spanish mortars, Richards observed and described their spherical chambers. He then reported and executed some sketches of these ordnances that unfortunately are no longer attached to the letters. But in Borgard's notebook, the mortar identified as "*Buda*" probably represents one of the 15-inch mortars examined by Richards (Figure 14.3). It is interesting to consider that working as Assistant in the Royal Artillery at Woolwich (a new position that was especially created for him) Borgard collaborated with Jacob Richard's elder brother, Michael (1673–1721), who was Surveyor of the Ordnance. Also

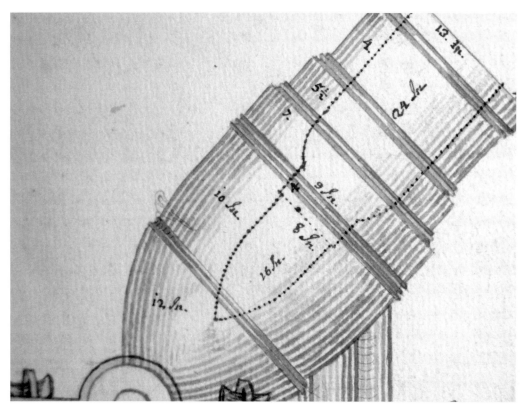

Figure 14.4. 13-inch mortar (JCL, MD/3026, Albert Borgard's notebook, plate 1).

Antonio Gonzalez was at Buda and when Richards arrived, the former had already set up his innovative mortars (*Memorias* 1802, 58). According to a contemporary report of the siege made by Federico Cornaro, then the Venetian ambassador, the devastating power of the Spanish (and Brandenburg) mortars was apparent to everybody. Richards also observed the improved Spanish shells and carcasses, developed by Gonzalez and examined their effects on buildings and fortifications. Thus it is reasonable to assume that the projectiles that Richards proposed to the Venetian government in 1687, when he was first contracted by that Republic, were based upon this experience (BL Stowe, ms 460).

With regard to the mortar, and particularly the mortar chamber, the English took advantage of the direct knowledge of the most advanced contemporary developments in Europe, but after a period of experiments they developed their own design. In his third edition of his *Treatise on Artillery*, Muller (1785, 66) said that each country had his own chamber design, spherical in Spain, conic, cylindrical bottled or concave in France, while the English preferred a frustum of a cone (Figure 14.4). Internal ballistics and the matter of the gas expansion were still quite unknown phenomena in the early 18th century, apart from the studies of Bigot de Morogues and Daniel Bernoulli and the connections between mathematical studies and experimental data made by B. Robins (*New Principles of Gunnery*, 1742). L. Euler authoritatively translated Robins' work in English (Gille 1980, 422; Hall 1952, 55) while of great importance was, according to Camara (1993, 239), the work of M. Belidor (*Le bombardier*

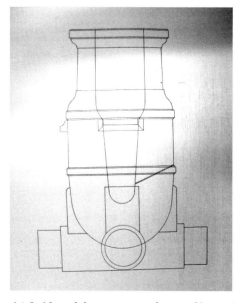

Figure 14.5. 13-inch brass mortar designed by A. Caruana after a drawing of Albert Borgard (JCL, MD/1501).

François, ou nouvelle method de jetter les bombes avec precision 1731). Regarding the influence of the chamber design in the velocity of the powder in catching fire, Euler preferred the spherical chamber, while Belidor preferred the conical shape. In 1732 the Royal Society carried out some experiments on ballistics, one of them regarded the shape of the chamber and the results promoted the idea that, given an identical volume, the more stretched the

Figure 14.6. Nine chambered bronze mortar, designed by Richard Leake and cast by William and Philip Whiteman, London 1687 (Tower of London, inv. XIX.131, © Board of Trustees of the Royal Armouries).

shape the more efficient the expansion of gases (Camara 1993, 271). The fact that grain size was the controlling factor in the velocity of inflammation of the powder was demonstrated before the Royal Society as late as 1779 (Caruana, MD 1501, box 14). Muller, speaking about the late general Borgard, said that he "*made his chambers conical, terminating in a circular form at the bottom*", but his 'qualifications as an inventor were but very moderate' (Muller 1768, 71) (Figure 14.5). Muller considered the cone as the best possible chamber: "*it is not the inward figure of the chamber but its entrance which produces its effect; because the smaller it is, the nearer it reduces the effect into the direction of the shell*" (Muller 1768, 75). On this theory the chambers were made spherical or pear-shaped, "*with a mouth of less diameter than the interior*" (JCL, MD 3026, notes on Borgard's notebook by RA Lieu-Colonel Miller 1867). Caruana made a more balanced evaluation of Borgard's work as gun designer, especially about brass ordnances.

Between 1677 and 1696 the Master Gunner of England Captain Richard Leake's open mind to innovations favoured experiments about mortars (Figure 14.6). He designed an innovative sea service mortar with nine chambers, now displayed at the Royal Armouries, an interesting evidence of this phase of experiments. Possibly more successful was Leake's method to fire the fuse of mortar bombs through the explosion of the charge. This novelty represented an important advance in terms of a safer use of mortars, since igniting the fuse and the charge separately, with a synchronised manoeuvre (the so-called *double fire* method), was obviously very dangerous. During the attack on St Malo in 1693, Leake made some experiments with the *Nicholas*

machines or *infernals,* a sort of fireship (Clowes 1966, 476). Two years later he took part in the preparation of another expedition against St. Malo (Hall 1952, 19), where Colonel Richards commanded five bomb vessels. During the French coast bombardment (1695–96), improved sea mortars were used. Colonel Martin Beckman, Colonel Richards and Albert Borgard, who joined the English service in 1692, took part in these actions. In 1702 Borgard, thanks to his experience in mortars, commanded a squadron of bomb vessels during the Cadiz expedition led by Admiral Rooke. At that time Borgard was possibly the finest expert on this subject: he had already fired mortars at the siege of Bon in 1689, at the battle of Landen in 1693, at Fort Knocke in 1695 and even at the siege of Namur. In the 1690s, bomb vessel design was far from satisfactory so the British decided to have recourse with a French Master Builder, Jean Fournier, who made his technical proposals in 1692–3. Four new bombs were subsequently built, one of them ship-rigged. How French design influenced this 1693 class of bomb vessels is unknown (Wray 1977), but of the four that were built, two were still in service in 1702 when they were employed in the siege of Cadiz and Vigo. The first big English innovation in bomb vessel design was a traversing mounting of the mortars that required less breadth and, by having the main mast stepped further forward, gave a better balanced sail plan; in France the bomb vessels had the mortars side by side (Ware 1994, 18, 84).

By the 1690s the problems of firing the mortars on board were not yet resolved. Mortars could not be used with the maximum possible charge of their chambers for the structure of the vessels would hardly resist the potent recoil (Peter 1995; Candiani 2008). During their first trials in 1684 for instance, three experimental Venetian crafts were destroyed by the recoil (Candiani 2008). The first scientific experiment to study recoil was made by Lord Brouncker in 1661 in the presence of the Royal Society and Charles II (Hall 1952, 66–67). While the French focused on heavier and heavier shells, even experimenting with 500lb bombs on 18-inch mortars (while the standard was 12-inch) but mainly relying on integral beds (Peter 1995, 137), the British concentrated on a separate wooden bed for the sea service mortar. Integral bed was initially designed to spread the load of the recoil produced by heavy charges that were necessary to contrast the inefficiency of the sea service mortar. Three different bed designs were developed in late 17th century (Figure 14.7): wooden bed, separate metal bed and integral bed. A technical committee that included Jean Fournier was organised at Deptford in 1694, partly formed by the Royal Navy (Captain Leake) and partly by the Board of Ordnance. On that occasion Jacob Richards proposed to mount mortars on turntables, in order to give them much more flexibility (in 1697 Richards affirmed that English mortars could be rotated by two men only), an innovation that became standard after 1702 (Ware, 1994, 88–89). The main British contributions can be represented by the revolving bed that made the two mortars independent, and then the adjustable elevation that also permitted to store the mortar during navigation and to lower the centre of gravity. The transition from fixed to adjustable elevation was effected between 1690 and 1728 (Wray 1979, 25). The *Terrible* of 1728 had these characteristics with the so-called trabucco-mortar, *i.e.* with trunnions at the breech.

The wooden bed was developed early in Britain and the wooden frame that sustained the weight and recoil of the mortar was later adapted as a bomb room that included a lifting system that was necessary to manoeuvre the 200lbs shells used in 13-inch mortars. This is clearly visible in a contemporary model at the Firepower Museum of Woolwich. According to Caruana the development of the wooden bed was made to accommodate the huge increase in weight of the mortars, a 13-inch could weigh almost 5 tons. This was made when the increase in power of the powder made stronger guns necessary. Adding metal, even if it was not understood that beyond a certain level this was useless, added weight. Therefore the wooden bed could help to balance this enormous burden on a vessel. The integral bed meant that the mortar was fixed at 45 degrees, the position of maximum range (Figure 14.8). Even if an integral bed 13-inch sea mortar was used at Vigo in 1719 on the *Speedwell* bomb vessel, the standard British sea service mortar bed became the wooden one. The *Granado* class (1742) shell room and oak-made mortar pit formed an integral part of the ship's structure and the regular complement for every vessel was three hundred bombs (Caruana 1994, 212). In terms of mortars, while the 12¼, 12½, 12¾ inch calibre were rather experimental ones, the 13 inch soon became standard for sea service. From 1689 to 1700 out of 116 mortars, 52 were destined to sea service, of which 39 were 13-inch. Eighteen mortars were cast in 1695 and nine bomb vessels built. In England the period 1675–1700 saw the production of at least twenty different calibres of mortars (shells were produced in 32

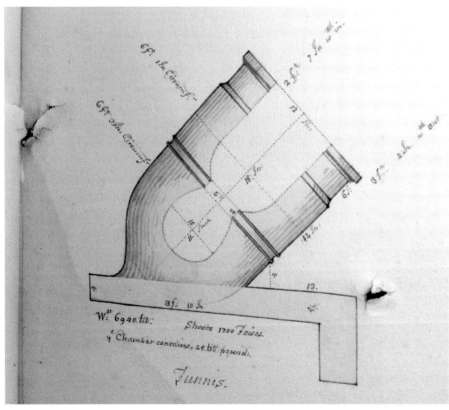

Figure 14.7. 12-inch brass mortar with integral bed marked Tunis (JCL, MD/3026, Albert Borgard's notebook, plate 13).

Figure 14.8. French bronze mortar, integral bed, Douai 1810 (Tower of London, XIX.137, © Board of Trustees of the Royal Armouries).

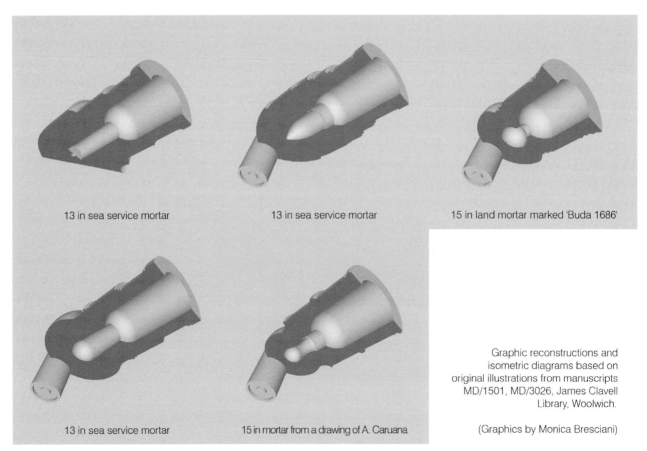

Figure 14.9. Different patterns of land and sea service mortar chambers from Albert Borgard's manuscripts.

different calibres) and since the mid-18th century, the bomb vessel mortars tended to be standardized in 10-inch and 13-inch. They were mostly produced in London by the Wightman and Morgan foundries. The two most important designers were Martin Beckman and Michael Richards who, according to Caruana, also designed an integral bed 13-inch mortar. An early 10-inch mortar, weighing 25 cwt (1,270 kg) did not turn out to be very successful, possibly because it did not achieve a sufficient range. The 10-inch mortars were used mostly on converted crafts and became the standard on bomb vessels later in the 18th century.

Conclusion

Probably more than any other military technologies, sea service mortar and its inseparable platform, the bomb vessel, were the result of a significant integration between naval and artillery knowledge and of an intense circulation of technologies activated, as in 1686 Buda, by a handful of European officers, who mastered them. Through the efforts of some 17th-century and 18th-century men, including Borgard, Richards, Gonzalez and Dummer, the sea-service mortar and the bomb vessel experienced a dynamic growth and development. The strong vertical recoil of more powerful mortars was contrasted by new beds and vessel reinforces. Each country developed its own theory about the shape of the chamber, effectively represented by Borgard (Figure 14.9). The integration between mortar and vessel development permitted to experience and develop a new form of warfare whose potential was immediately understood by the most advanced European navies.

Abbreviations

BL   British Library
JCL   James Clavell Library, Woolwich
TNA   The National Archives, Kew

References

Baigent, E. (2004) Borgard, Albert. In H. C. G. Matthew and B. Harrison (ed.) *Oxford Dictionary of National Biographies*, 658–659, Oxford, Oxford University Press.
Camara, H. (1993) Tendiendo puentes entre la teoría y la pràctica cientifica: el péndulo balístico. *Series Filosóficas* 2, 237–281.
Candiani, G. (2006) Un inglese a Venezia, unpublished article, by courtesy of the author.
Candiani, G. (2008) Novità tecnologica e pressione psicologica: l'introduzione delle galeotte a bombe nella marina veneziana (1685–1695), unpublished article, by courtesy of the author.
Caruana, A. B. (1992) Sea Service Mortars, unpublished article, James Clavell Library, Woolwich.
Caruana, A. B. (1994) *The History of English Sea Ordnances 1523–1875*. Vol. I. Rotherfield, East Sussex, J. Boudriot Publications.
Clowes, L. (1966) *The Royal Navy: A History from the Earliest Times to the Present*, II. New York, AMS Press Inc.
Duncan, F. (1879³) *History of the Royal regiment of artillery*. London.
Escuela de Palas o sea curso mathematic (1693), I, 204–205, Milan.
Gille, P. (1980) Ballistics. In M. Daumas (ed.) *A History of Technology and Invention*, III, 420–429, London, John Murray.
Goodwin, P. (1989) The bomb vessel *Granado*. London, Conway Maritime Press.
Hall, A. R. (1952) *Ballistics in the Seventeenth Century: A study in the relations of science and war with reference principally to England*. Cambridge University Press.
Hebbert, F. J. (1976) The Richards brothers. In *Irish Sword*, 12, 200–211.
Hime, H. W. L. (1885) An account of battles, sieges, &c wherein Lieut-General Albert Borgard hath served. With remarks, *Minutes of the Proceedings of the Royal Artillery Institution*, 13, 129–158.
Hogg, O. F. G. (1963) *English Artillery 1326–1716. Being the history of artillery in this country prior to the formation of the Royal Regiment of Artillery (with plates)*. London.
Ireland, B. (2000) *Naval warfare in the age of sail: War at sea 1756–1815*. London, HarperCollins.
Kennard, A. N. (1986) *Gunfounding and Gunfounders*. London, Arms and Armour Press.
Knight, R. (2005) *The Pursuit of Victory: The life and achievements of Horatio Nelson*. London, Penguin Books.
Memorias de la Real Academia de la Historia, IV, (1802), 482–496.
Moretti, T. (1672) *Trattato dell'Artiglieria*. Brescia.
Morin, M. (2002) Tre artiglierie veneziane a Copenaghen (e una a Parigi…). *Quaderni di Oplologia*, 14, 17–28.
Morin, M. (2006) Artiglierie navali in ambito veneziano: tipologia e tecnica di realizzazione, *Quaderni di Oplologia*, 23, 3–28.
Muller, J. (1768) *A treatise on Artillery*. London.
von Olsen, O. N. (1839) *Generallieutenant A. Borgaards Levnet og Bedrifter, tilligemed en kort Oversigt af de nærmest hermed i Forbindelse staaende Krigsbegivenheder. Særskilt aftrykt af "Militairt Repertorium"*. Kjøbenhavn.
Peter, J. (1995) *L'artillerie et les fonderies de la Marine sous Louis XIV*. Paris, Economica.
Ridella, R. G. (2005) Un cannone con l'effigie di Vincenzo I Giustiniani, Marchese di Bassano, nelle dotazioni d'artiglieria della Repubblica di Genova (XVIII secolo), *La Gazzetta Bassanese*, 105.
Rodger, N. A. M. (2004) *The Command of the Ocean: A naval history of Britain 1649–1815*. London, Penguin Books.
Royal Artillery Institution, (1885) *Minutes of the Proceedings of the Royal Artillery Institution*, XIII.
Ware, C. (1994) *The Bomb Vessel*. London, Conway Maritime Press.
Wray, D. (March 1977, September and December 1978, March 1979) Bomb Vessels. *Model Shipwrights*, 19, 25, 26 and 27.

15

Sixteenth-Century French Naval Guns

Max Guérout

During works undertaken in 1951/1952 in the commercial harbour of Toulon (France), a bronze gun was recovered. It bore on the reinforce the emblem of Francis I, king of France: a salamander surrounded by flames, the coat of arms of Louise of Savoy, the date of 1525 and the initials of the founder: a L and a C interlaced around the vent. The chase was decorated with series of *fleurs-de-lys* (Figures 15.1, 15.2).

The salamander appeared to have been cast on the gun at the time of manufacture, while the date and the coat of arms of Louise of Savoy had been engraved at a later date on the reinforce. These three indications are in fact quite redundant because the gun was probably cast at the end of the year 1524 or at the very beginning of the year 1525. When, in October 1524, Francis I started a new campaign in Italy, he appointed his mother, Louise of Savoy, as regent. The king was captured at the battle of Pavia (24 February 1525) and he recovered his liberty and his kingdom only in March 1526. We can easily understand that the coat of arms of Louise de Savoy was added during the captivity of the king.

The characteristics of the culverin (Figure 15.3) are as follows:

- Overall length   286.0 cm
- Standard length   262.5 cm
- Length of the chase   111.0 cm
- Length of the reinforce   151.5 cm
- Diameter at the muzzle astragal   22.4 cm
- Diameter at the rear end of the reinforce   37.6 cm
- Calibre   13.0 cm
- Diameter of the trunnions   12.4 cm

The gun has no weight mark, but its weight was calculated approximately from its volume and estimated to be of 1495 kg, or following the measure of the time 30, 6 quintals.

The gun has been identified as a culverin (a "*grande couleuvrine*" following French terminology) of the calibre of France (around 132 mm), firing shot with a diameter of around 125.5 mm and a weight of 15.6 pounds. However, due to its standard length, corresponding to about 20

calibres, in the Italian/Spanish and English terminology it would have been classed as a demi-cannon, rather than a culverin.

The length of about 8 feet (8.08 ft.) is shorter than the standard length of 9 or 10 feet, the weight being also below the standard.

The trunnions are disposed in a lowered position (below the level of the axis of the barrel). It is probably one of the first pieces of evidence of this disposition. This solution seems to have been adopted a little later for the English ordnance. The trunnions of an English bronze minion dated of 1527, in the collections of the Museum of the Order of St John in Clerkenwell, London (Caruana 1994, 7), are still level with the axis of the barrel, and the earliest surviving example with low trunnions from England is a bronze saker cast by Francisco Arcana in 1529 (Caruana 1994, 4).

It is highly likely that the gunfounder of the piece found in Toulon is Claude Laignel (Figure 15.4), who according to written sources cast bronze guns in the foundry of Marseille in the years 1520: "*Plus a bronze mortar with its pestle, newly made by Master Claude Laignel, founder and purveyor of a falcon...*" (Archives départementales des Bouches-du-Rhône, B 1260, Grande Maîtresse, inventaire du 26 novembre 1526, 88).

Having studied this gun we tried to discover if it came from a ship wrecked in the vicinity. The only reference concerning the loss of a vessel during this period was found in the chronicles written by Honorat de Valbelle (Valbelle1985, I, 247):

"This day, the great "nef" which was named the Grande Maîtresse was in the harbour of Toulon, when, ...on 26 September [1533], a rain and thunder storm occurs with the result that lightings fall down from the sky into the vessel which was burnt to the hull. It was a great loss, because this vessel was as big as a carrack, so well equipped with ordnance than no similar carrack was present in Genoa".

This ship's name means that it was owned by the Grand Master of France, René Bastard of Savoy, brother of Louise

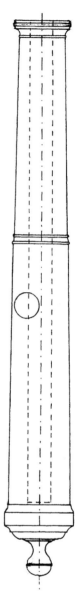

Figure 15.1 (top left). Toulon's Culverin – Gun n°M.M.5 AR 38: Musée national de la Marine – Toulon (Photo: GRAN/Guy Martin).

Figure 15.2 (top centre). Salamander, coat of arm of Louise de Savoie, date – Gun n°M.M.5 AR 38: Musée national de la Marine – Toulon (Photo: GRAN/Guy Martin).

Figure 15.3 (top right). Culverin found in the harbour of Toulon – Gun n°M.M.5 AR 38 : Musée national de la Marine – Toulon (Dessin: Max Guérout).

Figure 15.4 (left). Founder's mark LC – Gun n°M.M.5 AR 38: Musée national de la Marine – Toulon (Photo: GRAN/ Guy Martin).

of Savoy and uncle of Francis I. Although René had been killed at the battle of Pavia, and Anne de Montmorency a new Grand Master had been designated, the ship had kept her name when she sank. The *Grande Maîtresse* had been however bought by Louise of Savoy for the kingdom of France in 1526. The transaction led us to find and to publish a series of important manuscripts coming from different archives offices (Guérout and Liou 2001).

The study of 16th-century French naval ordnances is a difficult subject. Before the year 1628, when for the first time the Duke of Richelieu ordered artillery to be cast for the navy, guns are not made specially for the sea service, but could be used either on land or at sea. In spite of attempts to standardize ordnance the situation remains very confused, the changes coming in very fast and the characteristics of the guns spanning a very large spectrum. The vocabulary used to describe ordnance varies both in time and place, and it is always difficult to know the reality covered by a word, and so to have a general view of ordnances used in Europe.

On another hand, the manuscripts concerning the *Grande Maîtresse* give us the possibility to study the equipment of a royal "*nef*" in the year 1525, relying on very precise information: type of gun, description, weight and price. Even if the field of the study is narrow, we have there a first hand documentary source for the understanding of 16th-century naval ordnance, the more so as the cannon discovered in the harbour of Toulon gives us a concrete element of comparison.

Among the manuscripts concerning the *Grande Maîtresse*, there are four successive inventories of the ship.

– The first inventory was ordered by Louise of Savoy to the "*Lieutenant général de Provence*" it contains two parts with the same date: 25 November 1525. The first part contains the inventory of the ship and its equipments (Bibliothèque nationale, Fonds Clairambault, 325, f°41–44), the second one contains only the inventory of ordnance (Archives Départementales des Bouches-du-Rhône, B 1260, 74–80).

– The second inventory (Archives nationales, X^{1A} 8621, f°201v° – f°205v°) was ordered by Francis I to Pedro Navarre after the careening of the *Grande Maîtresse*; it is dated 10 July 1526. In comparison with the 1525 inventory, the number of guns is notably reduced. Pedro Navarre doing an evaluation of the amount to be paid by the King does not take into consideration a large number of the guns (all the bronze guns) which were already the property of the King.

The *Grande Maîtresse* was bought at the beginning of the month of September 1526.

– The third inventory (Archives Départementales des Bouches-du-Rhône, B 1450 f°262 (original) and Archives nationales, X^{1A} 8621, f°199v°–f°201v°

(copy)) is related to the appointment of Antoine d'Ancienville as captain of the ship on 5 September 1526.

– The fourth inventory (Archives Départementales des Bouches-du-Rhône, B 1260, p.81–89), in which a control of the Aix-en-Provence Parliament is made by Honorat Duché on 26 September 1526.

The inventory of November 1525 begins with a list of the King's ordnance, composed solely of bronze guns:

On board

– Five big serpentine cannons (*canons serpentins*) with the porcupine emblem remaining of seven guns which were formerly on board.
– Three demi culverins bastard (*couleuvrines bâtardes*) with the salamander emblem.
– Two minions (*couleuvrines moyennes*) with the salamander emblem remaining from the three which had formerly been on board.
– Four falcons.
– Forty-nine post hackbuts (*haquebutes à croc*).

Also on board:

– Two Venetian cannons with the emblem of St Mark, out of the Calibre of France.
– Two big serpentine cannons (*canons serpentins*).
– The following is the remainder of the ordnance landed and stored in different places:
– Two big Venetian cannons with the emblem of St Mark, of the calibre of France.
– Six minions (*couleuvrines moyennes*)
– Two falcons
– One saker
– One perier (*canon perrier*)
– Thirty-two post hackbuts (*haquebutes à croc*) and two hand hackbuts (*haquebutes à main*).

As a result the *Grande Maîtresse* was armed with 30 bronze guns and 83 hackbuts.

Before going on to discuss this inventory, it is good to have a better knowledge of what is called calibres of France.

In France the first attempts at standardization of ordnance was undertaken by Gaspart Bureau (Master of Ordnance between 1444 and 1469) in the reigns of Charles VII and Louis XI. He tried to lay down the principals of gun design and to standardize the calibres. This attempt continued during the reign of Charles VIII and Louis XII. We have found the first evidence of the use of these regulations in the logbook of Jacques Lion, keeper of the royal guns and ammunitions store at Marseille, (Archives Départementales des Bouches-du-Rhône, B 1232, Livre de Jacques Lion, f°3). He notes on 18 June 1512, the delivery of « *10 iron shots of the calibre of France* ». It was under the reign of Francis I, however, that the 6 calibres of France were officially adopted (Figure 15.5).

The characteristics of the six calibres of France, listed in a roll of 1537 are in Table 15.1.

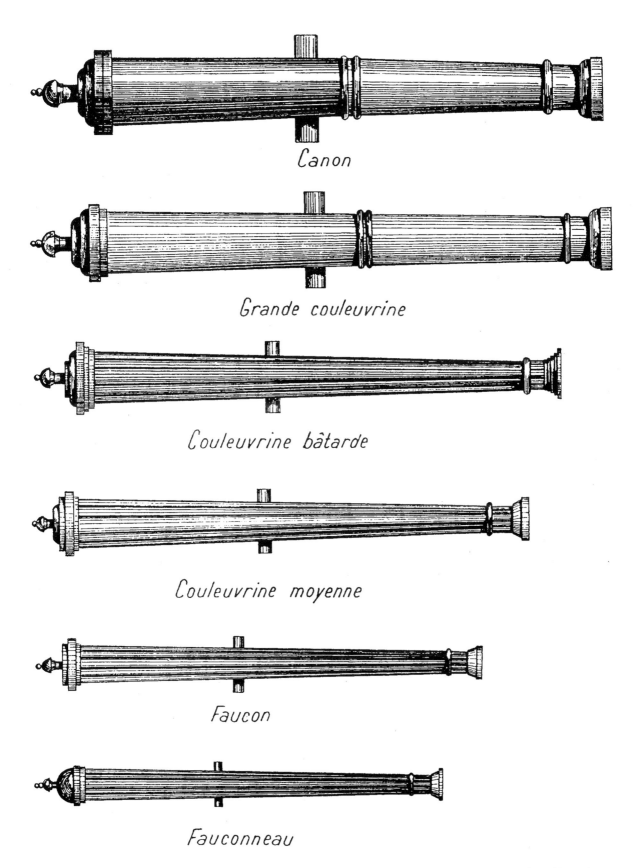

Canon

Grande couleuvrine

Couleuvrine bâtarde

Couleuvrine moyenne

Faucon

Fauconneau

Figure 15.5. The calibres of France, after Denoix, L. and Muracciole, J.-N. (1963), Historique de l'artillerie de Marine de ses origines à 1870. In Memorial de l'artillerie française, t. 37, 4e fascicule, 939.

Table 15.1.

Name English/French	Length in feet and inches	Calibre in inches and lignes	Weight in French pounds	Weight of shot in F. pound and ounce
Cannon / Canon	9 à 9-6	6-3 (169 mm)	5200 à 5400	33 à 33-4
Culverin Grande couleuvrine	9 à 10	4-11 (132 mm)	4000 à 4200	15-2 à 15-4
Bastard culverine Couleuvrine bâtarde	9	3-10 (103 mm)	2500	7-2 à 7-3
Demi culverin Couleuvrine moyenne	8	2-9 (74 mm)	1200 à 1250	2
Falcon / Faucon	6-10 à 6-4	2-4 (63 mm)	700 à 760	1-1
Falconet / Fauconneau	6-4	1-10 (49 mm)	410 à 420	0-14
Arquebus à croc Arquebuse à croc		(9,6 mm)		1/10

Figure 15.6. Venetian winged lion (Photo: G. Ridella).

Venetian cannons

The Venetian cannons bear the emblem of St Mark – the winged lion (Figure 15.6) – and a mark on the trunnion.

Two of them are at the calibre of France and their weight is 5000 and 3967 lb. Following their denomination, they would have fired 33 pound shots. This is probably true for the heavier one, as we can verify on the above table, but it is not clear for the other, the weight of which is close to that of a culverin.

The two other Venetian cannons do not correspond to the calibre of France. This information is confirmed by a weight of around 3200 lb which is between culverin and bastard culverin weight.

Valbelle gives us indications concerning the origin of these guns. During the Italian wars the French army won two battles in which Venetian troops were involved. The first took place at Agnadel near Cremona on 14 May 1509; the Venetians lost "*43 bronze guns*" (Valbelle 1985, I, 22) or "*20 heavy guns and numerous light guns*" (Guicciardini 1996, I 578). Later on, the ordnance captured at Agnadel reached Marseille:

> "*On 8 October of the same year [1511] captain Prégent arrives here with six armed galleys and ten new ones which had been built at Genoa and Savona. The new ones had not only their crew but were equipped with nice ordnance won by the King as well on the Venetians as during war with the Pope* (Valbelle 1985, I, 33).

The second battle occurred on 11 April 1512 at Ravenne:

> "*The French took all the ordnance...*" (Valbelle 1985 I, 42).

In 1512 the guns captured at Agnadel reached the Atlantic with Prégent de Bidoux whose galleys arrived at Brest to fight the fleet of Henri VIII, as described by Peter Martyr (Ep. 498, dated at Logroño on 3 September 1512, cited by (Spont 1897, 51)):

> "*Perijoannes, Galli regis praefectus maritimus, cum magnis quator armatis triremibus ad Oceanum tendit. Insunt triremibus basilici tres, in strage Venetorum habiti, machinae genus, quod uno ictu potis est nivim unam, quocumque illa sit perterebrare atque discerpere.*"

> "*Prégent, admiral of the King of France, is sailing into the Ocean with four big triremes. On these triremes are three basilics captured from the Venetians, this type of weapon is able, on a single shot, to run through and smash to pieces a ship, wherever it may be.*"

Serpentine cannons (canons serpentins)

The description of serpentines cannons is the following:

> "*Five big serpentine cannons with porcupine, sprinkled with fleurs-de-lys, one of which is sawn at the mouth,*

Figure 15.7. Crowned L – Gun n° 73 – Musée de l'armée – Paris (Photo: G. Ridella).

Figure 15.8. Crowned porcupine – Gun n° N 72 – Musée de l'armée – Paris (Photo: G. Ridella).

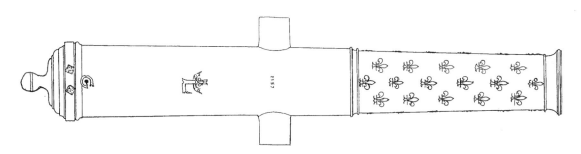

Figure 15.9. Bronze cannon found at Kalâa (Algeria). (Photo: Max Guérout).

weighing about 5 000 pounds, plus two serpentine cannons, one with porcupine and decorated with fleurs-de-lys and a crowned L on the reinforce weighing 52 quintals and a half and the other of same weight with a crowned L above also sprinkled with fleurs-de-lys."

All these guns decorated with porcupines (Figure 15.8) and crowned Ls (Figure 15.7) were cast during the reign of Louis XII (1498–1515); the name of *canons serpentins* was used before the adoption of the calibres of France. These guns could have fired shot of 24 *livres*. Diego Ufano (Diego Ufano 1614), giving a description of the guns of Charles VIII in 1494, speaks of serpentine firing shots of 24 *livres*. A 1534 report detailing the expenses for Royal ordnance speaks also of serpentine cannon weighing 4000 *livres* and firing shots of 24 *livres* (Denoix, Murraciole, 938).

However, guns cast in 1525 under the reign of Francis I are still often named serpentine, even when they are now firing 33 *livres* shot.

Three cannons of this design are displayed in the Musée de l'Armée (Paris). These guns also have a long story.

One of them (Musée de l'Armée: N. 72) with a crowned porcupine and the chase decorated with *fleurs-de-lys* was found by the French in the Arsenal of Algiers after the landing of the expedition in 1830. It is supposed to have been captured from the French at the battle of Pavia by the Spanish and then lost by them in turn on 31 August 1539 when Khayr ad-Dîn Barbarossa conquered the Algiers Peñon which had been occupied by the Spanish since 1509. This gun could have also been recovered from the Spanish ships sunk on the Algerian coast at the occasion of the expedition of Charles V in 1541. Supporting the Spanish thesis, engraved on the reinforce the weight of the guns is inscribed in Spanish measures: *quintal, arobe* and *libra*.

Another cannon bearing a crowned L on the reinforce with the chase decorated with *fleurs-de-lys*, was found in 1865 at Kalâa (Kabylie – Algéria) (Vaysette 1865, 31–39) and (Payen 1870, 300) (Figure 15.9).

These two cannon both have the gunfounder's mark G disposed around the vent, and were probably cast by Simon Gaidon. The presence of Simon Gaidon at Marseille in May 1512 is attested from written sources, describing how he cast eight cannons there (Archives Départementales des Bouches-du-Rhône, B 1232, Livre de Jacques Lion, f°3): « *To Master Simon Gaidon, to fire and test 8 cannons he have cast at Marseille: 24 iron shots* ». One of these guns was lost with the galley *Sainte-Claire* in the gulf of La Spezia on 3 June 1513 (Lion, f°23).

Six other guns cast by him under the reign of Francis I are also known.

A cannon (Musée de l'Armée N. 70) with a crowned porcupine and the chase decorated with fleurs-de-lys, from Rhodes, was presented to the French Emperor Napoleon III by the Sultan Abdul Azziz in 1862. This gun was probably given by Louis XII to the Order of St John with three others. Jacques Lion, keeper of the royal arsenal at Marseille notes (Archives Départementales des Bouches-du-Rhône, B 1232, Livre de Jacques Lion, f°34):

> "*On 7 September 1513, 200 iron shots were given to His Highness the captain of the bark of Rhodes, friar Liseron. These shots had a calibre fitting with two cannons made with a moor's head presented by the Admiral to the Great Master of Rhodes.*"

These guns were probably shipped in 1511 at Aigues Mortes by Jacques Gatineau, captain of the Great "nef" of Rhodes with two other ones (Chailan 1908, 9; Raybaud 1905, 48). One of which being probably the cannon presented by Abdul Azziz.

Demi culverins bastard (couleuvrines bâtardes)

> "*Three demi culverins bastard with the salamander weighting about 3000 livres...*"

The emblem of Francis I indicated here suggests the guns were cast between 1515 and 1525. The weight is a little heavier than the standard given in the above table. These guns were firing shot of about 7 *livres* with a diameter of 103 mm. A gun of this type is conserved in the Musée de l'Armée (Paris).

Minions (couleuvrines moyennes)

> "*Two demi- culverin with the salamander, out of three delivered by the keeper of the royal store, one of which was lost at sea....weighting about 1200 livres.*" A little further: "*Plus two demi-culverins, without mark weighing 1120 livres.*"

The difference of weight shows the limit of standardization due to the method of casting but also to the method used to weight guns.

Falcons (faucons), periers (canons perriers) and sakers (sacres)

Two falcons weighing 775 pounds and firing 1 pound lead shots, two guns which are not the *Calibre de France* are described as a bronze stone gun and a saker.

As its name indicates, stone gun fires stone shots. This type of gun is cast with a powder chamber whose diameter is narrower than the diameter of the bore. The powder charge needed is smaller, so that shot has a shorter range, but the gun is also lighter.

– The saker is recorded to weight 340 lb.
– The guns named saker had various characteristics depending on which country they were made for.

For instance the Spanish "*sacro*" used in the army of Charles V had a weight of 2650 *libras* and fired shot weighing 5 *libras* (Texier de Norbec 1792). However, two of the three bronze sakers recovered from the wreck of the *San Diego*, sunk off Manilla on 14th December 1600 (Decker 1991, 211), were lighter than that. Indeed, these pieces cast at Mechelen in 1555 and 1556 respectively, had a weight of 1963 and 1880 *libras*, a calibre of 91mm and fired iron shot of 5 *libras*. The third had a weight of 1826 *libras* and fired balls of 3 *libras* with a calibre of 77 mm.

– The Venetian saker shot balls weighing 8 *libre sottili* (Cataneo 1560).
– The English saker had a weight of 1400 pounds and fired 5.5 pounds shot (Monson 1610).
– The French saker of the time of Charles VIII fired 5 *livres* balls (Ufano 1592).
– The saker of the *Grande Maîtresse* is then a much lighter gun.

Wrought iron breech-loading guns (Figure 15.10)

This type of gun is recorded in the inventory of the 5 September 1526: "*Four big iron guns with five chambers*". These guns were not as prestigious as the bronze guns, but they were much cheaper. With the development of underwater archaeology numerous wrought iron guns have been recovered. The nearest chronologically are those found on the wreck of the *Lomellina* sunk in 1516 in the road of Villefranche-sur-mer. Other comparative cannons from archaeological sites include the wreck of the *Mary Rose* sunk in the Solent in 1545, and the unidentified wrecks of Anholt (Denmark) dated from the beginning of the century. These guns are made of a barrel build up with longitudinal iron rods forged to form a cylinder and reinforced by outside sleeves. The chamber is made of a single mass forging.

The other inventories show a constant variation in the number of guns carried by the ship. It is an illustration of the fact that when a ship is not in sail, the guns, being very expensive, are moved to where they are useful: on land or on other ships. By luck we can follow this story for the course of a year. However we must be aware of reading too much into and drawing conclusions from a single inventory and to generalize the result, a mistake already made with the inventories of the *Grande Maîtresse*.

After the last inventory, on November 1526, the *Grande Maîtresse* was ready to sail with the fleet. The King ordered the ordnance necessary to complete its armament to be sent up from Lyon. Bertrand Laurens keeper of the royal arsenal notes in his logbook (Archives Départementales des Bouches du Rhône, B 1260, 89) the delivery of: "*Three serpentine cannons, three culverins, three bastard culverins and three demy culverins*". The ordnance then carried was:

    5 serpentine cannons
    3 Venetian cannons
    4 iron guns
    2 stone guns

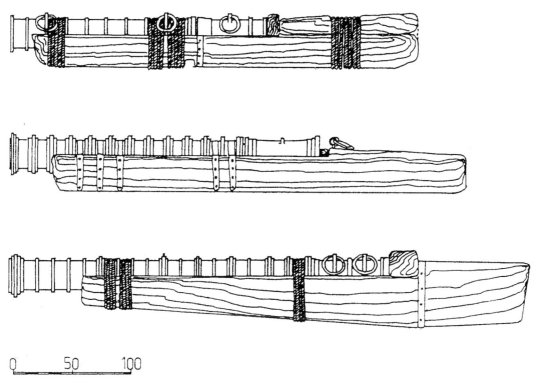

Figure 15.10. Wrought iron guns Lomellina (up) – Anholt – Mary Rose (down). (Design by the author).

4 culverins
3 bastard culverins
13 demy culverins
4 falcons
36 harquebuses à croc
10 hand harquebuses

In all 34 bronze guns, 4 iron guns and 46 harquebuses.

Short guns for sea service

During this period the guns are especially long, not only for practical or technical reasons, but also because it was considered a mark of prestige.

Luis Collado (Collado 1586, 27) compares Spanish saker (sacro) and demi-culverin (moyana) which have the same calibre, and remarks that the *mojana* is preferred to the saker for arming galleys and navy vessels because it is shorter and did not knock the masts on recoil. This remark throws light on a problem: the guns cast for sea service need to be shorter than land guns of the same calibre. Even though no firm evidence of a sea service standard has been found in the documentation available, in the practice its necessity seems to slowly emerge a long time before it was officially sanctioned. Several cases can be observed in the foundry of Marseille:

– The *grande coulevrine* found in the harbour of Toulon, cast by Claude Laignel, is 8 feet; one foot less than the standard length.
– One cannon cast by Simon Gaidon (Musée de l'Armée n°73) also has the same shorter length.

Casting shorter guns for sea service was probably adopted in reaction to the expeditious method sometime used to reduced their lengths. When a vessel needed to be armed in an emergency, when few guns were available, sometimes the muzzles of the longer guns could simply be sawn off. We have an example in the inventory of the *Grande Maîtresse* made on 25 November 1526 (Archives Départementales des Bouches-du-Rhône, B 1260, 74). "*Five big serpentine cannons with porcupine [emblems], strewn with fleur-de-lys, one of which is sawn at the muzzle*". Some time later, as inscribed in his logbook (Archives Départementales des Bouches-du-Rhône, B 1260, 34), Bertrand Laurens gives to Claude Laignel with other spare pieces of bronze: "*the muzzle mouth of a bronze gun which has been cut off*". A Spanish culverin recovered from the wreck of the *San Diego* was also sawn at the muzzle (Decker 1994, 206). The *San Diego* was armed in the hurry to sail out of the port of Manilla to fight the Dutch fleet of Olivier de Noort. Its armament was reinforced by guns taken from the walls of the town.

Gun foundry and royal store at Marseille

When reading the documents concerning the *Grande Maîtresse* we can observe the activities of the royal arsenal and gun foundry at Marseille.

In 1507, Master Patris de la Motte who was gunfounder at Domfront was sent by Louis XII to organise the foundry and prepare for the war in Italy. The foundry was built in the northern part of the "Place de Lenche" (Billoud 1951, 351). As we have seen, the installation of this foundry marks an important turning point in the development of naval ordnance.

During this period several gunfounders can be identified:

– Master Patris de la Motte (1507–1511)
– Master Michau (1512)
– Master Fcrri (1498 1515)
– Simon Gaidon (1512–1520?) founder mark G
– Claude Laignel (1525) founder mark L and C
– Girardin Castellan (1526)
– Imbert Batandier (1524–1526)

The royal arsenal was created in 1509 nearby in the tower of St Jean. The first keeper, a royal officer named Jacques Lion, was appointed by Louis XII on 23rd February 1509; his task was to keep and to manage the movements of guns, ammunition, sails and rigging. After the death of Jacques Lion in 1517, Bertrand Laurens was appointed as keeper.

If changes in the armament of the *Grande Maîtresse* during the period covered by the four inventories are difficult to understand, rules concerning the definition of a suitable armament for each type of ship did however exist. Two experienced sailors, Philippe de Clèves in 1508 (Paviot 1997) and Antoine de Conflans in 1516 (Conflans 1982) recommended guidelines for the armament of warships. Antoine de Conflans describes the ordnance suitable for the armament of 500 ton vessels. He recommends arming the vessel with 16 bronze guns and 10 stone guns. Philippe de Clèves, in describing how (Paviot 1997, 43) to arm an Admiral's ship (probably larger than 500 tons), is less precise concerning the type and the number of guns, but gives more details for the armament of the poop castle. He recommends arming an Admiral ship with 32 bronze guns heavier or equal to the falcon.

Armed with 30 bronze guns in 1525 and with 34 bronze guns when sailing from Marseille in September 1526, the *Grande Maîtresse* is not far off the number given by Philippe de Clèves.

As we can observe, these rules are, at best, an ideal, difficult to achieve because of administrative and technical difficulties, lack of discipline of the captains, and also profit. But the attention of the King himself shows that the impulse came from the top. The use of bronze was probably decisive, since bronze can be easily cast to display the arms of those in power. Therefore bronze ordnance becomes the symbol of power par excellence. The King demonstrates his control of metallurgy, of powder, of gunnery ballistic, in one word his control of fire, a fact very well illustrated by the emblem of Francis

I: the salamander surrounded by flames and his motto: "*Nutrisco et Extingo*" (*I feed the good fire and I extinguish the bad*).

References

Billoud, J. (1951) Histoire du commerce de Marseille de 1515 à 1599. In *Histoire du commerce de Marseille, III.* Paris. Plon, 169–563.
Caruana, A. (1994) The Age of Evolution, 1523–1715. In *History of English sea ordnance, 1523–1875.* Rotherfield. Jean Boudriot.
Cataneo, G. (1580) *Avvertimenti et essamini intorna a quelle cose che richiedono a un perfecto bombardiero cosi circa all' artiglieria come ave a fuochi artificiali.* Venice.
Chailan, Abbé. (1908) *L'ordre de Malte dans la ville d'Arles.* Bergerac.
Conflans, A. de (1982) *Le livre des faiz de la marine et navigaiges,* v. 1516–1520. In *Actes du 107ᵉ congrès national des sociétés savantes.* Brest, Michel Mollat du Jourdin et Florence Chillaud-Tontée.
Collado, Luis (1586) *Plática Manual de Artilleria.* Venice.
Decker, M. (1994) L'artillerie. In *Le San Diego, un trésor sous la mer.* Paris. Réunion des musées nationaux, 202–213.
Guérout, M., Liou, B. (2001) *La Grande Maîtresse, nef de François Ier.* Paris. Presse universitaire de Paris-Sorbonne.
Guicciardini. (1996) *Histoire d'Italie (1492–1534)* I. Paris. Laffont
Monson, W. (Sir) (1610) *Naval Tracts.*
Payen, Cdt. (1870) Notes archéologiques. In *Recueil des notices et mémoires de la Société d'archéologie de la province de Constantin,* 300–301 and pl. II and III. Constantine. Alessi.
Paviot, J. (1997) *Philippe de Clèves, seigneur de Ravestein, L'instruction de toutes manières de guerroyer (...) sur mer, édition critique du manuscrit français 1244 de la Bibliothèque nationale de France.* Paris. Honoré Champion.
Raybaud, J. (1905) *Histoire des prieurs et du prieuré de Saint-Gilles* 2, 48–50. Nîmes.
Spont, A. (1897) Letters and papers relating to the war with France, 1512–1513. *The Navy Record Society, vol. X.* Londres.
Texier de Norbec. (1792) *Recherches sur l'artillerie en général et particulièrement sur celle de la marine.* Paris.
Ufano, D. (1614) *Tratado de la artilleria y uso della, platicado por el capitan Diego Ufano en las guerras de Flandes.* Bruxelles.
Valbelle, Honorat de. (1985) *Histoires journalières (1498–1530),* V.L. Bourrily, R. Duchêne, L. Gaillard and Charles Rostaing, Aix-en-Provence, Université de Provence.
Vayssettes, E. (1865) Notice sur les canons de la Kalaa des Beni-Abbès. In *Recueil des notices et mémoires de la Société d'archéologie de la province de Constantine,* 31–39. Constantine. Alessi.